NOT TO
BE TAKEN
OUT OF
THE
LIBRARY

UNIVERSITY OF NOTTINGHAM

60 0267397 5

WITHDRAWN
FROM THE LIBRARY

KU-588-142

important reference books for businessmen and market researchers

Europe

Directory of European Associations: Part 1—National industrial, trade & professional associations.
Interests, activities and publications of c 7,500 organisations in Western and Eastern Europe. English French & German indexes.

European Companies: A Guide to Sources of Information.
Describes organisations and publications providing information about business enterprises in Western and Eastern Europe.

Statistics—Europe: Sources for Market Research.
Describes organisations and publications providing statistical information for market research in Western and Eastern Europe.

Current European Directories.
Guide to international, national and specialised directories covering all countries of Europe.

Great Britain & Ireland

Directory of British Associations.
Interests, membership, activities & publications of c 8,000 British and Irish organisations.

Current British Directories.
Describes c 2,500 directories and lists published in Great Britain, Ireland, the Commonwealth and South Africa.

Councils, Committees & Boards.
Constitution, activities and publications of executive, consultative and advisory authorities in Britain.

Overseas

Statistics—Africa: Sources for Market Research.
Describes organisations and publications providing statistical information for all countries of Africa.

Current African Directories.
Guide to directories and other sources of business information covering all countries of Africa.

Statistics—America: Sources for Market Research.
Describes organisations and publications providing statistical information for North, Central and South America.

Write for our complete descriptive catalogue

CBD Research Ltd
154 High Street, Beckenham, Kent, BR3 1EA, England
Telephone 01-650 7745.

 Member: European Association of Directory Publishers and Association of British Directory Publishers

STATISTICS

AMERICA

Sources for Market Research

(North, Central & South America)

Joan M. Harvey, FLA

Senior Lecturer at the School of Librarianship,
Loughborough Technical College

CBD Research Ltd
Beckenham, Kent, England

First published   1973.

Copyright   ©   Joan M Harvey.

Standard book number: 900246 13 8.

Price £6.00   (US & Canada $22.50).

 Member: European Association of Directory Publishers
Adhérent: Association Européenne des Editeurs d'Annuaires
Mitglied: Europäischer Adressbuchverleger Verband

 Members: Association of British Directory Publishers.

Printed in England by Page Bros (Norwich) Ltd., Norwich and London.

C O N T E N T S

v

essential information for all concerned with business in Europe

Directory of EUROPEAN ASSOCIATIONS

Part 1 : National industrial, trade & professional associations

trade and industrial associations, professional institutes, etc, classified by subject interest and subdivided by countries

giving their :
  name & authorised translations of name
  acronym or abbreviated name
  date of formation
  address, telephone & telex number
  membership data
  activities—especially conferences, information services, collection of statistics, etc
  publications

and with :
  subject indexes in English, French, German
  index of acronyms & abbreviated names and translations of names

coverage :
  all European countries except Great Britain and the Republic of Ireland

1st Edition, 1971.   SBN 900246 08 1.   450 pages, A4.   Price £12.00 ; $30.00

CBD Research Ltd
Beckenham · Kent · England

Gale Research Co
Detroit · Michigan · USA

1.   "Statistics – America: Sources for Market Research" is the third title to be published in a series of four volumes on sources of statistics for market researchers and others who need up-to-date information on statistical data throughout the world.   "Statistics – Europe" is in its second edition; "Statistics – Africa" was published in 1970; and the compilation of "Statistics – Asia & Australasia" will have been started before this present volume is published.

       Most statistical information is collected by governments, either directly or through trade associations and other organisations; it is usually published by the government departments concerned but, in the case of some Central and South American countries, much of the publication is done by the central banks.   In the more developed countries, the information is increasingly being collected and analysed with a view to its being used by market researchers and others as well as for official purposes, but in the developing countries the collection of statistics is mainly for use as a basis for economic planning.   Not all the information collected is published, either because it has been supplied on the understanding that it will be treated as confidential or because it is not considered of sufficient general interest to make publication worthwhile.   In the latter case it is often possible for enquirers to obtain the information from the organisation which collects it, perhaps in the form of computer printout.   The statistical information published by the United Nations, OECD and other international organisations is generally supplied by the governments of the countries concerned, and is often in a form suitable for national comparisons to be made.

       This guide describes the main sources of statistical information for each country in the American continent and adjacent islands.   Obviously, more information is available in some fields than in others; some countries publish very little, whilst others publish statistics on every conceivable topic and it has been necessary for the compiler to select items for inclusion.

2.   ARRANGEMENT

       The main body of the guide is arranged by countries in alphabetical order, and each entry, whether for the description of an organisation or of a publication, has been allocated a unique reference number.   The list of countries (page xi) indicates the first page number for each country.   A section on America as a whole precedes the individual countries.   Each section contains:

(1)   the name, address and telephone number of the central statistical office of the country, and of other important organisations that collect and publish statistical material useful for market research; this is followed by some information on the organisation and work of each agency, the facilities it provides, its publications, etc;

(2)   the principal libraries in the country where collections of statistical material may be consulted by the public;

(3)   libraries and information services in other countries (particularly English-speaking countries) where the country's statistical publications may be consulted;

(4)   the principal bibliographies of statistics; only reasonably current bibliographies have been included, and sales lists are mentioned because of the general dearth of special bibliographies in this field; national bibliographies (e.g. the British National Bibliography) are not included, but should not be overlooked as a means of tracing statistical titles.

(5)   the major statistical publications, arranged in the following standard groups:

¶   A   General
¶   B   Production
¶   C   External trade
¶   D   Internal distribution
¶   E   Population
¶   F   Standard of living.

3.   NOTES ON THE GROUPS

¶ A   Titles listed in group A are useful only for general indications of overall patterns, and are not usually sufficiently detailed for market research into a particular industry or product.

¶ B   Group B includes statistics of both industrial and agricultural production. Censuses are usually devoted more to the structure (finance, labour, machinery, power, etc) of the industry than to the quantity and value of goods produced.

¶ C   The classification schemes used for the tabulation of foreign trade statistics follow closely similar patterns for most countries, often being based on the Standard International Trade Classification (SITC) or correlated to it.   Many countries classify their imports and exports in more detail than the SITC and sometimes publish their own schemes; alternatively, a useful key to the classification used in a particular country can be the International Customs Journal (Bulletin International des Douanes), which is obtainable from the International Customs Tariff Bureau, rue de l'Association 38, Bruxelles, Belgium, or from sales agents.   It comprises about 200 volumes, each containing the customs tariff of a single country, and is kept up-to-date by supplements and new editions as required.

¶ D   There are very few publications providing statistics of internal distribution, although the number is increasing, so this section is relatively small.

¶ E   Group E includes only censuses of population and some demographic surveys and projections, references to more up-to-date figures are made to the statistical yearbooks and bulletins.

¶ F   Group F contains publications likely to be useful in gauging the standard of living in each country, and consists mainly of sources of retail price indices, reports of household budget surveys, and the like.

4.   FORM OF ENTRY

The entry for each publication comprises:

(1)   serial number;

(2)   title, English translation of title is the original is not in English, and name of responsible organisation (sometimes omitted when the name of the organisation is a part of the title);

(3)   name and address of the publisher or of other agency or sales office from which the publication can be obtained;

(4)   date when first published (omitted in cases where it is difficult to determine because of changes of title, responsible organisation, etc); date of latest issue seen by compiler (not necessarily the latest published), except in a very few cases where it has not been possible to locate copies, if published annually or less frequently; price (generally given in local currency); number of pages or volumes of the latest issue of an annual or less frequent publication;

(5)   description of contents;

(6)   indication of the lapse of time between the latest data included and the date of the publication (as the actual date is seldom cited in the publication and seldom coincides with the normal date of an issue, part or edition, this information has been obtained mainly by observation of dates of receipt in libraries, and should be treated with caution);

(7)   language(s) of the text, indicated by the symbol § followed by international symbols (BS 3862).

5. REFERENCES

References have been made wherever necessary to relevant publications in other groups within each country section or in the section for another individual country, but NOT from individual countries to the general section of America as a whole, except in one or two special cases. It will, therefore, often be worthwhile to consult the appropriate group in the general section if no suitable material is found in a particular country section.

6. CHANGES OF TITLE

Only the latest title of each publication is given. Many statistical publications have a long history of title variations, and it would be impracticable to list all the changes. The librarian, sales agent, or publisher will be able to advise prospective users and purchasers of earlier issues if titles have changed.

7. ACKNOWLEDGEMENTS

The compiler would like to thank everyone who has helped in the preparation of this volume. She has had the most generous help and co-operation from most of the statistical offices, libraries, diplomatic posts, and other organisations; and has appreciated the easy access she has been allowed to the many libraries she has used, particularly the Statistics and Market Intelligence Library of the Department of Trade and Industry where most of the material has been examined. Finally, but by no means of least importance, she would like to thank Gillian and David Wiltshire for the help they have given her in translating correspondence into and from Latin-American Spanish and Portuguese.

LOUGHBOROUGH
July 1972

ABBREVIATIONS & SYMBOLS

§	language of text
(A)	published annually
c	circa
De	German
ed	edition
En	English
Es	Spanish
Fr	French
(irreg)	irregular publication
(M)	published monthly
Nl	Dutch
OECD	Organisation for Economic Co-operation & Development
Pt	Portuguese
(Q)	published quarterly
Ru	Russian
SITC	Standard International Trade Classification
t	telephone number
tg	telegraphic address
tx	telex number
vol	volume
yr	per annum (annual subscription)

LIST OF COUNTRIES - TABLE DES PAYS - LÄNDERVERZEICHNIS

STATISTICS:

Sources for Market Research

Joan M. Harvey

A series of four separate works:

Statistics—Europe
(covering both Western & Eastern Europe)
2nd Edition, 1972. 265 pages. £5.00 (US $18.00)

Statistics—Africa
(covering the whole continent & adjacent islands)
1st Edition, 1970. 186 pages. £4.00 (US $15.00)

Statistics—America
(covering North, Central & South America)
1st Edition, 1973. 220 pages. £6.00 (US $22.50)

Statistics—Asia & Australasia
In preparation, for publication in 1973.

giving, for each country:

    central statistical office: address, description
      of work, facilities offered

    other important organisations that collect &
      publish statistics

    principal libraries of statistical material

    information services provided in other countries,
      particularly the UK, the USA, Canada & Australia

    bibliographies of statistics

    descriptions of major published sources, arranged
      in a standard grouping: General — Production —
      External trade — Internal distribution —
      Population — Standard of living.

CBD Research Ltd.

154 High Street, Beckenham, Kent, England

01-650 7745

Some international organisations publishing statistics

001   United Nations,
             New York, NY, USA.
             t   754 1234.

        The Statistical Office of the United Nations collects and publishes data from as many countries as possible in periodic as well as ad hoc publications.   On the basis of these statistics, the Statistical Office computes a large number of economic indicators in the form of global and regional aggregates and index numbers.   It also publishes methodological studies, guides and manuals, and assists governments in implementing statistical practice recommended by the Statistical Commission.   The Statistical Office is part of the United Nations Department of Economic and Social Affairs.

        Publications other than those described in the following pages include:

             Yearbook of the United Nations.
             Everyman's United Nations.   (every three years).
             National accounting practices in sixty countries.
             Standard international trade classification, revised.
             International standard industrial classification of all economic activities.
             World economic survey.   (A).
             Recommendations for the 1973 world programme of industrial statistics.

002   United Nations Economic Commission for Latin America,
             Edificio Naciones Unidas, Avenida Dag Hammarskjöld, Vitacura 3030, Santiago, Chile.
             t   48 50 5I.

        Established in 1948 to promote and facilitate action for the economic and social development of Latin America; to maintain and strengthen the economic relations of Latin American countries between themselves and throughout the world; to undertake and sponsor research, studies and investigations on economic and technical problems of development.   The Commission collects, evaluates and disseminates economic, technological and statistical information.

        Publications other than those described in the following pages include:

             Boletín economica de America Latina.   [Economic bulletin for Latin America].

003   Food and Agriculture Organisation of the United Nations,
             via delle Terme di Caracalla, 00153 Roma, Italy.
             t   (06) 5797   tx   61181.

        Created to raise the levels of nutrition and standards of living, to secure improvements in the efficiency of production and distribution of all agricultural products, and to better the conditions of rural populations.   To help achieve these aims, the FAO provides an intelligence service of facts and figures relating to nutrition, agriculture, forestry and fisheries, and also appraisals and forecasts of production, distribution and consumption in these industries.

        Statistical publications other than those described in the following pages include:

             Yearbook of forest product statistics.
             World grain statistics.   (A).
             Commodity bulletin series.   (irregular).

004   Organisation of American States,
           Pan American Union, 17th Street and Constitution Avenue N.W., Washington, D.C. 20006, USA.
           t   EX 3-8450   tx   89-503   cables PAN-WASH-DC.

           The Organisation of American States is a regional agency within the United Nations which aims
to strengthen the peace and security of the continent; to prevent possible causes of difficulties and to
ensure the pacific settlement of disputes among member states; to provide common action in the event
of aggression; to seek the solution of political, juridical and economic problems that may arise among
the member states; and to promote, by co-operative action, their economic, social and cultural
development.

           An outgrowth of the International Union of American Republics, created in 1890, the Organisation
nowadays operates through a large number of agencies and institutions throughout the Western Hemisphere.
The Pan American Union, with headquarters in Washington, is the permanent organ and general secretariat
of the Organisation of American States.

           Member countries of the O.A.S. are Argentina, Barbados, Bolivia, Brazil, Chile, Colombia,
Costa Rica, Cuba, Dominican Republic, Ecuador, Guatemala, Haiti, Honduras, Jamaica, Mexico,
Nicaragua, Panama, Paraguay, Peru, El Salvador, Trinidad and Tobago, United States of America,
Uruguay, and Venezuela.

005   Inter-American Statistical Institute.   Instituto Interamericano de Estadística.
           1725 1st Avenue N.W., Washington, D.C. 20006, USA.
           t   EX 3-3450.

           Established in 1940, mainly because the International Statistical Institute was unable to function
adequately during the 1939-1945 war, it is a professional organisation affiliated to the Organisation of
American States and its Secretariat, the Pan American Union, whereby it is able to assist in the economic
and social development of the Americas.   The Institute seeks to stimulate improved methodology in the
collection, tabulation, analysis and publication of both official and unofficial statistics, to encourage
measures designed to improve the comparability and availability of economic and social statistics among
the nations of the Western Hemisphere, to provide a medium for professional collaboration among statisticians, and to co-operate with national and international organisations in advancing the science and
administration of statistics.

           Many of the Institute's publications are issued jointly with the Organisation of American States
and the Pan American Union.   Publications of the Institute not described in the following pages include:
           Statistical vocabulary.   Vocabulario estadística.   2nd ed.
           Bibliography of statistical textbooks and other teaching material.   Bibliografía de tratados
                y demás material de enseñanza de estadística.   2nd ed.
           Actividades estadísticas de las Naciones Americanas.   [Statistical activities of the American
                countries].   2nd ed.
           Quarterly consolidated report on statistical consulting in the Western Hemisphere and some
                statistical training programmes for Latin Americans.
           Estadística: journal of the Inter-American Statistical Institute.   (Q).

006   Asociación Latinoamericana de Libre Comercio (ALALC).   [Latin-American Free Trade Association],
           Cebollati 1461, Casilla de Correo 577, Montevideo, Uruguay.
           t   40-11-21   tx & cables   ALALC.

           The Association was established in 1960, and evolved between 1962 and 1966, "to establish a
continent-wide institutional basis for economic co-operation among countries that share a common
political history and cultural values and have similar productive structures".   Member countries of
ALALC are Argentina, Bolivia, Brazil, Colombia, Chile, Ecuador, Mexico, Paraguay, Peru, Uruguay,
and Venezuela.

           Publications other than those described in the following pages include:
           ALALC Sintesis mensual.   [Monthly synthesis].
           Industrias de la zona.   [Industries of the area].   (A series of separate bulletins on individual
                industries, but including very few statistics).

007   Caribbean Free Trade Area (CARIFTA),
             Georgetown, Guyana.

       Established in May 1968 between Antigua, Barbados, Guyana and Trinidad & Tobago; joined in
July 1968 by Dominica, Grenada, St Kitts-Nevis-Anguilla, St Lucia and St Vincent; and in August
1968 by Jamaica and Montserrat.

       Note: included as an important organisation, although it has not as yet published any statistical
              data.

008   Secretaría Permanente del Tratado General de Integración Económica Centroamericana (SIECA).
             [Permanent Secretariat of the General Treaty on Central American Economic Integration],
             4 a, Avenida 10-25, Zona 14, Guatemala City, Guatemala.

       Established in December 1960 in Managua on the signing of the treaty by representatives of the
governments of Guatemala, El Salvador, Honduras, Nicaragua, and Costa Rica.   Aims are to promote
integration of Central American economies and to co-ordinate economic policies.   It is also concerned
with efforts to develop a Central American Common Market, as originally planned by the United Nations
Economic Commission for Latin America.

Libraries and information services

       Many national, university and public libraries throughout the world are deposit libraries for
United Nations publications (a "List of depository libraries receiving United Nations material" was
published by the United Nations Secretariat in 1971 as ST/LIB/12/Rev. 5, and it is also included
annually in the Cumulative Index to the "United Nations documents index"); such libraries should
have unrestricted documents and publications available for reference.   United Nations Information
Centres usually have the more recent UN publications available.

       It is usual for the official statistical offices of countries to exchange their publications with
other national statistical offices, and these publications are often, if not always, stored in the
libraries of the statistical offices.   These libraries are often accessible to those who wish to consult
this type of material, even when not generally open to the public.

United Kingdom

       The most accessible large collection of the publications referred to in this guide is at the
Department of Trade and Industry's Statistics and Market Intelligence Library, Export House,
50 Ludgate Hill, London EC4M 7HU (t 01-248 5757, ext 368); the Statistics Library at Warwick
University, Coventry (t   0203 24011) is building up a large collection of this kind of material, but
has not, as yet, a great deal for Central and South American countries, so that it is suggested that
enquiries be made before visiting this library regarding the holdings of the material required and the
conditions laid down for the use of the library by those outside the university.   Other large collections
are housed in the British Library of Political & Economic Science, Houghton Street, London WC2
(t   01-405 7686), which is the library of the London School of Economics;   and in the State Paper Room
of the British Museum, London WC1 (t   01-687 1555), where much material is housed elsewhere because
of lack of space and may take up to 24 hours to produce.

       The larger public libraries are deposit libraries for United Nations publications and take OECD
material; they often also take a selection of statistical yearbooks for the larger countries overseas
(probably only for the United States and Canada in the area covered by this volume) but one or two
have much larger collections of statistical yearbooks, although none takes the more detailed statistical
publications described in this guide.

Libraries and Information Services,   continued

Australia

The two largest collections of statistical publications, including those of international organisations and of individual overseas countries, are in the National Library of Australia, Wentworth Avenue, Kingston, Canberra (t   9 0301), and the Commonwealth Bureau of Census and Statistics, Treasury Buildings, Newlands Street, Parkes, Canberra (t   63 9111).

There are also collections of this type of material in the State libraries, situated in each capital city, and in some university libraries, particularly the University of Sydney.   The Australian National University Library at Canberra has a collection of statistical material to support its research in demography.

The United Nations Information Centre at 44 Martin Place, Sydney, NSW (t   28 5141) has a collection of United Nations publications available for reference.

Canada

The Library of Statistics Canada at Ottawa (t   232 8311) has an extensive collection of statistical material, including publications of the international organisations and of individual overseas countries, and these may be consulted by the public.

Many of the larger university, government department and state libraries in Canada are deposit libraries for United Nations publications but do not collect statistical publications of individual countries outside North America to any extent.

New Zealand

Both the Library of the Department of Statistics, BMA Building, 26 The Terrace, Wellington C1 (t   70 599) and the National Library of New Zealand, 35 Sydney Street West, Wellington C1 (t   48 850) have large collections of statistical material, including publications of international organisations and of individual overseas countries.

Some material is also held in the public libraries of the main and secondary cities and in the libraries of certain other government departments, such as the Department of Industries and Commerce.   Much of the material available in New Zealand is accessible for loan through a public library.

United States of America

The Library of the Bureau of the Census, Room 2455, Federal Office Building No. 3, Washington 25, D.C., maintains a collection of censuses, statistical yearbooks, bulletins, etc, including those of other American countries and of international organisations, which may be consulted for research purposes in the library during office hours.   The Library of Congress in Washington, D.C., the Library of the United Nations in New York, and the Library of the Inter-American Statistical Institute in Washington, D.C., also have collections of this type of material.

A large number of the university and public libraries throughout the USA are deposit libraries for United Nations publications, and the United Nations Information Center at Suite 714, 1028 Connecticut Avenue N.W., Washington 6, D.C. (t   296 5370) has a collection of publications of the United Nations.

Bibliographies

009 United Nations document index (United Nations).

    Sales Section, United Nations, New York, NY 10017; or from sales agents.

    1950-   (M). £10.42 or $25.00 yr.

    Lists all unrestricted documents and publications of the United Nations arranged by issuing
      department of the UN.   An annual cumulative checklist and cumulative subject index are
      included in the subscription and are issued some considerable time after the end of the year
      covered.

010 United Nations publications: a reference catalogue (United Nations).

    Sales Section, United Nations, New York, NY 10017; or from sales agents.

    A comprehensive list of the publications of the UN issued for sale since 1945.   The issue for
      1945-1963, published in 1964, has been followed by annual volumes.

011 Bibliography of industrial and distributive-trade statistics (United Nations, Department of
      Economic and Social Affairs).

    Sales Section, United Nations, New York, NY 10017; or from sales agents.

    1967. £1.10 or $3. 144 pages.

    Issued as "Statistical papers, series M, no. 36, rev. 3", this is now rather out of date but lists
      the information which was then being collected by each reporting country, mentioning the
      publications in which the information appeared.

012 Catalogue of publications (OECD).

    Organisation for Economic Co-operation and Development, 2 rue André-Pascal, 75 Paris 16, France.

    A sales list, annotated, which is published annually.

Statistical publications

¶ A - General

013 Statistical yearbook (United Nations Statistical Office).

    Sales Section, United Nations, New York, NY 10017; or from sales agents.

    1947- 1970. £6.56; $22. 816 pages.

    Main sections:

World summary	Transport
Population	Communications
Manpower	Consumption
Land	Balance of payments
Agriculture	Wages & prices (including consumer price indices)
Forestry	National accounts
Fishing	Finance
Industrial production (index numbers)	Public finance
Mining & quarrying	International capital flow
Manufacturing	Health
Construction	Housing
Energy	Education
Internal trade	Culture
External trade	

[continued next page

¶ A, continued

013, continued

An annex contains information on conversion coefficients and factors.

Time factor: the 1970 edition, published mid-1971, contains tables with figures for many years up to 1969 or 1970 (provisional).

§ En & Fr.

014 Monthly bulletin of statistics (United Nations Statistical Office).

Sales Section, United Nations, New York, NY 10017; or from sales agents.

1947- £1.31 or $3.00; £10.42 or £25.00 yr.

Provides monthly statistics on a range of subjects similar to those covered by item 013 above, together with special tables illustrating important economic developments. Included twice a year (June and December in 1972) ia a table "Retail price comparisons to determine salary differentials of United Nations officials", which indicates the cost of living in various capitals of the world.

Time factor: most tables include data for about seven years, and at least the last 12 months to to two or three months prior to the date of issue.

§ En & Fr.

015 Statistical yearbook (UNESCO).

UNESCO, Place de Fontenoy, 75 Paris 7; or from sales agents.

1963- 1970. £10.50 or $26. 788 pages.

Includes data on population, education, libraries, museums, book production, paper consumption, films, cinema, radio and television for more than 200 territories. The 1970 edition also has data on scientific and technological manpower, and expenditure for research and experimental development.

Time factor: the 1970 edition, published late 1971, has data for 1970 and some earlier years.

§ En & Fr.

016 Annuaire de statistique internationale des grandes villes. International statistical yearbook of large towns (Institut Internationale de Statistique).

Office Permanent de l'Institut Internationale de Statistique, 2 Oostduinlaan, Den Haag, Netherlands.

1927- 1968. Fl 40. xxxiv, 290 pages.

Main sections:

Population by sex	Civil air transport
Births	Urban transport
Deaths	Telephones, radio and television
Newly constructed dwellings classified by number of rooms	Theatres
	Libraries
Railways, sea-borne shipping and inland waterway transport	Sports grounds and covered sports courts

Time factor: the 1968 edition was published in 1970, and shows the latest information available.

§ Fr; En.

Note: A series "International statistics of large towns" is also issued, each volume dealing with a particular subject, such as population and vital statistics, housing and building statistics, economic data, public utilities and transport, and cultural and sports statistics.

¶   A,   continued

017   Boletín estadístico de America Latina.   Statistical bulletin for Latin America   (United Nations.
               Economic Commission for Latin America).

               United Nations Economic Commission for Latin America, Edificio Naciones Unidas,
                    Avenida Dag Hammarskjöld, Vitacura 3030, Santiago, Chile; or from sales agents.

               1964-   2 per annum.   £2.10; $5 a copy.

               Contains regional and national statistics on population, demography, agriculture, mining,
                    manufacturing, construction, electricity, prices (wholesale and consumer), foreign trade,
                    and transport.

               Time factor: each issue has runs of figures for several years to about a year prior to the date of
                    issue.   Data prior to 1964 was included in the "Economic bulletin for Latin America".

               §   En & Es.

018   Economic survey of Latin America   (United Nations.   Economic Commission for Latin America).

               United Nations Economic Commission for Latin America, Edificio Naciones Unidas,
                    Avenida Dag Hammarskjöld, Vitacura 3030, Santiago, Chile; or from sales agents.

               1948- 1970.   £2.60; $6.   approx. 400 pages.

               Includes a section on the economic situation in selected countries containing financial and foreign
                    trade statistical tables.

               Time factor: the 1970 edition, published late in 1971, has data for several years to 1969 and
                    some provisional 1970 figures.

               §   En.

019   Statistical abstract of Latin America   (University of California: Latin American Center).

               University of California: Latin American Center, Los Angeles, California, USA.

               1955- 1970. $12 hard cover; $8 paper cover.   c. 300 pages.

               Contains a comprehensive collection of statistics on the cultural, economic, financial, political
                    and social structures of individual Latin American countries.   There is also to be an irregular
                    series of supplements, the first of which was published in 1970 and is titled "Cuba 1968:
                    a supplement ... ".

               Time factor: Published every two years.   The 1970 edition of the abstract was published in 1972.

               §   En.

020   America en cifras   [America in figures]   (Organización de los Estados Americanos and Instituto
               Interamericano de Estadística).

               Organisation of American States, Washington, D.C. 20006; or from sales agents.

               1960- 1970. $1.00 per volume.   9 vols.

               The volumes are:

                    Situación demográfica   [the demographic situation].
                    Situación económica   [the economic situation].
                         This volume is divided into five parts:
                              1. Agriculture, livestock, forestry, hunting and fishing.
                              2. Industry.
                              3. Commerce, services, transport, communications and tourism.
                              4. Balance of payments, national income and product, and finance.
                              5. Prices, wages, consumption and other economic aspects.
                    Situación sociale   [the social situation (including housing, social assistance, health, and
                         employment)].

[continued next page

7

¶ A, continued

020, continued

Situación cultural [the cultural situation (including education)].
Supplemento: indice general de materias, indice analitico general, bibliografía general [Supplement: general contents, general analytic index, general bibliography].

The data is for each of the O.A.S. member countries, Canada and Guyana.

Time factor: the 1970 edition, published in 1971 and 1972, has data for several years to 1968 or 1968/69. A new issue, with varying number of volumes, is published every two or three years.

§ Es, with separate English translations of the text of each volume. The supplement is in En & Es.

021   Compendio estadístico de America [Statistical compendium of the Americas] (Organización de los Estados Americanos and Instituto Interamericano de Estadística).

Organisation of American States, Washington, D.C. 20006; or from sales agents.

1968- 1969. £1.00. vii, 116 pages.

A pocket-book with selected statistical data for all the O.A.S. countries, Canada and Guyana on territory, climate, population, agriculture, industry, electricity, foreign trade, transport and communications, balance of payments, national income and national product, public finance and money, prices, wages and labour, housing, and education.

Time factor: the 1969 edition, published in 1969, has data for 1967 or 1968 and one or two previous years.

§ Es. There is also an English edition.

022   Boletín estadístico [Statistical bulletin] (Organización de los Estados Americanos and Instituto Interamericano de Estadística).

Organisation of American States, Washington, D.C. 20006; or from sales agents.

1965- (M). not priced.

Up-dates "America en cifras" (item 020). Information varies with each issue and can be national or international. Subjects covered include consumer price indices, foreign trade, finance, population, social security, production, and preliminary figures for censuses of population and agriculture. In the main, the data is for the countries of the O.A.S.

§ Es.

023   World almanac and book of facts (Newspaper Enterprises Association Inc).

Newspaper Enterprise Association Inc, 230 Park Avenue, New York, NY 10017, and 1200 West Third Street, Cleveland, Ohio 44113, USA.

1868- 1971. $3.95. 952 pages.

A general reference book, mainly on the United States of America, but including general statistical data on general and economic topics for most countries, USA and Canadian cities, etc.

§ En.

¶ A, continued

024   AID economic data book: Latin America   (Agency for International Development).

Agency for International Development, Bureau for Program on Policy Coordination, Office of
Statistics and Reports, Washington, D.C. 20503, USA.

Revised ed, July 1971. $6.00.   328 pages (various paging).

Issued as PB-201589 report, this book contains basic economic, demographic and social information
and trend data on the individual countries of Latin America, including agricultural and industrial
production, national accounts, prices, government finances, foreign trade, balance of payments,
external debt and national reserves, natural resources, population, labour force, health,
education, transport and power.

Time factor: the revised edition dated July 1971 has data for several years to 1969, 1970 or 1971
according to country.

§   En.

025   BOLSA review   (Economic Intelligence Department, Lloyds & Bolsa International Bank Ltd).

Lloyds & Bolsa International Bank Ltd, 40-66 Queen Victoria Street, London EC4P 4EL.

1967- (M).   not priced.

Each issue contains one or two articles relating to Latin America or individual Latin American
countries, economic and political news from each country, and a statistical section.
Statistical tables include total and regional trade , commodity prices, cost of living,
economic indicators, and exchange rates.

§   En.

026   Series estadísticas seleccionadas de Centroamérica y Panamá: indicadores económicos   [Economic
indicators of Central American countries and Panama]   (SIECA).

Secretaría Permanente del Tratado General de Integración Económica Centroamericana (SIECA),
4a, Avenida 10-25, Zona 14, Guatemala City, Guatemala.

1967- no.12.   not priced.

Contains mainly financial statistics, including public finance, money, foreign trade, production of
certain items, and consumer prices, for Guatemala, El Salvador, Honduras, Nicaragua,
Costa Rica and Panama.

Time factor: published at irregular intervals, no.12 was issued in July 1971.

§   Es.

027   West Indies and Caribbean yearbook.   Anuario comercial de las Antilles y paises del Caribe
(Thomas Skinner Directories).

Thomas Skinner Directories, RAC House, Lansdowne Road, Croydon CR9 2HH, England.

1930- 1971.   £5.00; $17.00.   1013 pages.

Contains a few statistics of population, agriculture, trade and commerce, etc, among the more
general information about Bermuda, Bahamas, Barbados, British Honduras, British Virgin Islands,
Cayman Islands, Turks & Caicos Islands, Guyana, Jamaica, Leeward Islands, Trinidad & Tobago,
Windward Islands, Canal Zone (Panama), Costa Rica, El Salvador, Guatemala, Honduras,
Nicaragua, Colombia, Cuba, Dominican Republic, French Guyana, French West Indies of
Guadeloupe and Martinique, Haiti, Netherlands Antilles, Panama, Puerto Rico, Surinam,
Venezuela, and the Virgin Islands of the US.

§   En.

¶ A, continued

028   Allgemeine Statistik des Auslandes: Länderberichte   [General foreign statistics: reports on foreign countries]   (Statistisches Bundesamt).

W Kohlhammer GmbH, Postfach 2727, 65 Mainz, Germany.

A series of reports, each on a particular foreign country, containing statistics on the climate, population, health, education, labour, agriculture, forestry, fisheries, production, foreign trade, transport, tourism, finance, prices and wages, etc. The reports are supported by a series of more brief reports: "Allgemeine Statistik des Auslandes: Länderkurzberichte". American countries for which there are reports are Argentina, Bolivia, Brazil, Canada, Chile, Colombia, Costa Rica, Cuba, Ecuador, Guatemala, Haiti, Honduras, Jamaica, Mexico, Nicaragua, Panama, Peru, Trinidad & Tobago, Uruguay, USA and Venezuela.

Time factor: the reports are published at varying intervals and contain the latest data available for each country.

§   De.

029   Main economic indicators   (Organisation for Economic Co-operation and Development).

OECD, 2 rue André-Pascal, 75 Paris 16; or from sales agents.

1965- (M). £0.77 or £8.35 yr; $2.25 or $24 yr; Fr 10 or Fr 110 yr, including supplements.

A rapid guide to recent economic developments and a basic source of international statistical data, but including data for Canada and the USA only on the American continent. Contains tables and charts on national income and product, industrial production indices, deliveries, stocks and orders, construction, retail sales, and labour. There are separate supplements on industrial production, consumer prices, and historical statistics. 'Sources and methods', published at intervals, describes the methodology used by the national authorities to compile their economic indicators.

Time factor: most of the tables in the monthly issues contain data for the last four years, and quarterly figures and monthly figures for the last twelve months to one or two months prior to the date of the issue.

§   En & Fr.

030   Yearbook of national accounts statistics   (United Nations Statistical Office).

Sales Section, United Nations, New York, NY 10017; or from sales agents.

1957- 1969. Vol 1 $12.50; £5.46. Vol 2 $3.50; £1.52½. 2 vols.

The detailed statistical data and tables provide comparisons between the situation in the 120 countries and regions covered. Vol 1 has individual country data on gross product by type of expenditure and industrial origin, national income by distribution shares, finance and composition of gross domestic capital formation, composition of private consumption expenditure, etc. Vol 2 has international tables, including estimates of total and per capita national income, gross domestic product and gross national product in US$ for comparison.

Time factor: the 1969 edition, published in October 1970, has data for 1969.

§   En.

¶   B - Production

031   The growth of world industry   (United Nations Statistical Office).

Sales Section, United Nations, New York, NY 10017; or from sales agents.

1938/61- 1969.   Vol I £4.20 or $10.   Vol II £4.37½ or $10.

Volume I contains general industrial statistics, including the basic national data for each country, and also a selection of main indicators showing global and regional trends in industrial activity. Volume II contains detailed information on world production of 315 industrial commodities.

Time factor: both volumes of the 1969 edition were published in 1971 and carry data for 1960-1968 and 1960-1969 respectively.

§   En & Fr.

032   Production yearbook   (Food and Agriculture Organisation of the UN).

FAO, via delle Terme di Caracalla, 00153 Roma, Italy; or from sales agents.

1947- 1970.   £4.00; $10.00.   840 pages.

Contains data on land use, holdings, population, index numbers of agricultural production, crops, livestock, food supply, means of production, prices, wages and freight rates for each continent and individual reporting countries.

Time factor: the 1970 edition, published Autumn 1971, contains data for 1969/70 and some earlier years.

§   En, Fr, Es.

033   Monthly bulletin of agricultural economics and statistics   (Food and Agriculture Organisation of the UN).

FAO, via delle Terme di Caracalla, 00153 Roma, Italy; or from sales agents.

1952-   £0.24 or £2.40 yr; $0.60 or $6.00 yr.

Each issue contains an article, commodity notes, and statistical tables.   Statistical data includes production, trade and prices for agricultural products of reporting countries.

Time factor: each issue has data for about six years and several months or quarters up to between two and six months prior to publication.

§   En.

034   Report on the 1960 world census of agriculture   (Food and Agriculture Organisation of the UN).

FAO, via delle Terme di Caracalla, 00153 Roma, Italy; or from sales agents.

The report is being published in several volumes including:

Vol I   Census results by country.   (In 3 parts, $11.00 or £4.40 each part).
Vol II   Programme, concepts and scope.   ($8.00 or £3.30½).
Vol V   Analysis and international comparisons of census results.   ($5.00 or £2.40).

Time factor: the reports have been appearing from 1966 onwards.

§   En.

035   Indices of agricultural production for the Western Hemisphere excluding the United States and Cuba. (US Department of Agriculture, Economic Research Service).

Economic Research Service, Department of Agriculture, Washington, D.C. 20250, USA.

Time factor: includes data from 1961 through 1969 and preliminary data for 1970.   Published in April 1971.

§   En.

¶ **B,**   continued

036   Agricultural commodity projections, 1970-1980   (Food and Agriculture Organisation of the UN).
             FAO, via delle Terme di Caracalla, 00153 Roma, Italy; or from sales agents.
             Contents:
                 Vol I, part 1   General outlook
                         part 2   Projections by commodities
                 Vol II, part 1   General methodology
                         part 2   Statistical appendix
             Time factor: published in 1971.
             §   En, Fr & Es editions.

037   Grain crops: a review of production, trade, consumption and prices relating to wheat, wheat flour,
                 maize, barley, oats, rye and rice.   (Commonwealth Secretariat).
             Commonwealth Secretariat, Marlborough House, Pall Mall, London SW1Y 5HX.
             Vol 14, 1971.   £2.00.   203 pages.
             Time factor: the 1971 edition, published in 1971, covers various years to 1968 and 1969.
             §   En.

038   Fruit: a review of production and trade relating to fresh, canned, frozen and dried fruit, fruit
                 juices and wine   (Commonwealth Secretariat).
             Commonwealth Secretariat, Marlborough House, Pall Mall, London SW1Y 5HX.
             Vol 18, 1970.   £2.00.   358 pages.
             Time factor: the 1970 edition, published in 1970, has long runs of figures to 1967 and 1968.
             §   En.

039   Meat: a review of production, trade, consumption and prices relating to beef and veal, mutton
                 and lamb, poultry meat, offal, pig meat, and canned meat   (Commonwealth Secretariat).
             Commonwealth Secretariat, Marlborough House, Pall Mall, London SW1Y 5HX.
             Vol 18, 1969.   £1.50.   143 pages.
             Time factor: the 1969 edition, published in 1969, has data from 1962 to 1968, and is up-dated
                 by the monthly "Meat and dairy produce bulletin" (£12.00 yr).
             §   En.

040   Plantation crops: a review of production, trade, consumption and prices relating to coffee, cocoa,
                 tea, sugar, spices, tobacco and rubber   (Commonwealth Secretariat).
             Commonwealth Secretariat, Marlborough House, Pall Mall, London SW1Y 5HX.
             Vol 13, 1968.   £2.00.   298 pages.
             Time factor: published in 1970, and kept up-to-date by "Tropical Products Quarterly" and
                 "Tobacco Intelligence".
             §   En.

¶ B, continued

041   Vegetable oils and oilseeds: a review of production, trade, utilisation and prices relating to groundnuts, soya beans, sunflower seed, rape seed, copra, oil palm products, linseed, and other major oilseeds and oils.   (Commonwealth Secretariat).

Commonwealth Secretariat, Marlborough House, Pall Mall, London SW1Y 5HX.

Vol 20, 1971.   £2.00.   197 pages.

Time factor: contains data for the years 1962 to 1969 generally.

§   En.

042   Sugar yearbook   (International Sugar Council).

International Sugar Council, 28 Haymarket, London SW1.

1947- 1970.   £2.00.   371 pages.

Contains statistics of production, imports, exports, consumption, stocks, prices, etc of sugar.

Time factor: the 1970 edition, with data for several years to 1970, was published mid-1971.

§   En.

043   Statistical bulletin   (International Sugar Council).

International Sugar Council, 28 Haymarket, London SW1.

1947- (M).   £0.75; £7.50 yr.

Up-dates the information in the annual issue (see item 042 above).

§   En.

044   Annual coffee statistics   (Pan American Coffee Bureau).

Pan American Coffee Bureau, 1350 Avenue of the Americas, New York, NY 10019, USA.

1934- 1970.   not priced.   x, 106 + 96 pages.

The annual review of coffee statistics, including price movements, world production, world trade, as well as foreign exchange rates, barter and compensation agreements.   Information is also given for individual countries.

Time factor: the 1970 edition, with data for 1970 and earlier years, was published in 1971.

§   En.

045   Cocoa statistics   (Food and Agriculture Organisation of the UN).

FAO, via delle Terme di Caracalla, 00153 Roma, Italy; or from sales agents.

1958- (Q) with supplements (M).   £0.30 or £1.00 yr; $0.75 or $2.50 yr.

Includes data on production, imports and exports of beans, butter, powder, paste, chocolate and chocolate products; prices of beans; and stocks of beans.   Both producing countries and importing countries are names.

Time factor: the dates vary with each table.

§   En, Fr, Es.

¶ B, continued

046   Cocoa statistics   (Gill & Duffus Ltd).

Gill & Duffus Ltd, 23 St Dunstan's Hill, London EC3R 8HR.

(A) 1971.   not priced.   36 pages.

Contains statistics of production and grindings of raw cocoa, imports and exports, supply and demand, and market prices. There is also data for cocoa butter and cocoa powder.

Time factor: the 1971 edition, published mid-1971, has long runs of statistics to 1970.

§   En.

047   South America's tobacco industry   (US Department of Agriculture. Foreign Agricultural Service).

Foreign Agricultural Service, Room 5918 So., Department of Agriculture, Washington, D.C. 20250.

Not priced.   22 pages.

Includes a statistical appendix of production and foreign trade statistics with data for several years to 1970.

Time factor: published early 1972.

§   En.

048   The state of food and agriculture   (Food and Agriculture Organisation of the UN).

FAO, via delle Terme di Caracalla, 00153 Roma, Italy; or from sales agents.

1957- 1971. $10.00; £4.00.   236 pages.

Includes a world review and a regional review on production of agriculture, fisheries, forestry, foreign trade, prices, water pollution, policies and programmes.

Time factor: the 1971 edition, published late 1971, has data for a number of years up to 1969 and provisional 1970 figures.

§   En.

049   Yearbook of fishery statistics   (Food and Agriculture Organisation of the UN).

FAO, via delle Terme di Caracalla, 00153 Roma, Italy; or from sales agents.

1942- 1970.   £3.60 or $9.00 each volume.   2 vols.

One volume contains data on catches and landings, and the other on fishery commodities.

Time factor: the 1970 edition, published in 1972, has data for 1968, 1969 and 1970.

§   En, Fr, Es.

050   Statistical summary of the mineral industry: world production, exports and imports   (Natural Environment Research Council. Institute of Geological Sciences. Mineral Resources Division).

H M Stationery Office, P.O.Box 569, London SE1 9NH.

1913/20- 1964/69.   £1.50.   412 pages.

Contains data on quantities produced, imported and exported of the following minerals for all countries so far as the information is available: abrasives, aluminium, antimony, arsenic, asbestos, barium minerals, bentonite, beryl, bismuth, borates, bromine, cadmium, cement, china clay, chrome ore and chromium, coal, coke and by-products, cobalt, copper, diamonds, diatomaceous earth, feldspar, fluorspar, fuller's earth, gold, graphite, gypsum, iodine, iron and steel, lead, lithium minerals, magnesite & dolomite, manganese, mercury, mica, molybdenum, nickel, nitrogen compounds, petroleum & allied products, phosphates, platinum, potash minerals, pyrites, rare earth and thorium minerals, salt, selenium, sillimanite, silver, strontium minerals, sulphur, talc,

[continued next page

¶ B, continued

050, continued tantalum & niobium minerals, tungsten, uranium minerals, vanadium, vermiculite, zinc, zirconium minerals, other minerals and metals.

      Time factor: the 1964/69 edition, containing data for those years, was published in June 1971.

      §   En.

051   Minerals yearbook: vol IV – area reports: international   (US Bureau of Mines).

      Government Printing Office, Washington, D.C. 20402, USA.

      1969. $6.00.   c. 1000 pages.

      Contains detailed textual and statistical data on the mineral industry in each country of the world.

      Time factor: the 1969 edition was published early 1971 and contains data for several years to 1969.

      §   En.

052   BP statistical review of the world oil industry   (British Petroleum Co Ltd).

      British Petroleum Co Ltd, Britannic House, Moor Lane, London EC2Y 9BU.

      (A) 1971.   not priced.   24 pages.

      Contains data on reserves, production, consumption, trade, refining, tankers, and energy.

      Time factor: the 1971 edition, published early 1972, has data for 1971 and 1970.

      §   En.

053   Oil: world statistics   (Institute of Petroleum).

      Institute of Petroleum, 61 New Cavendish Street, London W1M 8AR.

      Contains statistics of production, refining capacity, consumption, tanker tonnage, etc of oil by countries.

      (A) 1971.   £0.05.   9 pages.

      Time factor: the 1971 edition, published in September 1971, has data for 1937, 1950, 1960, 1969 and provisional figures for 1970.

      §   En.

      Note: Others in this series, not mainly statistical, include "Oil: North America", "Oil: Latin America" and "Oil; the world's reserves".

054   Twentieth century petroleum statistics   (De Golyer and MacNaughton).

      De Golyer and MacNaughton, 5625 Daniels Avenue, Dallas, Texas 75206, USA.

      1945– 1971. $10.00.   98 charts (in book form).

      Contains statistics, graphs, etc, of crude oil production, gas production, crude oil reserves, refined products, capacity, demand, tanker ships, etc for all oil-producing and prospective oil-producing states of the US and 52 foreign countries.

      Time factor: the 1971 edition, published late 1971, has data for 1970 and long runs of figures in some cases.

      §   En.

055   Metal statistics   (Metallgesellschaft AG).

Metallgesellschaft AG, 6 Frankfurt/Main, Germany.

1913- 1960-70.   not priced.   viii, 316 pages.

A world survey of production and consumption of aluminium, lead, copper, zinc, tin, cadmium, nickel, mercury and silver. There are comparisons by continents, and detailed surveys of the situation in producing countries.

Time factor: the 1960-70 edition, covering those years, was published in 1971.

§   En. There is also a German edition.

Note: Similar publications in France and Italy are "Statistiques... cuivre, plomb, zinc, étain, antimoine, cadmium, cobalt, nickel, aluminium, magnesium, mercure, argent, or", issued annually by Minerais et Métaux SA, 61 avenue Hoche, 75 Paris 8, France; and "Metalli non ferrosi e ferroleghe: statistiche", issued by Ammi SpA, via Malise 11, Roma, Italy.

056   Metal bulletin handbook   (Metal Bulletin Ltd).

Metal Bulletin Ltd, 46 Wigmore Street, London W1H 0BJ.

1913- 1970.   £4.   1048 pages.

Contains data on production, consumption, deliveries, exports and prices of non-ferrous metals and of iron and steel.

Time factor: the 1970 edition, published late 1970, contains data for the period 1966 to 1969.

§   En.

057   World metal statistics   (World Bureau of Metal Statistics).

World Bureau of Metal Statistics, 6 Vicarage Road, Edgbaston, Birmingham B15 3EY
     or 6 Bathurst Street, Sussex Square, London W2 2SD.

1948- (M).   £22 yr; $62.00 yr.

Contains data on production, consumption, trade, stocks, etc of metals (aluminium, antimony, cadmium, copper, lead, nickel, tin, zinc).

§   En.

058   Metal statistics   (The American Metal Market).

The American Metal Market, 320 Campus Drive, Somerset, NJ 08873, USA.

1908- 1970. $7.50.   463 pages.

Includes statistical data on the production, consumption, stocks, prices, foreign trade, etc, for all metals in the United States of America and in the world.

Time factor: the 1970 edition, published in 1971, has data for several years to 1968.

§   En.

059   Yearbook of the American Bureau of Metal Statistics.

American Bureau of Metal Statistics, 50 Broadway, New York, NY 10004, USA.

1921- 1969. $6.   c. 150 pages.

Includes statistics of mine production, smelter production, consumption, imports and exports, etc, on a world-wide basis for copper, lead, zinc, nickel, aluminium, bauxite, gold, silver, tin, antimony, cadmium, cobalt, magnesium, molybdenum, platinum, etc.

Time factor: the 1969 edition, published June 1970, contains data for 1969 and earlier years.

§   En.

¶ B,   continued

060   Statistical handbook   (British Steel Corporation).

         British Steel Corporation, P.O.Box 403, 33 Grosvenor Place, London SW1X 7JG.

         1959- 1969.   2 loose-leaf vols.

         Contains a section for every iron and steel producing country, for each of which is given data on
             the production of the various types of iron and steel, imports and exports.

         Time factor: the 1969 edition, which commenced publication in 1969 (the loose-leaf pages are
             distributed as the information is received and printed) contains data for 1968 and some earlier years.

         §   En.

061   The iron and steel industry   (Organisation for Economic Co-operation and Development).

         OECD, 2 rue André-Pascal, 75 Paris 16; or from sales agents.

         1954- 1970.   £1.15; $3.25; Fr 15.   104 pages.

         Analyses developments with regard to demand and trade, production, prices and investment in the
             iron and steel industry in OECD countries, including Canada and USA.

         Time factor: the 1970 edition, published January 1972, contains final data for 1970 and trends
             for 1971.

         §   En.

062   Anuario estadístico de la siderurgia y minería del fierro de América Latina   [Statistical yearbook on
             the mining and manufacture or iron and steel]   (Instituto Latinoámericano del Fierro y del Acero
             [Latin American Institute for Iron and Steel]).

         Instituto Latinoámericano del Fierro y del Acero, Santiago de Chile.

         1967- 1970.   not priced.

         §   Es.

063   Statistical yearbook: tin, tinplate, canning   (International Tin Council).

         International Tin Council, 28 Haymarket, London SW1Y 4ST.

         1959- 1968.   £4.00.   281 pages.

         Contains data on production, exports, imports, stocks, consumption, trade in manufactures,
             and labour for each country.

         Time factor: published every other year, with supplements in intervening years; the 1968 edition
             contains data generally for the period 1964 to 1968 and was published in 1970.

         §   En.

064   Statistical bulletin   (International Tin Council).

         International Tin Council, 28 Haymarket, London SW1Y 4ST.

         1959- (M).   £0.50; £5.00 yr.

         Up-dates the yearbook (see item 063 above).

         §   En.

¶ B, continued

065 The non-ferrous metals industry (Organisation for Economic Co-operation and Development).

    OECD, 2 rue André-Pascal, 75 Paris 16; or from sales agents.

    1954- 1970. £0.90; $2.75; Fr 12. 82 pages.

    Contains four series of statistical tables dealing with production, consumption, trade and uses at the first processing stages of the principal non-ferrous metals, and end-uses of aluminium in OECD countries, including Canada and USA.

    Time factor: the 1970 edition, published Autumn 1971, contains data for 1970 and some earlier years.

    § En & Fr.

066 The cement industry (Organisation for Economic Co-operation and Development).

    OECD, 2 rue André-Pascal, 75 Paris 16; or from sales agents.

    1954- 1970. £0.62; $1.75; Fr 8. 40 pages.

    Contains data on production and labour force, production capacity, consumption and prices, international trade, and investment in OECD countries, including Canada and USA.

    Time factor: the 1970 edition, published Autumn 1971, has statistics for 1970 and trends for 1971.

    § En & Fr.

067 The chemical industry (Organisation for Economic Co-operation and Development).

    OECD, 2 rue André-Pascal, 75 Paris 16; or from sales agents.

    1953- 1969/70. £2.30; $8.00; Fr 36. 52 pages.

    Contains data on general trends in the industry, and on production, demand, raw materials, employment, prices, investments, foreign trade, and the outlook for the future. There are also country studies (including Canada and USA) and sector studies (devoted to particular types of chemicals).

    Time factor: the 1969/70 edition, published March 1971, has data for 1969 and trends for 1970.

    § En.

068 Annual fertiliser review (Food and Agriculture Organisation of the UN).

    FAO, via delle Terme di Caracalla, 00153 Roma, Italy; or from sales agents.

    1951/54- 1970. £2.00; $5.00. 196 pages.

    Contains data on world production, consumption, trade and prices of fertilisers.

    Time factor: the 1970 edition, with data for that year, was published in mid-1971.

    § En.

069 Fertiliser demand and supply projections to 1980 for South America, Mexico and Central America (United Nations Industrial Development Organisation (UNIDO), Vienna).

    Sales Section, United Nations, New York, NY 10017; or from sales agents.

    £0.65; $1.50. 80 pages.

    Time factor: published late 1971 as no. 6 in the 'Fertiliser industry series'.

    § En.

¶ B, continued

070   Pulp and paper industry in the OECD member countries   (Organisation for Economic Co-operation
          and Development).

       OECD, 2 rue André-Pascal, 75 Paris 16; or from sales agents.

       1954- 1970/71.   £1.37; $4.00; Fr 18.   182 pages.

       A statistical report on the situation in the pulp and paper markets of the OECD countries, including
          Canada and USA.

       Time factor: the 1970/71 edition, published late 1971, contains data for 1970-71 and trends for 1972.

       §   En & Fr.

071   Industrial fibres: a review of production, trade and consumption, relating to wool, cotton and man-
          made fibres, silk, flax, jute, sisal and other hemps, mohair and kapok   (Commonwealth
          Secretariat).

       Commonwealth Secretariat, Marlborough House, Pall Mall, London SW1Y 5HX.

       Vol 19, 1969.   £2.00.   254 pages.

       Includes details of production, consumption, stocks, trade and prices for the commodities mentioned
          in the title.

       Time factor: the 1969 edition, published mid-1970, has data for 1969 and several earlier years.

       §   En.

072   Textile industry in the OECD countries   (Organisation for Economic Co-operation and Development).

       OECD, 2 rue André-Pascal, 75 Paris 16; or from sales agents.

       1953- 1969/70.   £1.37; $4.00; Fr 18.   188 pages.

       Contains general trends in the textile industry of production, trade, consumption, competition,
          prices, manpower, orders, stocks, outlook, etc in OECD countries, including Canada and USA.

       Time factor: the 1969/70 edition, published mid-1971, contains data to 1969/70.

       §   En & Fr.

073   Textile organon.

       Textile Economics Bureau Inc, 10 East 40th Street, New York, NY 10016, USA.

       1930- (M). $0.50 or $5.00 yr (Jan 1958 and Jan 1962 issues $1.50 each).

       Contains world-wide information on man-made fibres and wool. The January 1958 and January 1962
          numbers are "basic book issues" which the monthly tables up-date.

       Time factor: each issue contains statistical data for about 10 years and monthly figures for 12 months
          up to one or two months prior to the date of the issue.

       §   En.

¶ B, continued

074   Cotton - world statistics: quarterly bulletin of the International Cotton Advisory Committee.

International Cotton Advisory Committee, South Agriculture Building, Washington, D.C. 20250, USA.

$4.50 yr to member countries; $20 yr to non-member countries.

Contains world tables and country tables on the supply, distribution, production, consumption, imports and exports, stocks and prices of cotton; also production, imports and exports of cotton yarn, cotton cloth and rayon cloth.

Time factor: the latest figures available for each country.

§   En.

Note: Also published by the International Cotton Advisory Committee and included in the subscription is "Cotton: monthly review of the world situation".

075   International cotton industry statistics   (International Federation of Cotton and Allied Textile Industries).

International Federation of Cotton and Allied Textile Industries, 29 am Schanzengraben, Postfach 289, CH-8039 Zürich, Switzerland.

(A) 1969.   not priced.   16 pages.

Contains statistical data on spinning (numbers of spindles, hours worked, consumption of raw materials) and weaving (number of looms, hours worked) sub-divided geographically.

Time factor: the 1969 edition, with data for 1969, was published mid-1971.

§   En.

076   Quarterly statistical review   (The Textile Statistics Bureau).

The Textile Statistics Bureau, 10 Blackfriars Street, Manchester M3 5DR.

1946-   £1.50; £5.00 yr.

Apart from detailed United Kingdom statistics, the review contains figures for world production of yarn and cloth, and world imports and exports.

Time factor: each issue includes long runs of figures to the latest available on each subject.

§   En.

077   Motor industry of Great Britain   (Society of Motor Manufacturers' and Traders).

SMMT, Forbes House, Halkin Street, London SW1X 7DS.

1947- 1971.   £5.00.   375 pages.

Contains detailed statistics of production of cars and commercial vehicles, tractors, etc in the United Kingdom and overseas, registrations or numbers of cars in use in the United Kingdom and overseas, and overseas trade of the United Kingdom and overseas countries.

Time factor: the 1971 edition, with data for 1970 and some earlier years, was published late 1971.

§   En.

¶ B, continued

078   World automotive market   (Automobile International, New York).

Johnson International Publishing Corporation, 386 Park Avenue South, New York, NY 10016, USA.

1966- 1971. $5.00.   44 pages.

Includes data on world production and trade of motor vehicles.

Time factor: the 1971 edition, published early 1971, has data for 1969 and 1970.

§   En.

079   World motor vehicle production and registration   (US Department of Commerce. Business & Defence Services Administration).

Superintendent of Documents, US Government Printing Office, Washington, D.C. 20402, USA.

(A) 1969/70. $0.10.   8 pages.

Time factor: the 1969/70 edition, with data for 1969 and 1970, was published in March 1971.

§   En.

080   World energy supplies   (United Nations Statistical Office).

Sales Section, United Nations, New York, NY 10017; or from sales agents.

1952- 1965-68. $2.00; £0.87$\frac{1}{2}$.   112 pages.

A study on energy supplies, which includes statistics on production, trade and consumption of solid fuels, petroleum and its products, gas and electricity (thermal, hydro and nuclear) for approximately 150 countries, with regional and global totals. Summary data for 1958-1968 is also included.

Time factor: the 1965-1968 edition, issued as Statistical Paper, Series J, no.13 in July 1970, has statistical data for 1965 to 1968.

§   En.

¶ C - External trade

081   Yearbook of international trade statistics   (United Nations Statistical Office).

Sales Section, United Nations, New York, NY 10017; or from sales agents.

1950- 1969.   £6.09; $12.75.   936 pages.

A general compilation of national tables showing annual figures, including value of merchandise imported and exported in national currency and US$; trade in gold; quantum and unit value indexes; currency conversion factors; trade in principal commodities; and trade by principal countries of provenance and destination.

Time factor: the 1969 edition, published late 1971, has data for 1969.

§   En.

B

¶ C, continued

082   Commodity trade statistics   (United Nations Statistical Office).

Sales Section, United Nations, New York, NY 10017; or from sales agents.

(Q).   £12.50 or $30.00 yr.

Issued in fascicules of about 250 pages each as quarterly data becomes available from the reporting countries. Each country's imports and exports are shown in the 625 sub-groups of the SITC, subdivided by countries of origin and destination. Values have been converted to US$ and quantities are in metric units. In front of each fascicule is an index showing in which issue appeared the latest data for each country. American reporting countries are Argentina, Barbados, Brazil, Canada, Chile, Costa Rica, Fr Guyane, Guadeloupe, Guatemala, Honduras, Martinique, Mexico, Netherlands Antilles, Nicaragua, El Salvador, Trinidad & Tobago, and USA.

Time factor: varies for each country. Data is cumulated January-March, January-June, January-September and January-December (data for January-March is not always published).

§   En.

083   World trade annual   (Walker & Co, by agreement with the UN Statistical Office).

Walker & Co, 720 Fifth Avenue, New York, NY 10019, USA.

1963- 1969.   5 vols at $30.00 each; 5 supplementary vols of which Vol II costs $69.00.

The main volumes contain statistics of foreign trade in each of 1,312 items of the SITC as reported by 24 principal countries, including the USA and Canada. The data are in commodity order, subdivided by countries of origin and destination. Vol I deals with food; beverages; crude materials, inedible, except fuels; mineral and vegetable oils and fats. Vol 2 deals with mineral fuels, lubricants and related materials, and chemicals. Vol 3 deals with manufactured goods classified chiefly by material. Vol 4 deals with miscellaneous manufactured articles. Vol 5 deals with machinery and transport equipment, and commodity transactions not classified according to kind.

Supplementary volume II (titled "World trade annual supplement: Trade of the industrialized nations with Eastern Europe and the developing nations, Vol II: South and Central America, including the Caribbean") carries statistics of imports and exports which are often more up-to-date than those of the individual countries concerned because they have been taken from the reports of the countries with which they trade as well as from their own reports. Countries included are Argentina, Bahamas, Barbados, Bermuda, Bolivia, Brazil, Chile, Colombia, Costa Rica, Cuba, Dominican Republic, Ecuador, French Guyana, Guatemala, Guyana, Haiti, Honduras, Jamaica, Martinique and Guadeloupe, Mexico, Netherlands Antilles, Nicaragua, Panama, Panama Canal Zone, Paraguay, Peru, El Salvador, Surinam, Trinidad & Tobago, Uruguay, Venezuela, the sterling area of the Caribbean as a whole, and the Latin American Free Trade Area (LAFTA).

Time factor: the 1969 edition, covering that year, was published in 1971.

§   En.

084   Handbook of international trade and development statistics   (UNCTAD).

Sales Section, United Nations, New York, NY 10017; or from sales agents.

1964- 1972. $8.00; £3.50.   xiv, 367 pages.

Provides a basic collection of statistical data on world trade and development, primarily for the use of delegates to the UN Conference on Trade and Development.

Time factor: the 1972 edition, normally has data from 1955 to 1969 with some 1970 figures, and was published in 1972.

§   En.

¶ C, continued

085   Estadística de comercio exterior de la ALALC   [Foreign trade of ALALC]   (Asociación Latinoamericana de Libre Comercio).

ALALC, Calle Cebollatí 1461, Montevideo, Uruguay.

1961/1967-   not priced.

The 1961/67 edition is kept up-to-date on a quarterly basis with separate annual sheets for each
member country's intrazonal trade with other members and the rest of the world.

§   Es.

086   Intercambio intrazonal ALALC   [Interzonal trade of ALALC countries]   (CENCI, Uruguay).

CENCI, Misiones 1361, Montevideo, Uruguay.

1962- 1967.   not priced.   287 pages.

Main tables show statistics of imports and exports arranged by commodity and subdivided by
ALALC countries.

Time factor: the 1967 edition, with data for 1967, was published in 1969. There is also a
supplement for 1968 published late 1970.

§   Es.

087   Trade yearbook   (Food and Agriculture Organisation of the UN).

FAO, via delle Terme di Caracalla, 00153 Roma, Italy; or from sales agents.

1947- 1970.   £2.80; $7.00.   612 pages.

Contains data on imports and exports of agricultural commodities and agricultural requisites, classified
by SITC, for each reporting country. Data is in US$ and metric quantities.

Time factor: the 1970 edition, published mid-1971, contains data for several years to 1969, and is
kept up-to-date by tables in item 033.

§   En, Fr.

088   World grain trade statistics: exports by source and destination   (Food and Agriculture Organisation
of the UN).

FAO, via delle Terme di Caracalla, 00153 Roma, Italy; or from sales agents.

(A) 1969/70.   £0.80.   80 pages.

Time factor: the 1969/70 edition, published in 1971, has data for 1969/70 and earlier figures from
1958 for some tables.

§   En, Fr, Es.

089   Statistics of world trade in steel   (United Nations Economic Commission for Europe).

Sales Section, United Nations, New York, NY 10017; or from sales agents.

1913/59- 1970.   £0.44; $1.00.   60 pages.

Contains data on the exports of the various semi-finished and finished steel products by regions and
countries of destination. Exporting countries include the USA and Canada.

Time factor: the 1970 edition, containing data for that year, was published late 1971.

§   En.

¶ C, continued

090   Bulletin of statistics on world trade in engineering products   (UN Economic Commission for Europe).

Sales Section, United Nations, New York, NY 10017; or from sales agents.

1964- 1969.   £1.31; $3.00.   284 pages.

Time factor: the 1969 edition, with data for 1969, was published early 1971.

§   En, Fr, Ru.

¶ D – Internal distribution

091   Preise, Löhne, Wirtschaftsrechnungen – Reihe 9: Preise im Ausland. I Grosshandelspreise
[Prices, wages and family budget surveys – Series 9: Prices in foreign countries. I Wholesale
prices]   (Statistisches Bundesamt).

W Kohlhammer GmbH, Postfach 1150, 65 Mainz, Germany.

(Q).   DM 3 or DM 10 yr.

Contains data on wholesale prices and price indices for most countries, arranged in three volumes for
each issue.   The first volume covers food and beverages; the second textiles, skins, leather,
rubber, mineral oils, building materials, plastics, wood, paper, resins and waxes; the third
coal, ores and minerals, iron and steel, non-ferrous metals, chemicals and fertilisers.

Time factor: each issue has data for the period of the issue and the current year to date, and also
averages for the last eight years.

§   De.

Note: this title is supplemented by a monthly "Weltmarktpreise ausgewählter Waren"   [World market
prices of selected goods]   DM 1 or DM 10 yr.

092   World record markets   (EMI Ltd).

EMI Ltd, 20 Manchester Square, London W1A IES.

2nd ed, 1971.   £2.50.   112 pages.

The following statistical information is given for each country of the world, so far as this information
has been collected: Total populations, and population by age groups; family units; area; per
capita income and average weekly income of households; record companies; pressing plants;
recording studios; record labels; distributors; retail outlets; record clubs; juke boxes; record
players; records (singles and albums); and tapes, etc.

Time factor: the data included is the latest available to the compilers and is usually for 1968 or 1969.

§   En.

¶ D, continued

093   The world's telephones   (American Telephone and Telegraph Company).

Overseas Administration, American Telephone and Telegraph Company, 32 Avenue of the Americas, New York, NY 10013, USA.

1912- 1971.   not priced.   26 pages.

Contains, for the principal cities of the world, the numbers of telephones in use, numbers in each city as a percentage of the number in the world, number in each city as a percentage of the population, and the number that are automatic.

Time factor: the 1971 edition, which has data as at January 1971, was published in December 1971.

§   En.

Refer also to 013, 014 and 020.

¶ E - Population

094   Demographic yearbook   (United Nations Statistical Office).

Sales Section, United Nations, New York, NY 10017; or from sales agents.

1948- 1970.   £9.24; $18.00.   840 pages.

Includes population figures for about 250 geographic areas of the world, including tables by age and sex, the population of capital cities and cities over 100,000 inhabitants, and totals from latest censuses.

Time factor: the 1970 edition, published early 1972, contains the latest information available for each country.

§   En, Fr.

095   Population and vital statistics report   (United Nations Statistical Office).

Sales Section, United Nations, New York, NY 10017; or from sales agents.

(Q).   £0.55 or £1.67 yr; $1.00 or $3.00 yr.

Contains data from the latest census returns and demographic statistics for all reporting countries.

§   En.

096   Demographic trends ... in Western Europe and North America   (Organisation for Economic Co-operation and Development).

OECD, 2 rue André-Pascal, 75 Paris 16; or from sales agents.

1951/71- 1965/80.   £0.75; $2.50; Fr 10.   116 pages.

Total and active population projections for 1965 to 1980, established by means of questionnaires. Contains a general report and analyses by country.

§   En, Fr.

¶ E, continued

097   Datos básicos de población en América Latina, 1970 [Basic data of the population of Latin
    America, 1970] (Organisation of American States).

    Organisation of American States, 17th Street and Constitution Avenue N W, Washington,
    D.C. 20006, USA.

    Time factor: published in 1971.

    § Es.

    Refer also to 013, 014, 017, 020, 021 and 022.

¶ F – Standard of living

098   Compendium of social statistics (United Nations Statistical Office).

    Sales Section, United Nations, New York, NY 10017; or from sales agents.

    1963- 1967. £3.83; $8.75. 662 pages.

    An international compendium presenting basic national statistical indicators required for describing
    the major aspects of the social situation in the world, as well as changes and trends in levels of
    living. It is organised into eight sections as follows: population and vital statistics, health
    conditions, food consumption and nutrition, housing, education and cultural activities, labour
    force and conditions of employment, income and expenditure, consumer prices.

    Time factor: published every four years, the 1967 edition contains data available at 1 November
    1966 and appeared in 1968.

    § En, Fr.

099   Income distribution in Latin America (United Nations Economic Commission for Latin America).

    Sales Section, United Nations, New York, NY 10017; or from sales agents.

    £1.05; $2.50. 148 pages.

    Has data on the general aspects of the income distribution structure; a comparison of Latin America
    with the Western industrial countries; variations within regions – Argentina, Venezuela, Mexico,
    Brazil and El Salvador; and more specific aspects of income distribution studies. Tables are
    included in the text.

    Time factor: published late 1971.

    § En.

100   Yearbook of labour statistics (International Labour Office).

    Bureau International du Travail, rue de Lausanne 154, CH-1211 Genève, Switzerland.

    1941- 1970. £5.12; $14.00. xxiii, 919 pages.

    Contains data on the active population, employment and unemployment, hours of work, labour,
    productivity, wages, consumer prices, industrial accidents, and industrial disputes. Indices of
    consumer prices include general indices, food indices, fuel and light indices, clothing indices,
    and rent indices.

    Time factor: the 1970 edition, published early in 1971, contains data for the ten years to 1970.

    § En, Fr.

¶   F,   continued

101   Bulletin of labour statistics   (International Labour Office).

Bureau International du Travail, rue de Lausanne 154, CH-1211 Genève, Switzerland.

(Q), with supplements (M).   £0.70 or £2.20 yr; $1.75 or $5.50 yr; Fr 7 or Fr 22 yr.

Includes data on general consumer price indices and food price indices.

Time factor: varies with each country.   Tables contain monthly, quarterly and half-yearly data
    for the last three years.

§   En, Fr.

102   Preise, Löhne, Wirtschaftsrechnungen - Reihe 9: Preise im Ausland. II Einzelhandelspreise
    [Prices, wages and family budget surveys - Series 9. Prices in foreign countries. II Retail prices]
    (Statistisches Bundesamt).

W Kohlhammer GmbH, Postfach 1150, 65 Mainz, Germany.

(Q).   DM 4 or DM 14 yr.

Contains data on retail prices and price indices for most countries.

§   De.

103   Preise, Löhne, Wirtschaftsrechnungen - Reihe 10: Internationaler Vergleich der Preise für die
    Lebenshaltung   [Prices, wages and family budget surveys - Series 10: International comparison
    of consumer prices]   (Statistisches Bundesamt).

W Kohlhammer GmbH, Postfach 1150, 65 Mainz, Germany.

Monthly: DM 1 or DM 10 yr; annual issues: DM 7.

Compares the cost of living in about 50 countries, including Bolivia, Brazil, Canada, Chile,
    Colombia, Costa Rica, Dominican Republic, Guatemala, Mexico, Panama, Paraguay, Peru,
    USA, Uruguay and Venezuela.

Time: latest figures published are often those for the month of issue, depending on the subject of
    the tables, and four earlier months' figures are also included.

§   De.

Refer also to 013, 014, 017, 020, 021 and 022.

Antigua, onr of the Leeward Islands, now has self-government in association with Britain, which retains powers and responsibilities for defence and external affairs. There is no central statistical office, but enquiries about statistical data could be made to the Minister of Trade, Production and Labour at St John's, or to the Antigua Chamber of Commerce, St Mary's Street, St John's.

Statistical publications

¶   A - General

104   Antigua: report for the year ...   (Foreign and Commonwealth Office).
            H M S O, P.O.Box 569, London SE1 9NH.
            1955/56- 1963/64.   £0.32$\frac{1}{2}$.   61 pages.
            Mainly textual, but includes some statistics of population, employment, commerce, tourism,
                production, etc.
            Time factor: published 1966.
            §   En.

¶   B - Production

            Refer to item 104.

¶   C - External trade

105   Annual trade report   (Ministry of Trade and Production).
            Ministry of Trade and Production, St John's, Antigua.
            1958- 1967.   not priced.   134 pages.
            Main tables show imports and exports arranged by commodity subdivided by countries of origin and
                destination.
            Time factor: the 1967 edition, with data for 1967, was issued in 1968.
            §   En.

¶   D - Internal distribution

            Refer to item 104

¶ E – Population

106   West Indies population census, 1960   (Department of Statistics, Jamaica).
Department of Statistics, 23½ Charles Street, Kingston, Jamaica.
Includes data on the population of Antigua.
§   En.

Refer also to 104.

Central statistical office

107   Instituto Nacional de Estadística y Censos   [National Institute of Statistics and Censuses],
           Hipólita Yrigoyen 250, piso 12, Buenos Aires.
           t   27 7556.

        The Instituto Nacional de Estadística y Censos is responsible for the collection, analysis and
publication of official economic statistics of Argentina.
        Unpublished statistical information can be provided if available, and a fee is charged based on
the amount of work to be done.   A photocopying service is also available.

        Publications other than those described in the following pages include:
                Edificación   [Building]   (Q & A).
                Costo de la construcción   [Cost of construction]   (M)
                Navigación comercial Argentina   [Commercial shipping of Argentina]   (A)
                Hechos demograficos   [Demographic data]   (5 yearly).
                Estadística telefónica, 1960-1969   [Telephone statistics, 1960-1969]
                Transporte automotor de pasajeros   [Passenger road transport]
                Aeronavegación comercial Argentina, 1960-1969   [Commercial aviation of Argentina,
                    1960-1969].

Libraries

        The Instituto Nacional de Estadística y Censos, referred to above, has a library which is open to
the public for reference to statistical publications.   Banco Central de la República Argentina, Reconquista
266, Buenos Aires (t   40-0181) also has a library containing statistical publications.

Libraries and information services abroad

        Argentine Embassies abroad receive copies of statistical publications for reference, including:
        United Kingdom   Argentine Embassy, 111 Cadogan Gardens, London SW3 2RQ.   t   01-730 4388.
        USA   Argentine Embassy, 1600 North H Avenue N W, Washington, D.C.
                                  t   DE2 7100.
        Canada   Argentine Embassy, 211 Stewart Street, Ottawa.   t   236-2351.

Bibliographies

108   The Instituto Nacional de Estadística y Censos issues a 'Lista de publicaciones', the latest issue of
           which was published in 1970, and is kept up-to-date by supplements.

Statistical publications

¶   A - General

109   Boletin de estadística   [Statistical bulletin]   (Dirección General de Estadística y Censos).
           Instituto Nacional de Estadístico y Censos, Hipólita Yrigoyen 250, piso 12, Buenos Aires.
           1956-   (Q). $10.00 (US$3.50); $40.00 (US$14.00) yr.
           Includes data on demography, foreign trade, wages, cost of living and price indices,
                agriculture and livestock, fishing industry, transport and communications, business,
                industry, and finance.
           Time factor: each issue has data for the period of the issue, cumulated figures for the year
                to date, and some earlier years, and is published about three months later.
           §   Es.

110   Boletin estadístico   [Statistical bulletin]   (Banco Central de la República Argentina).
           Banco Central de la República Argentina, Reconquista 266, Buenos Aires.
           1937-   (M).   not priced.
           Includes mainly banking and financial statistics, but also data on the gross national product and
                income.   There are also occasional supplements on various subjects.
           §   Es.

111   Informe economico   [Economic report]   (Ministerio de Economía y Trabajo).
           Ministerio de Economía y Trabajo, Buenos Aires.
           1968-   (Q).   not priced.
           Includes a statistical appendix containing data on world supply and demand; prices, costs and
                indicators of income; balance of payments; public finance; money and credit.
           §   Es.

112   Business conditions in Argentina   (Ernesto Tornquist & Cia Ltda).
           Ernesto Tornquist & Cia Ltda, Bartolome Mitre 559, Buenos Aires.
           1884-   (Q).   not priced.
           Contains data on Argentine economic conditions and a few statistics, including banking, building,
                agricultural products, hides and meat, cost of living indices, foreign affairs and foreign trade,
                domestic affairs and finance, shipping, stock exchange, transport and communications.
           §   En & Es editions.

113   Review of the River Plate (incorporating the Times of Argentina).
           Review of the River Plate, Casilla de Correo 18 (suc. 25-B), Austria 1828, Buenos Aires.
           1892- 3 per month. $3.00 (abroad $3.50); $99.00 (abroad $114.00) yr.
           A journal dealing with Argentine financial, economic, agricultural and shipping affairs,
                including some statistical data.
           §   En.

¶ A, continued

114   Plan nacional de desarrollo, 1970-1974 [National development plan]   (Secretaría del Consejo Nacional de Desarrollo).

Secretaría del Consejo Nacional de Desarrollo, Buenos Aires.

Not priced.   7 vols.

The seven volumes are devoted to a global analysis, a plan for public national investment, the agricultural sector, the industrial sector, the foreign sector, the economic infrastructure, and the social infrastructure.

Time factor: published in 1970.

§   Es.

¶ B - Production

115   Censo nacional económico: industria manufacturera [National economic census: manufacturing industry]   (Instituto Nacional de Estadística y Censos).

Instituto Nacional de Estadística y Censos, Hipólita Yrigoyen 250, piso 12, Buenos Aires.

1963- 1963. $3.50 (US$2.00) or $5.00 (US$3.50) each volume.

The volumes containing the final results are:
     General results
       Part 1 - Federal Capital
       Part 2 - Gran Buenos Aires
       Part 3 - Tierra del Fuego
       Part 4 - Regional totals
     Primary materials used and products improved.

§   Es.

116   Estadística industrial [Industrial statistics]   (Instituto Nacional de Estadística y Censos).

Instituto Nacional de Estadística y Censos, Hipólita Yrigoyen 250, piso 12, Buenos Aires.

1937- 2 per annum.   1965/1969. $2.00 (US$1.00).   1st half 1970. $2.50 (US$1.50).

Contains data on production, employment, hours of work, wages, etc.

Time factor: the 1965/1969 edition, with data for those years, was published in 1970. It is up-dated by half-yearly issues, with monthly figures, the issue covering the year 1970 being published late 1971.

§   Es.

117   Censo nacional económico: minería, construcción, electricidad y gas [National economic census: mining, construction, electricity and gas]   (Instituto Nacional de Estadística y Censos).

Instituto Nacional de Estadística y Censos, Hipólita Yrigoyen 250, piso 12, Buenos Aires.

1963- 1963. $3.50 (US$2.00).

§   Es.

¶   B,   continued

118   Estadística minera de la República Argentina, producción – exportación – importación
        [Mineral statistics of Argentina, production – exports – imports]   (Dirección Nacional de
        Promoción Minera   [National Institute of Geology and Mining]).

        Dirección Nacional de Promoción Minera, Buenos Aires.

        1960/65– 1969.   not priced.   xvii, 255 pages.

        Contains figures on production, exports and imports of minerals, and other supplementary details
            of the mining industry.   Data is given for the country as a whole and for the provinces, and
            includes types of exploitation, power installed, personnel employed, transport of materials,
            (Minerals includes minerals, petroleum, natural gas and natural gasoline).

        Time factor: the 1969 edition, published in 1971, has data for 1969.

        §   Es.

119   Censo nacional de agropecuario   [National census of agriculture & stockbreeding]   (Instituto
            Nacional de Estadística y Censos).

        Instituto Nacional de Estadística y Censos, Hipólita Yrigoyen 250, piso 12, Buenos Aires.

        1960– 1960.   3 vols.

        The definitive results were published in three volumes, and there are also 21 volumes each
            dealing with a province or large town.

        §   Es.

        Note: A later census was taken in 1969 and the provisional results are now available (free) with
            comparative figures for 1969 and 1960.

        Refer also to 109.

¶   C – External trade

120   Comercio exterior argentino   [Argentine foreign trade]   (Instituto Nacional de Estadística y Censos).

        Instituto Nacional de Estadística y Censos, Hipólita Yrigoyen 250, piso 12, Buenos Aires.

        1887– 1969. $35.00 (US$15.00).   3 vols.

        Contents:
            Vol I   General summary
            Vol II   Exports, arranged by commodity and subdivided by countries of origin and destination,
                        and arranged by country subdivided by commodities.
            Vol III   Imports, arranged by commodity subdivided by countries of origin and destination, and
                        arranged by country subdivided by commodities.

        Time factor: the 1969 edition, with data for 1969, was published early 1971.

        §   Es.

¶   C,   continued

121   Comercio exterior   [Foreign trade]   (Instituto Nacional de Estadística y Censos).

Instituto Nacional de Estadística y Censos, Hipólita Yrigoyen 250, piso 12, Buenos Aires.

1915-   (Q). $3.50 (US$2.50); $14.00 (US$10.00) yr.

Main tables show imports and exports arranged by commodity.

Time factor: each issue covers the period of the issue and cumulated figures for the year to date, together with some earlier figures, and is published about six months later,

§   Es.

122   A.L.A.L.C.: intercambio comercial argentino con los países de la Asociación Latinoamericana de Libre Comercio   [ALALC: foreign trade of Argentina with the countries of the Latin American Free Trade Association]   (Instituto Nacional de Estadística y Censos).

Instituto Nacional de Estadística y Censos, Hipólita Yrigoyen 250, piso 12, Buenos Aires.

1962-   (Q). $3.00 (US$1.50); $12.00 (US$6.00) yr.

Contains brief foreign trade statistics arranged by commodity and subdivided by countries of origin and destination.

§   Es.

Refer also to 082, 083 and 109.

¶   D - Internal distribution

123   Censo nacional economico: comercio y prestación de servicios   [National economic census: distribution and service trades]   (Instituto Nacional de Estadística y Censos).

Instituto Nacional de Estadística y Censos, Hipólita Yrigoyen 250, piso 12, Buenos Aires.

1963- 1963. $3.50 (US$2.00) or $5.00 (US$3.50) per volume.

The volumes containing the final results are:
     General results
          Volumes for the Federal Capital, Gran Buenos Aires, and each province (8 volumes).

§   Es.

124   Comercio interior   [Internal trade]   (Instituto Nacional de Estadística y Censos).

Instituto Nacional de Estadística y Censos, Hipólita Yrigoyen 250, piso 12, Buenos Aires.

1963-   (Q). $2.00 (US$1.00) per issue.

Contains tables showing index numbers of cost of living, wholesale and retail prices.

§   Es.

Refer also to 109.

¶ E – Population

125   Censo nacional de población [National census of population]   (Instituto Nacional de Estadística
        y Censos).

        Instituto Nacional de Estadística y Censos, Hipólita Yrigoyen 250, piso 12, Buenos Aires.

        1960.   9 vols. $10.00 each volume

        Contents:

Vol I	General Results	Vol VI	Chaqueña
Vol II	Gran Buenos Aires	Vol VII	Noroeste
Vol III	Pampeana	Vol VIII	Cuyana
Vol IV	Central	Vol IX	Patagónica
Vol V	Mesopotámica		

        §   Es.

        Note: a census of population, families and housing was taken in 1970 and the provisional results
        have been published ($5.00).

126   Proyección quinquenal de la población, 1965–2000 [Five-yearly projection of the population,
        1965–2000]   (Instituto Nacional de Estadística y Censos).

        Instituto Nacional de Estadística y Censos, Hipólita Yrigoyen 250, piso 12, Buenos Aires.

        Not priced.   93 pages.

        §   Es.

        Refer also to 109.

¶ F – Standard of living

127   Costo de vida [Cost of living]   (Instituto Nacional de Estadística y Censos).

        Instituto Nacional de Estadística y Censos, Hipólita Yrigoyen 250, piso 12, Buenos Aires.

        1963–   (M). $3.00 (US$1.25); $36.00 (US$15.00) yr.

        Contains the cost of living index in the Federal Capital and in the country generally, retail
        prices of articles and services included in the compilation of the cost of living index, and
        wages in various industries.

        §   Es.

        Refer also to 109, 111 and 112.

Central statistical office

128   Department of Statistics,
Cabinet Office, P.O.Box 3904, Nassau.
t   22847-9.

The Department collects statistical information, directly or through other government departments, analyses and publishes it.
Unpublished statistical information may be supplied on request, and usually there is no fee.

Publications other than those described in the following pages include:
    Shipping and aviation statistics report. (A).

Libraries

The Department of Statistics has a library but it is not open to the public, and there are no other libraries in the Bahamas where statistical publications may be consulted.

Libraries and information services overseas

Publications of the Department of Statistics are available for consultation in the Bahamas Commissioner's Office, 39 Pall Mall, London SWI.

Statistical publications

¶   A - General

129   Commonwealth of the Bahamas statistical abstract   (Department of Statistics).

Department of Statistics, Cabinet Office, P.O.Box 3904, Nassau.

1969- 1969.   B$7.50.   xiv, 140 pages.

Main sections:

Geography & climate	Post Office
Demography	Health, prisons, court cases
Tourism & migration	Education
External trade	Motor vehicles & drivers' licences
Building & construction	Agriculture, forestry & fisheries
Public utilities	Banking, finance & insurance
Traffic	Labour
Aviation and shipping	Retail price index

Time factor: the 1969 edition, published early 1971, has data for the years 1959 to 1969.

§   En.

¶ A, continued

130   Development plan of New Providence Island and the city of Nassau   (Institute of Urban Environment
            and the Division of Urban Planning of the School of Architecture of Columbia University, for the
            Government of the Bahamas Islands).

        Cabinet Office, P.O.Box 3904, Nassau
                or   H M S O, P.O.Box 569, London SE1 9NH.

        £12.50   348 pages.

        Time factor: published late 1971.

        §   En.

131   Basic data on the economy   (US Department of Commerce, Bureau of International Commerce).

        US Department of Commerce, Sales and Distribution Branch, Washington, D.C. 20230, USA.

        US$0.15.   8 pages.

        Issued as 71-032 in the series "Overseas business reports", this report presents selected basic data
            useful in the analysis of the Bahamas as a market for US exports.   Data include statistics of
            population, structure of the economy, agriculture, manufacturing, construction, power, etc.

        Time factor: published in January 1971, the report contains data for several years to 1969.

        §   En.

132   Commonwealth of the Bahamas statistical summary   (Department of Statistics).

        Department of Statistics, Cabinet Office, P.O.Box 3904, Nassau.

        1971-   (Q).   B$2.00 per copy.

        Includes statistical tables on meteorology, population and vital statistics, tourism, external trade,
            building and construction, public utilities, traffic, aviation, health, agriculture, forestry,
            fishing, finance, labour and prices.

        §   En.

¶ B - Production

133   Company statistics report   (Department of Statistics).

        Department of Statistics, Cabinet Office, P.O.Box 3904, Nassau.

        1970- 1970.   B$2.00.   v, 27 pages.

        Contains data on the number of registered companies, their authorised capital classified by economic
            activity, subdivided by town or geographical area.

        Time factor: the data in the 1970 edition is for 31.12.70, published mid-1971.

        §   En.

        Refer also to 129 and 132.

¶   C - External trade

134   External trade statistics report   (Department of Statistics).

Department of Statistics, Cabinet Office, P.O.Box 3904, Nassau.

1918- 1970.   not priced.   233 pages.

Main tables show statistics of imports and exports arranged by commodity and sub-divided by
    countries of origin and destination, and by countries of origin and destination sub-divided by
    commodities.

Time factor: the 1970 edition, published Autumn 1971, has data for 1970.

§   En.

135   External trade statistics report   (Department of Statistics).

Department of Statistics, Cabinet Office, P.O.Box 3904, Nassau.

(Q).   not priced.

Main tables show imports and exports arranged by commodity and subdivided by countries of
    origin or destination.

Time factor: each issue has data for the quarter of the issue and cumulated totals for the year
    to date, being published about 3 months after the end of the period covered.

§   En.

Refer also to 129 and 132

¶   E - Population

Refer to 129 and 132

¶   F - Standard of living

136   Index of retail prices ...   (Ministry of Finance).

Ministry of Finance, Nassau.

(Q).   not priced.

§   En.

Refer also to 129 and 132

BARBADOS - BARBADE

Central statistical office

137   Statistical Service,
The Garrison, St Michael, Barbados.
t   77841.

The Statistical Service is responsible for the collection, analysis and publication of statistics for Barbados.

Publications other than those described in the following pages include:

        Census of tourism   (A).
        Financial statistics   (A).
        Selected monthly indicators.

Statistical publications

¶   A - General

138   Quarterly digest of statistics   (Statistical Service).

Statistical Service, The Garrison, St Michael.

1956-.   EC $0.25 per copy.

Supplements the 'Abstract of statistics', the latest edition of which is no.5, 1965.
    Main sections:

Population	Banking
Vital statistics	Currency
Migration	Visible trade
Social conditions	Distribution of trade (i.e., foreign trade)
Manufacturing	Retail prices
Building	Transport
Service industries (electricity & gas)	Tourism
	Selected remittances from abroad

Time factor: each issue has annual data for five or six years and quarterly data for three years to the date of the issue, and is published about six months later.

§   En.

139   Barbados economic surveys   (Economic Planning Unit).

Economic Planning Unit, Office of the Prime Minister, Bridgetown.

1962- 1969.   not priced.   75 pages.

Included in the text are statistical tables on foreign trade, population and migration, gross domestic product, industry, agriculture and fisheries, tourism, construction, public utilities, external communications, banking and finance, public finance, and the index of retail prices.

Time factor: the 1969 edition, published late 1969, refers to 1968 and earlier years.

§   En.

¶ B – Production

Refer to 138 and 139.

¶ C – External trade

140   Overseas trade

Statistical Service, The Garrison, St Michael.

1896– 1969.   EC $3.00.   ix, 398 pages.

Main tables show detailed imports and exports arranged by commodity and subdivided by countries of origin and destination.

Time factor: the 1969 issue, with data for 1969, was issued early 1971.

§   En.

141   Quarterly overseas trade report   (Statistical Service).

Statistical Service, The Garrison, St Michael.

1957–.   EC 25¢ per copy.

Up-dates the information given in the annual volume (see above).

Time factor: each issue contains data for the period of the issue, and is published about six-nine months later.

§   En.

Note: The Statistical Service also issues 'Statement of imports and exports by countries of origin and destination', a quarterly 2-page leaflet which appears in advance of the more detailed report.

Refer also to 082, 083, 138 and 139.

¶ E – Population

142   Population census   (Central Statistical Office, Port of Spain).

Government Printer, 2 Victoria Avenue, Port of Spain, Trinidad.

1960.   TT $1.50 each vol.

The census covered the whole of the Eastern Caribbean within the British Commonwealth. Vol I Part A is a description of the census and methods used; Vol I Part C contains a comprehensive description of each enumerative district of Barbados; Vol II contains summary tables including Barbados; Vol III contains the major tabulations of the whole census with less geographical detail.

§   En.

Refer also to 138 and 139.

¶   F – Standard of living

Refer to 138 and 139.

There is no central statistical office in Bermuda, but enquiries about statistical data could be made to the Department of Tourism and Trade Development of the Bermudan Government, or to the Bermuda Chamber of Commerce, both at Hamilton.

Statistical publications

¶   A - General

143   Bermuda: report for the year   (Foreign and Commonwealth Office).

H M S O, P.O.Box 569, London SE1 9NH.

1970.   £1.05.   92 pages.

Includes an appendix of statistical tables on population, employment, commerce, tourism, etc.

Time factor: the 1970 edition was published in January 1972.

§   En.

144   Basic data on the economy   (US Department of Commerce, Bureau of International Commerce).

US Department of Commerce, Sales and Distribution Branch, Washington, D.C. 20230, USA.

$0.15.   8 pages.

Issued as 68-95 in the series "Overseas business reports", this report presents selected basic data useful in the analysis of Bermuda as a market for US exports.   Data include statistics of population, structure of the economy, agriculture, manufacturing, construction, power, etc.

Time factor: published in November 1968, the report contains data for several years to 1967.

§   En.

¶   C - External trade

145   Report of the Customs imports and exports   (Customs).

H M Customs, Hamilton.

1952- 1970/71.   not priced.   125 pages.

Main tables show imports and exports arranged by commodity and subdivided by countries of origin and destination.

§   En.

Note: A 2-page 'Monthly import analysis' and a 'Quarterly exports return', both showing trade by country only, are also available from H M Customs.

¶ E – Population

146   Census of Bermuda   (Bermuda Government).

Bermuda Government, Hamilton.

1960.   not priced.   136 pages.

Combines the report of the census and the statistical tables relating to the population.

Time factor: published in 1961.

§   En.

Refer also to 143.

Central statistical office

147   Instituto Nacional de Estadística   [National Institute of Statistics],
Ministerio de Finanzas [Ministry of Finance], Pliegos Oficiales, La Paz.

        The Instituto Nacional de Estadística, formerly known as "Dirección General de Estadística y Censos" is responsible for the collection, analysis and publication of official economic statistics for Bolivia.
        Publications other than those described in the following pages include:
            Anuario demográfico   [Demographic annual].
            Balanza comercial de Bolivia: comercio exterior   [Balance of payments of Bolivia: foreign trade]   (A).
            Censo demográfico, 1950   [Demographic census, 1950].
            Censo agropecuario, 1950   [Census of agriculture and stockbreeding].

Statistical publications

¶   A - General

148   Estadísticas económicas de Bolivia   [Economic statistics of Bolivia]   (División Económica y Oficina de Programación, US Agencia International de Desarrollo (USAID)).

US Agencia International de Desarrollo (USAID), La Paz.

(A) 1970.   not priced.

Contains data on demographic and social indicators, national income, production, energy, transport, foreign trade, balance of payments, money, credit, banking, public finance, aid, etc.

Time factor: the 1970 edition, published in 1970, has data for 10 years.

§   Es.

149   Boletín estadístico   [Statistical bulletin]   (Instituto Nacional de Estadística).

Instituto Nacional de Estadística, Ministerio de Finanzas, Pliegos Oficiales, La Paz.

1901- (Q).   not priced.

Contains data on population, production, consumption, foreign trade, etc.

§   Es.

150   Memoria anual   [Annual report]   (Banco Central de Bolivia).

Banco Central de Bolivia, La Paz.

1929- 1970. not priced.   157 + 52 pages.

The report is concerned with the main economic and banking events of the previous year, as well as having a statistical appendix with data on balance of payments, currency movements, basic economic statistics, etc.

§   Es.

¶   A,   continued

151   Boletín estadístico   [Statistical bulletin]   (Banco Central de Bolivia).

Banco Central de Bolivia, La Paz.   .

1922-   (Q).   not priced.

Contains data on banking and finance, and also statistics of exports of minerals and oil,
       consumer price index, etc.

§   Es.

152   Suplemento estadístico   [Statistical supplement]   (Banco Central de Bolivia).

Banco Central de Bolivia, La Paz.

1943-   every two months.   not priced.

A statistical summary of vital statistics, money in circulation, gold reserves, activities of
       various Bolivian banks, mineral exports, world production and consumption of tin,
       foreign exchange activities in Bolivia, petroleum statistics, industrial production, etc.

§   Es.

153   Basic data on the economy   (US Department of Commerce, Bureau of International Commerce).

US Department of Commerce, Sales and Distribution Branch, Washington, D.C. 20230, USA.

US$0.15.   8 pages.

Issued as 69-36 in the series "Overseas business reports", this report presents selected data
       useful in the analysis of Bolivia as a market for US exports.   Data include statistics of
       population, structure of the economy, agriculture, manufacturing, construction, power, etc.

Time factor: published in July 1969, the report contains data for several years to 1968.

§   En.

¶   B – Production

154   Revista minera BaMin   [Mineral review of BaMin (Banco Minero de Bolivia)].

Banco Minero de Bolivia, Calle Comercio no.1290, Casilla Correo 1410, La Paz.

1965-   (M).   not priced.

Mainly text, but includes some statistics on mining, refining, exports, etc of minerals.

§   Es.

Refer also to 148, 149, 152 and 153 for production generally.

¶ C – External trade

155   Anuario de comercio exterior   [Yearbook of foreign trade]   (Instituto Nacional de Estadística).
         Instituto Nacional de Estadística, Ministerio de Finanzas, Pliegos Oficiales, La Paz.
         1912– 1968.   not priced.   2 vols.
         Volume I contains data on imports and volume II on exports.   Both have main tables which show
            statistics of imports and exports arranged by commodity subdivided by countries of origin and
            destination.
         Time factor: the 1968 edition, with data for 1968, was published in 1971.
         §   Es.

         Refer also to 148, 149, 151 and 152.

¶ E – Population

         Refer to 149 and 152.

¶ F – Standard of living

         Refer to 151.

Central statistical office

156 Instituto Brasiliero de Geografía e Estatística   [Brazilian Institute of Geography and Statistics],
Av. Franklin Roosevelt 166, Rio de Janeiro.
t   242 5770.

The institute is responsible for the organisation of the national plan for basic statistics, statistics
essential for socio-economic planning.   A subordinate organisation, CENDIE (Centro de Documentação
e Informações Estatística) is responsible for disseminating statistical information and for providing
statistical information services.

Publications other than those described in the following pages include:
Movimento bancário do Brasil, segundo as praças   [Banking movement, by trading centres] (A).
Veiculos licenciados   [Licensed vehicles]   (A) .
Indústria da construção   [Construction industry]   (M & A).
Inquérito nacional de preços   [National survey of prices]   (M).
Revista Brasiliera de estatística   [Brazilian review of statistics]   (Q) .

Another important organisation publishing statistics

157 Centro de Informações Econômico-Fiscal   [Centre for Economic and Financial Information],
Ministério da Fazenda, Avenida Presidente Antonío Carlos, 375-90 andar, Rio de Janeiro.
t   252 3605.

The Centre is responsible for the collection, analysis and publication of statistics of foreign trade.

Libraries

The Biblioteca Waldemar Lopes, an integral part of the Institute Brasileiro de Geografía e
Estatística, is a library of about 120,000 volumes of theoretical and applied statistics, including the
publications of the institute and foreign statistical compilations.   It is open to the public, and has
photocopying facilities.   There are also libraries in each of the branches of the institute throughout
Brazil.

Libraries and information services abroad

Brazilian embassies abroad have copies of Brazil's statistical publications for reference, including:
United Kingdom   Brazilian Embassy, Brazilian Trade Centre, 15 Berkeley Street,
London W1.   t   01-499 6706.
USA   Brazilian Embassy, 3007 Whitehaven N W, Washington, D.C.
t   CO5-9880.
Canada   Brazilian Embassy, 450 Wilbrod Street, Ottawa.   t   237-1090.
Australia   Brazilian Embassy, 55 Mucca Way, Red Hill, Canberra.   t   9 2680.

Bibliographies

158   Catálogo de periódicos e publicações seriadas da Biblioteca Waldemar Lopes   [Catalogue of periodicals and serial publications in the Waldemar Lopes Library]   (Fundação IBGE – Instituto Brasileiro de Estatística).

Volume I of the preliminary issue was published in 1971, and contains a list of holdings of serials (including annuals) of Brazilian publications in the library.

159   Boletim trimestral da Biblioteca Waldemar Lopes   [Quarterly bulletin of the Waldemar Lopes Library] (Fundação IBGE – Instituto Brasileiro de Estatística).

The accessions list of the library, which to some extent up-dates the catalogue referred to above for Brazilian periodicals and serial publications.

160   A list of publications (sales list) of the Instituto Brasileiro de Estatística is published at irregular intervals in English and with prices in US dollars.

Statistical publications

¶   A – General

161   Anuário estatístico do Brasil   [Statistical yearbook of Brazil]   (Instituto Brasileiro de Estatística).

Instituto Brasileiro de Estatística, Fundação IBGE, Avenida Franklin Roosevelt 166, Rio de Janeiro.

1908- 1970.   US$ 10.00.   771 pages.

Main sections:
        Geographical situation
        Demography
        Economy (forestry, hunting, fishing, farming, industry, commerce, insurance, services, transport, communications, money and finance, companies, consumption, national accounts)
        Social situation (housing, public services, employment, health, social assistance and security, associations and co-operatives, religion)
        Culture (including education)
        Administrative and political affairs (including public finance and justice).

Time factor: the 1970 edition, published in 1971, has data mainly for 1968, sometimes 1969, and also earlier figures in some tables.

§   Pt.

Note: Statistical yearbooks are currently issued by the local statistical offices for Acre, Amapá, Espérito Santo, Rio de Janeiro, Rio Grande do Sul, São Paulo, Manáus and São Luís.

¶ A, continued

162 Sinopse estatística do Brasil [Statistical summary for Brazil]   (Instituto Brasileiro de
    Estatística).

    Instituto Brasileiro de Estatística, Fundação IBGE, Avenida Franklin Roosevelt 166, Rio de Janeiro.
    1968- 1971. US$8.00. 436 pages.

    Main sections:

Geography	Communications
Population	Money & finance
Demography	Price indices
Forestry	Consumption
Hunting	National accounts
Fishing	Housing
Agriculture	Employment
Industry	Health
Commerce	Education
Transport	Public finance

    Time factor: the 1971 edition has data for several years to 1969 or 1970.

    § Pt & En.

163 Brasil - séries estatísticas retrospectívas [Brazil - retrospective statistics] (Instituto Brasileiro de
    Estatística).

    Instituto Brasileiro de Estatística, Fundação IBGE, Avenida Franklin Roosevelt 166, Rio de Janeiro.
    1970- 1970. US$8.00. 280 pages.

    Follows the general pattern of the statistical yearbook (157) but attempts to illustrate the changes
    in economic and social fields and the recent situation in Brazil.

    Time factor: the 1970 edition covers a ten-year period to 1968.

    § Pt.

164 Boletim estatístico [Statistical bulletin] (Instituto Brasileiro de Estatística).

    Instituto Brasileiro de Estatística, Fundação IBGE, Avenida Franklin Roosevelt 166, Rio de Janeiro.
    1943- (Q). Cr$3.00 or US$2.00; Cr$10.00 or US$5.00 yr.

    Contains data on population, industrial production, agricultural production, transportation,
    prices, banking, cost of living index, foreign trade, etc. As well as statistical information,
    there are studies and commentaries.

    Time factor: each issue contains data for the last three years and 12 to 15 months to about a year
    prior to the date of the issue.

    § Pt.

165 Conjuntura econômica [Economics situation] (Fundação Getúlio Vargas).

    Albertino Ferro da Silva, Praia de Botofogo 188, Rio de Janeiro. (CP 21-120-ZC-05).
    1947- (M). Cr$5.00; Cr$50.00 yr.

    Economic and business articles include some statistical tables, and also included are national
    and regional economic indices of prices, foreign trade, building permits, transport, and
    wholesale prices of domestic products, etc.

    § Pt. A brief international edition, "Economics and business in Brazil", is also available.

¶   B - Production

166
Produção industrial   [Industrial production]   (Instituto Brasileiro de Estatística).

Instituto Brasileiro de Estatística, Fundação IBGE, Avenida Franklin Roosevelt 166, Rio de Janeiro.

1952- 1969.   US$20.00.   1034 pages.

Following a summary of economic activity, there are statistical data on capital involved in each industry; numbers of employees and wages; fluctuations of employment; charges and expenses of various kinds, including industrial operations of production and improvement of goods; distribution of products; and production of selected products.   Data are available for Brazil as a whole and by region.

Time factor: the 1969 edition, with data for 1969, was published in 1971.

§   Pt.

167
Indústria de transformação   [Improvement industry]   (Instituto Brasileiro de Estatística).

Instituto Brasileiro de Estatística, Fundação IBGE, Avenida Franklin Roosevelt 166, Rio de Janeiro.

1967- (M).   US$10.00 yr.

Contains data for each region on production, employment, etc, in particular industries.

Time factor: each issue has data for the month of issue and cumulated figures for the year to date. It is published about two months later.

§   Pt.

168
Produção agrícola   [Agricultural production]   (Ministério da Agricultura).

Ministério da Agricultura, Esplanada dos Ministérios, Bloco 8 - 6° andar, Brasilia, D.F.

1939- 1969.   not priced.   57 pages.

Contains data on the area cultivated, quantities and values of crops produced in each region of Brazil.

Time factor: the 1969 edition, with data for that year, was published in 1971,   Preliminary estimates have also been produced annually since 1964, "Estimativa preliminar na produção agrícola", and these are available sooner.

§   Pt.

Note: the Ministry also publishes a monthly 'Informativo da produção agrícola' since 1969.

169
Produção florestal   [Forestry]   (Ministério da Agricultura)

Ministério da Agricultura, Esplanada dos Ministérios, Bloco 8 - 6° andar, Brasilia, D.F.

1941- 1969.   not priced.   30 pages.

Contains data on forestry and forest products.

Time factor: the 1969 edition, with data for that year, was published in 1971.

§   Pt.

170
Produção extrativa vegetal   [Vegetable products]   (Ministério da Agricultura).

Ministério da Agricultura, Esplanada dos Ministérios, Bloco 8 - 6° andar, Brasilia, D.F.

1938/42- 1969.   not priced.   23 pages.

Contains data on vegetable products.

Time factor: the 1969 edition, with data for that year, was published in 1971.

§   Pt.

¶   B,   continued

171   Pecuária, avicultura, apicultura e sericicultura   [Stockbreeding, poultrykeeping, beekeeping and silk production]   (Ministério da Agricultura).

Ministério da Agricultura, Esplanada dos Ministérios, Bloco 8 - 6° andar, Brasilia, D.F.

1939- 1969.   not priced.   21 pages.

Contains data on numbers of cattle and fowls, beehives and honey production, and silkworm production.

Time factor: the 1969 edition, with data for that year, was published in 1971.

§   Pt.

172   Indústria pesqueira   [Fish industry]   (Ministério da Agricultura).

Ministério da Agricultura, Esplanada dos Ministérios, Bloco 8 - 6° andar, Brasilia, D.F.

1939- 1969.   not priced.   26 pages.

Contains data on the fish industry by area.

Time factor: the 1969 edition, with data for that year, was published in 1971.

§   Pt.

173   Pesca   [Fishing]   (Ministério da Agricultura).

Ministério da Agricultura, Esplanada dos Ministérios, Bloco 8 - 6° andar, Brasilia, D.F.

1939- 1969.   not priced.   20 pages.

Contains data on the fishing industry.

Time factor: the 1969 edition, with data for that year, was published in 1971.

§   Pt.

174   Carnes, derivados e subprodutos   [Meat and meat products]   (Ministério da Agricultura).

Ministério da Agricultura, Esplanada dos Ministérios, Bloco 8 - 6° andar, Brasilia, D.F.

1940/42- 1969.   not priced.   61 pages.

Contains data on slaughter of animals and production of meat and its derivative products.

Time factor: the 1969 edition, with data for that year, was published in 1971.

§   Pt.

175   Oleos e gorduras vegetais   [Vegetable oils and fats]   (Ministério da Agricultura).

Ministério da Agricultura, Esplanada dos Ministérios, Bloco 8 - 6° andar, Brasilia, D.F.

1935/45- 1969.   not priced.   46 pages.

Contains data on the production of vegetable oils and fats.

Time factor: the 1969 edition, with data for that year, was published in 1971.

§   Pt.

¶ B,   continued

176   Anuário estatístico do arroz   [Statistical yearbook of rice]   (Instituto Rio Grandense do Arroz).
             Instituto Rio Grandense do Arroz, Av. Júlio de Castilhos, 585, 1° andar, Porto Alegre,
                 Rio Grande do Sul.
             1944- 1971.   not priced.   130 pages.
             Contains data on the production, commerce and foreign trade, and cost of production of rice.
             Time factor: the 1971 edition has data for several years to the crop year 1969/70.
             §   Pt.

177   Anuário estatístico do café   [Statistical yearbook of coffee]   (Ministério da Industria e do
                 Comércio. Instituto Brasileiro do Café).
             Instituto Brasileiro do Café, Av. Rodrigues Alves, 129 - térreo, Rio de Janeiro.
             1939/40- 1968/70.   not priced.   146 pages.
             Contains data on the production, export, consumption in Brazil, import and prices of coffee.
             Time factor: the 1968/70 edition, with data for that period, was published in 1971.
             §   Pt.
             Note: the Institute also issues a monthly news bulletin, 'Boletim informativo e estatístico'.

178   Produção extrativa mineral   [Mining production]   (Servico de Estatística da Produção).
             Servico de Estatística da Produção, Brasilia, D.F.
             1947- 1967.   not priced.   approx. 20 pages.
             Contains data on mining and production of minerals for the country as a whole and for regions.
             Time factor: the 1967 edition, with data for 1967, was published late in 1968.
             §   Pt.

             Refer also to 161, 162, 163 and 164.

¶ C - External trade

179   Comércio exterior do Brasil   [Foreign trade of Brasil]   (Instituto Brasileiro de Estatística).
             Instituto Brasileiro de Estatística, Fundação IBGE, Avenida Franklin Roosevelt 166, Rio de Janeiro.
             1901- 1969.   Vol I US$6.00; Vol II US$4.00.
             Contains detailed tables of the foreign trade of Brazil arranged by commodity subdivided by countries
                 of origin and destination, and also arranged by countries of origin and destination subdivided by
                 commodities.   Volume I contains data on imports, and volume II on exports.
             Time factor: the 1969 edition, with data for that year, was published early in 1971.
             §   Pt.

¶ C, continued

180   Boletim do comércio exterior   [Foreign trade bulletin]   (Secretaria da Receita Federal: Centro de Informações Econômico-Fiscais).

Secretaria da Receita Federal: Centro de Informações Econômico-Fiscais, Avenida Presidente Antonío Carlos, 375 - 90 andar, Rio de Janeiro.

1970-   (Q).   not priced.

Contains detailed data on imports and exports arranged by commodity.   There are also some less detailed tables arranged by countries for some commodities.

Time factor: cumulative figures for the year to date and for the corresponding period for the previous year.

§   Pt.

181   Foreign trade of Brazil (CIEF).

Centre de Informações Econômico-Fiscais (CIEF), Ministério da Fazenda, Rio de Janeiro.

1955/56- 1969.   not priced.   2 vols.

Volume 1 contains data on imports and volume 2 on exports.   Main tables show detailed foreign trade by country subdivided by commodity.

Time factor: the 1969 edition, with data for 1969, was published late 1970.

§   En.   There is also a Portuguese edition.

Refer also to 082 and 083.

¶ D - Internal distribution

Refer to 161, 162 and 163.

¶ E - Population

182   Recenseamento geral do Brasil   [General census of Brazil]   (Instituto Brasileiro de Estatística).

Instituto Brasileiro de Estatística, Fundação IBGE, Avenida Franklin Roosevelt 166, Rio de Janeiro.

1970.

The preliminary reports for Brazil and for each province have now been published (Brazil: US$5.00; each province: US$4.00) and the final reports will no doubt begin to appear shortly.

Time factor: the 1970 census is the 8th, the 7th having been taken for 1960.

§   Pt.

Refer also to 161, 162, 163 and 164.

c

BRAZIL, continued

¶   F – Standard of living

        Refer to 162, 164 and 165.

Central statistical office

183   Planning Unit,
        Ministry of Finance and Economic Development, Belmopan.

        The Unit's responsibilities include the preparation of the annual abstract and the economic survey described in the following pages.

        Unpublished statistical information will be supplied on request if available.

Another important organisation collecting and publishing statistics

184   Department of Customs and Excise,
        Custom House, Fort George, Belize City.
        t   3416.

        The Department compiles the annual trade report described in the following pages, and will also supply available but unpublished foreign trade statistical information on request.

Statistical publications

¶   A – General

185   Annual abstract of statistics   (Central Planning Unit, Ministry of Finance and Economic Development).
        Government Printer, 1 Church Street, Belize City.
        1961– 1967.   BH$1.00.   107 pages.
        Main sections:
                Population   Medical statistics
                Vital statistics   Education
                Trade   Transport & communications
                Finance   Miscellaneous
                Agriculture and land
        Time factor: the 1967 edition, published in 1967, has data for the years 1960 to 1966.
        §   En.

186   Basic data on the economy   (US Department of Commerce, Bureau of International Commerce).
        US Department of Commerce, Sales and Distribution Branch, Washington, D.C. 20230, USA.
        US$0.15.   12 pages.
        Issued as 70-88 in the series "Overseas business reports", this report presents selected basic data
            useful in the analysis of British Honduras as a market for US exports.   Data include statistics
            of population, structure of the economy, agriculture, manufacturing, construction, power, etc.
        Time factor: published in December 1970, the report contains data for several years to 1969.
        §   En.

¶   B - Production

Refer to 185 for agricultural production.

¶   C - External trade

187   Trade report   (Department of Customs and Excise).
             Government Printer, 1 Church Street, Belize City.
             1920- 1968.   not priced.   various pagings.
             Main tables show imports and exports arranged by commodity and subdivided by countries of origin
                 and destination.
             Time factor: the 1968 edition has data for 1968 and was published in 1970.
             §   En.

¶   E - Population

188   West Indies population census, 1960   (Department of Statistics, Jamaica).
             Department of Statistics, 23½ Charles Street, Kingston, Jamaica.
             Includes data on the population of British Honduras.
             §   En.

             Refer also to 185.

The Islands are now governed by an Administrator who is responsible for defense and internal security, external affairs, the public service, and courts and finance. There is no central statistical office, but enquiries on statistical matters concerning the Islands could be made to the Administrator at Tortola.

Statistical publications

¶ A - General

189
British Virgin Islands: report for the year   (Foreign and Commonwealth Office, London).
H M Stationery Office, P.O.Box 569, London SE1 9NH.
1955/56- 1965-1969. £0.45. 64 pages.
Mainly text but includes some statistics on public finance, education, health, labour, justice, etc.
Time factor: the 1965-1969 edition, dealing with those years, was published in April 1971.
§   En.

190
Basic data on the economy   (US Department of Commerce, Bureau of International Commerce).
US Department of Commerce, Sales and Distribution Branch, Washington, D.C. 20230, USA.
US$0.15. 7 pages.
Issued as 71-027 in the series "Overseas business reports", this report presents selected basic data useful in the analysis of the British Virgin Islands as a market for US exports. Data include statistics of population, structure of the economy, agriculture, manufacturing, construction, power, etc.
Time factor: published in October 1971, the report contains data for several years to 1970.
§   En.

¶ C - External trade

191
Summary of imports and exports of the British Virgin Islands   (Customs Department).
Customs Department, Tortola.
(A) 1970. not priced. 38 pages.
Contains data on imports, exports and re-exports arranged by commodity and subdivided by countries of origin and destination.
Time factor: the 1970 edition, with data for 1970, was published early in 1971.
§   En.

¶ E - Population

192
The West Indies population census, 1960   (Department of Statistics, Jamaica).
Department of Statistics, Kingston, Jamaica.
This census included the British Virgin Islands.
§   En.

Central statistical office

193   Statistics Canada.   Statistiques Canada,
Ottawa K1A OT6, Ontario.
t   (613) 992 2959   telex 013-424.

The Dominion Bureau of Statistics became Statistics Canada in May 1971 and the new title is being progressively phased in as the issuing authority of former DBS publications (please note that to avoid confusion the new name is used in connection with the publications on the following pages, even though some were published before May 1971).

The duties of Statistics Canada are to collect, compile, analyse, abstract and publish statistical information relating to the commercial, industrial, financial, social, economic and general activities and conditions of the people; to collaborate with Canadian government departments in the collection, compilation and publication of statistical information, including statistics derived from the activities of those departments; to take the censuses of population and agriculture of Canada; to endeavour to avoid duplication of collection of information; and generally to promote and develop integrated social and economic statistics pertaining to the whole of Canada and each province.

It is possible to request certain unpublished statistical information from Statistics Canada which may require a special tabulation. Depending on the nature of the request, the availability of the information, and the time taken to prepare it, there may be a charge based on the time and costs involved.

Publications other than those described in the following pages include:

      Annual report of Statistics Canada.
      Canada; the official handbook ...   (A).
      Wheat review   (M).
      Oilseeds review   (Q).
      Canada's international investment position, 1926 to 1967.
      Systems of national accounts: financial flow accounts   (Q).
      Medium-term capital investment survey   (A).
      Private and public investment in Canada: outlook ... and regional estimates   (A).
      Wages, salaries and hours of labour   (A).
      Dairy statistics   (A).
      Vital statistics   (A).
      Hospital statistics   (A).
      Federal government expenditure on scientific activities   (A).
      Input-output structure of the Canadian economy, 1961.
      General review of the manufacturing industries of Canada   (A).

Libraries

Statistics Canada (referred to above) has a large reference library at headquarters in Ottawa as well as smaller libraries in each of the seven regional offices located in St John's, Halifax, Montreal, Toronto, Winnipeg, Edmonton and Vancouver. The headquarters library has a complete collection of all reports published by Statistics Canada from 1918 to the present day, and also an extensive collection of publications of foreign governments and agencies. The libraries are open to the public during normal working hours and a limited photocopying service is available to users free of charge.

Canadian university libraries maintain extensive holdings of the publications of Statistics Canada for reference and research work, and most large public libraries in the major Canadian cities maintain a large assortment of such publications.

Libraries and information services abroad

Canadian embassies abroad stock only those publications which they feel are necessary for local reference, and the number at each embassy varies considerably.

Bibliographies

194

Catalogue   (Statistics Canada).

The 1971 edition of the catalogue, which is kept up-to-date by occasional supplements, is
divided into two parts: part I containing data on publications and part II on data files and
unpublished information.   This is a sales list and is available free from Statistics Canada.

§   En; Fr (bilingual).

195

Statistical observer   (Statistics Canada).

This is a quarterly free publication started in 1968 which is designed to contribute towards
informing economists, statisticians and related professionals about selected research and
development undertaken in Statistics Canada, in other Federal departments and agencies,
in provincial departments, in universities and in business and independent research
organisations.

§   En; Fr (separate editions).

196

Federal services for business   (Department of Industry, Trade and Commerce).

Summarises the range of services and information available from Federal government departments
and agencies.   The revised edition was published in 1970.

§   En.

Statistical publications

¶   A - General

197

Canada yearbook: official statistical annual of the resources, demography, institutions and
social and economic conditions of Canada   (Statistics Canada).

Publications Distribution, Statistics Canada, Ottawa K1A OT6; or from sales agents.

1905- 1970-71.   Can$6.00 or £2.89.   vii, 1408 pages.

Main sections:

Physiography & related sciences	Electric power
Constitution & government	Manufactures
Population	Capital expenditure, construction, housing
Immigration & citizenship	Labour
Vital statistics	Transport
Health, welfare & social security	Communications
Education	Domestic trade & prices
Scientific & industrial research	Foreign trade
Crime & delinquency	Government finance
Land use & renewable resources development	Trends in economic aggregates
	Banking, other commercial finance & insurance
Agriculture	Defence
Forestry	Official sources of information &
Fisheries & furs	miscellaneous data.
Mines & minerals	

Time factor: the 1970-71 edition, published in December 1970, has data for long periods up to
1968 and 1969.

§   En; Fr (separate editions).

¶   A,   continued

198   Annuaire du Québec.   Quebec yearbook   (Quebec Bureau of Statistics).

The Quebec Official Publisher, Parliament Buildings, Quebec.

1921- 1971.   Can$6.00.   xvi, 835 pages.

Main sections:
    Physical milieu
    Human milieu
    Resources of the Quebec economy (labour, wages, salaries, agriculture, forests,
        fisheries and game, mines, power and fuel, industrial production, construction)
    Trade (transport & communications, prices, domestic trade, foreign trade)
    Finance.

Time factor: the 1971 edition has data for several years to 1969, and was published in 1971.

§   En & Fr (bilingual).

199   Ontario statistical review   (Economics Analysis Branch, Economic and Statistical Services Division,
        Department of Treasury and Economics).

Economic Analysis Branch, Economic and Statistical Services Division, Department of Treasury and
    Economics, Frost Building, Queen's Park, Toronto 182.

1971- 1971.   not priced.

Contains economic indicators covering the 1949-70 period, the basic tables for Ontario's input-
    output model, selected regional economic developments, and estimates of the major components
    of the gross product for Ontario for 1957 to 1969.   Supplements the bi-monthly "Ontario
    economic review".

Time factor: the 1971 edition was published in July 1971.

§   En.

200   Canadian statistical review.   Revue statistique du Canada   (Statistics Canada).

Publications Distribution, Statistics Canada, Ottawa K1A OT6.

1926- (M), with weekly and annual supplements.   Can$0.50; $5.00 yr.

Contains economic articles and a summary of current economic indicators, including population,
    national accounts, labour, prices (including the cost of living index), manufacturing, fuel,
    power, mining, construction, food & agriculture, domestic trade, external trade, transport
    and finance.

Time factor: each issue has data for a period up to about three months prior to the date of the issue.

§   En & Fr (separate editions, except for the annual supplements which are bilingual).

201   Bank of Canada review.   Revue de la Banque du Canada.   (Statistics Canada).

Publications Distribution, Statistics Canada, Ottawa K1A OT6.

(M).   Can$1.00; $10.00 ($12.00 abroad) yr.

Contains charts and statistical tables on banking, capital markets and interest rates, financial
    institutions, general economic statistics (population, national accounts, gross national
    expenditure, real domestic product, employment, construction, mortgages, consumer price
    index, etc), external trade and international statistics.

Time factor: each issue has data for a period up to the month previous to the date of the issue.

§   En & Fr (bilingual).

¶ A, continued

202
Market research handbook. Manual statistique pour études marché   (Statistics Canada).

Publications Distribution, Statistics Canada, Ottawa K1A OT6.

1931- 1969.   Can$5.00.   xv, 545 pages.

Contains data on selected economic indicators, merchandising, advertising & media, population characteristics, personal income & expenditure, housing, motor vehicles, household facilities & equipment, and small area market data.

Time factor: the 1969 edition has data for 1966, 1967 and 1968 compared with that of the last edition of the handbook published in 1961.   Having been published every ten years in the past, the handbook is to be published every five years in future.

§   En & Fr (bilingual).

203
Survey of markets   (The Financial Post).

Maclean-Hunter Ltd, 481 University Avenue, Toronto 2 or 2055 Peal Street, Montreal 2.

1925- 1971.   Can$11.00.   322 pages.

An annual market survey of the newest facts of Canada's provinces, cities and towns, plus special review of the major economic and business indicators of the nation.

Time factor: the most recent actual figures are given and also forecasts for the future, the 1971 edition being published towards the end of that year.

§   En.

204
Canadian business chartbook   (The Conference Board of Canada).

The Conference Board of Canada, 615 Dorchester Boulevard West, Montreal 101.

1957- 1970.   Can$30.00 (includes data service).   39 pages.

Includes statistical data on national accounts and expenditure, employment, unemployment, prices, production, housing, retail trade, orders and shipments, profits, money and credit, foreign trade, balance of payments and reserves, and data on international companies.

Time factor: the 1970 edition, with data up to 1969, was published late 1970.

§   En.

205
Annual report of the Economic Council of Canada.

Information Canada, Publishing Division, Ottawa, Ontario.

1964- 1970.   Can$2.50.   109 pages.

Each annual issue has a different title, the title of the 1970 edition being 'Patterns of growth'. Dealing mainly with the economic situation of the country, it usually includes a statistical section on the main topic of the edition.

§   En.

206
OECD economic surveys: Canada   (Organisation for Economic Co-operation and Development).

OECD, 2 rue André-Pascal, 75 Paris 16, France; or from sales agents.

1962- 1971/72.   £0.35; US$1.00.   68 pages.

An analysis of the economic policy of the country which includes statistics showing recent developments in demand, production, wages and prices, conditions in the money and capital markets, and developments in the balance of payments.

Time factor: the 1971/72 issue was published late 1971.

§   En; Fr (separate editions).

¶ A, continued

207   System of national accounts - national income and expenditure accounts   (Statistics Canada).

Publications Distribution, Statistics Canada, Ottawa K1A OT6.

(Q) & (A).   Quarterly issues Can$0.75; $3.00 yr.   Annual issue $3.00.

Contains summary tables of income and expenditure, data, sector accounts, industrial distribution
    of gross domestic product, geographical distribution of personal income, etc.

§   En.

¶ B - Production

208   Manufacturing industries of Canada.   Industries manufacurières du Canada   (Statistics Canada).

Publications Distribution, Statistics Canada, Ottawa K1A OT6.

1968.   Can$3.50 (prices for single parts vary).   8 vols.

The separate volumes are:

    Section A   Summary for Canada
    Section B   Atlantic provinces
    Section C   Quebec
    Section D   Ontario
    Section E   Prairie provinces
    Section F   British Columbia, Yukon and Northwest Territories
    Section G   Geographical distribution (principal statistics of industries for census divisions or
                    counties or municipalities)
    Type of organisation and size of establishments
    Products shipped by Canadian manufacturers*

The principal statistics in the general reports include numbers of establishments, cost at plant of
    materials used, value of shipments of goods manufactured, value added by manufacturer,
    production workers, total employees, salaries and wages for all manufacturing industries,
    industry groups, leading industries, etc.
There are also some 135 annual reports on individual industries, containing statistics of quantities
    and values of products shipped and of materials used by individual industry, together with
    certain additional industrial information and the principal statistics carried in the general reports.

Time factor: the 1968 edition basic data was first issued in preliminary reports and the final reports
    were issued in 1971.

§   En & Fr editions (except item marked * which is in En only).

209   [Reports for individual industries]   (Statistics Canada).

Publications Distribution, Statistics Canada, Ottawa K1A OT6.

These are separate monthly, quarterly or annual publications not issued within a series.   The contents
    of each report are similar in character and include such principal statistics as number of establish-
    ments, number and type of employees and their salaries and wages, cost of fuel and electricity,
    value of shipments of goods of own manufacture, and value added.
The reports issued currently are listed below in broad subject groupings:

    Food, beverage and tobacco industries:
        Biscuit manufacturers   (A) $0.50   c. 7 pages.
        Bakeries   (A) $0.50   c. 10 pages.
        Breweries   (A) $0.50   c. 10 pages.
        Distilleries   (A) $0.50   c. 7 pages.
        Wineries   (A) $0.50   c. 8 pages.
        Soft drink manufacturers   (A) $0.50   c. 10 pages.
        Dairy factories   (A) $0.50   c. 12 pages.   [continued next page

¶ B,   continued

209,   continued   Canned and frozen processed foods   (A) $0.25   c. 7 pages.
Confectionery manufacturers   (A) $0.50   c. 11 pages.
Feed manufacturers   (A) $0.50   c. 10 pages.
Flour mills   (A) $0.50   c. 10 pages.
Fish products industry   (A) $0.25   c. 6 pages.
Fruit and vegetable canners and preservers   (A) $0.50   c. 14 pages.
Slaughtering and meat processors   (A) $0.50   c. 10 pages.
Sugar refineries   (A) $0.50   c. 10 pages.
Vegetable oil mills   (A) $0.25   c. 6 pages.
Miscellaneous food industries   (A) $0.50   c. 14 pages.
Tobacco products industries   (A) $0.50   c. 12 pages.
Monthly production of soft drinks $0.10; $1.00 yr.
Dairy factory production   (M) $0.10; $1.00 yr.
Grain milling statistics   (M) $0.10; $1.00 yr.
Oils and fats   (M) $0.20; $2,00 yr.
Stocks of dairy and poultry products   (M) $0.20; $2.00 yr.
Stocks of fruit and vegetables   (M) $0.20; $2.00 yr.
Pack, shipments and stocks of selected canned fruits and vegetables   (M) $0.20; $2.00 yr.
Stocks of meat products   (M) $0.30; $3.00 yr.
Sugar situation   (M) $0.10; $1.00 yr.
Tobacco and tobacco products statistics   (Q) $0.50; $2.00 yr.
Bread and other bakery products   (Q) $0.25; $1.00 yr.
Biscuits and confectionery   (Q) $0.25; $1.00 yr.
Fruit and vegetable preparations   (Q) $0.25; $1.00 yr.
Miscellaneous food preparations   (Q) $0.25; $1.00 yr.
Breweries   (M) $0.10; $1.00 yr.
Selected meat and meat preparations   (M) $0.10; $1.00 yr.
Distilled beverage spirits and industrial ethyl alcohol   (M) $0.10; $1.00 yr.

Leather and rubber products:
Leather tanneries   (A) $0.25   c. 6 pages.
Shoe factories and boot & shoe findings manufacturers   (A) $0.50   c. 10 pages.
Leather glove factories   (A) $0.25   c. 6 pages.
Miscellaneous leather products manufacturers   (A) $0.50   c. 10 pages.
Rubber industries   (A) $0.50   c. 16 pages.
Raw hides, skins and finished leather   (M) $0.10; $1.00 yr.
Footwear statistics   (M) $0.20; $2.00 yr.
Consumption, production and inventories of rubber   (M) $0.20; $2.00 yr.

Textiles and apparel:
Canvas products industry   (A) $0.50   c. 9 pages.
Cordage and twine industry   (A) $0.50   c. 12 pages.
Cotton and jute bag industry   (A) $0.25   c. 6 pages.
Cotton yarn and cloth mills   (A) $0.50   c. 9 pages.
Textile dyeing and finishing plants   (A) $0.25   c. 5 pages.
Synthetic textile mills   (A) $0.50   c. 8 pages.
Wool mills   (A) $0.50   c. 18 pages.
Miscellaneous textile industries   (A) $0.75   c. 44 pages.
Foundation garment industry   (A) $0.25   c. 6 pages.
Fur goods industry   (A) $0.25   c. 6 pages.
Hosiery and knitting mills   (A) $0.50   c. 20 pages.
Men's clothing industry   (A) $0.50   c. 18 pages.
Women's and children's clothing industries   (A) $0.50   c. 30 pages.
Other clothing industries (including fabric glove manufacturing and the miscellaneous clothing
     industry)   (A) $0.50   c. 12 pages.
Fibre preparing mills   (A) $0.50   c. 8 pages.
Carpet, mat and rug industry   (A) $0.25   c. 8 pages.
Garment shipments   (Q) $0.25; $1.00 yr.
Foundation garment shipments   (Q) $0.25; $1.00 yr.

Wood products:
Hardwood flooring industry   (A) $0.50   c. 8 pages.
Sawmills and planing mills   (A) $0.50   c. 24 pages.
Sash, door and other millwork plants   (A) $0.50   c. 16 pages.   [continued next page

¶ B, continued

209, continued

Veneer and plywood mills   (A) $0.50   c. 10 pages.
Miscellaneous wood industries   (A) $0.50   c. 14 pages.
Wooden box factories   (A) $0.25   c. 6 pages.
Coffin and casket industry   (A) $0.50   c. 8 pages.
Household furniture industry   (A) $0.50   c. 22 pages.
Office furniture industry   (A) $0.25   c. 8 pages.
Miscellaneous furniture industries   (A) $0.50   c. 12 pages.
Electric lamp and shade industry   (A) $0.25   c. 6 pages.
Shipments of prefabricated buildings of own manufacture   (A) $0.25   c. 6 pages.
Peeler logs, veneers and plywoods   (M) $0.20; $2.00 yr.
Production, shipments and stocks on hand of sawmills east of the Rockies   (M) $0.20; $2.00 yr.
Production, shipments and stocks on hand of sawmills in British Columbia   (M) $0.20; $2.00 yr.
Quarterly shipments of flush type doors (wood) by Canadian manufacturers
     (Q) $0.25; $1.00 yr.
Quarterly shipments of selected furniture products $0.25; $1.00 yr.

Paper products and printing:
Printing, publishing and allied industries   (A) $0.75   c. 62 pages.
Pulp and paper mills   (A) $0.50   c. 16 pages.
Asphalt roofing manufacturers   (A) $0.50   c. 8 pages.
Miscellaneous paper converters   (A) $0.50   c. 12 pages.
Paper and plastic bag manufacturers   (A) $0.50   c. 9 pages.
Manufacture of corrugated boxes   (A) $0.25   c. 8 pages.
Manufacture of folding cartons and set-up boxes   (A) $0.50   c. 9 pages.
Hardboard   (M) $0.10; $1.00 yr.
Rigid insulating board   (M) $0.10; $1.00 yr.
Particle board   (M) $0.10; $1.00 yr.

Metal (manufactures):
Iron and steel mills   (A) $0.50   c. 24 pages.
Aluminium rolling, casting and extruding   (A) $0.25   c. 6 pages.
Fabricated structural metal industry   (A) $0.25   c. 6 pages.
Hardware, tool and cutlery manufacturers   (A) $0.50   c. 8 pages.
Scrap iron and steel   (A) $0.25   c. 4 pages.
Smelting and refining   (A) $0.50   c. 12 pages.
Metal rolling, casting and extruding   (A) $0.50   c. 8 pages.
Wire and wire product manufacturers   (A) $0.50   c. 8 pages.
Steel pipe and tube mills   (A) $0.25   c. 6 pages.
Ornamental and architectural metal industry   (A) $0.50   c. 11 pages.
Boiler and plate works   (A) $0.50   c. 8 pages.
Copper and alloy rolling, casting and extruding   (A) $0.25   c. 6 pages.
Heating equipment manufacturers   (A) $0.50   c. 9 pages.
Iron foundries   (A) $0.25   c. 6 pages.
Metal stamping, pressing and coating industry   (A) $0.50   c. 12 pages.
Miscellaneous metal fabricating industries   (A) $0.50   c. 8 pages.
Primary iron and steel   (M) $0.30; $3.00 yr.
Steel ingots and pig iron   (M) $0.10; $1.00 yr.
Iron castings and cast iron pipes and fittings   (M) $0.10; $1.00 yr.
Stoves and furnaces   (M) $0.20; $2.00 yr.
Steel wire and specified wire products   (M) $0.10; $1.00 yr.
Non-ferrous scrap metal   (Q) $0.25; $1.00 yr.
Oil burners and oil-fired water heaters   (M) $0.10; $1.00 yr.

Machinery and transport equipment:
Agricultural implement industry   (A) $0.50   c. 10 pages.
Aircraft and parts manufacturers   (A) $0.50   c. 9 pages.
Boatbuilding and repair   (A) $0.25   c. 6 pages.
Shipbuilding and repair   (A) $0.25   c. 6 pages.
Machine shops   (A) $0.25   c. 5 pages.
Motor vehicle manufacturers   (A) $0.50   c. 8 pages.
Motor vehicle parts and accessories manufacturers   (A) $0.25   c. 6 pages.
Railroad rolling stock industry   (A) $0.50   c. 8 pages.
Miscellaneous vehicle manufacturers   (A) $0.25   c. 6 pages.   [continued next page

209, continued   Miscellaneous machinery and equipment manufacturers (A) $0.50 c. 6 pages.
Commercial refrigeration and air conditioning equipment manufacturers (A) $0.50. c. 8 pages.
Office and store machinery manufacturers (A) $0.50. c. 8 pages.
Truck body and trailer manufacturers (A) $0.50. c. 8 pages.
Preliminary report on the production of motor vehicles (M) $0.10; $1.00 yr.
Motor vehicle shipments (M) $0.10; $1.00 yr.

Electrical equipment:
    Manufacturers of small electrical appliances (A) $0.50. c. 8 pages.
    Manufacturers of major appliances (electric and non-electric) (A) $0.50. c. 8 pages.
    Manufacturers of household radio and television receivers (A) $0.50. c. 8 pages.
    Communications equipment manufacturers (A) $0.50. c. 12 pages.
    Manufacturers of electrical industrial equipment (A) $0.50. c. 14 pages.
    Manufacturers of electric wire and cable (A) $0.50. c. 8 pages.
    Manufacturers of miscellaneous electrical products (A) $0.50. c. 8 pages.
    Domestic refrigerators and freezers (M) $0.10; $1.00 yr.
    Domestic washing machines and clothes dryers (M) $0.10; $1.00 yr.
    Specified domestic appliances (M) $0.10; $1.00 yr.
    Radios and television receiving sets, including record players (M) $0.20; $2.00 yr.
    Factory sales of electric storage batteries (M) $0.10; $1.00 yr.
    Air conditioning and refrigeration equipment (Q) $0.10; $1.00 yr.

Non-metallic mineral products:
    Abrasive manufacturers (A) $0.50. c. 7 pages.
    Cement manufacturers (A) $0.50. c. 8 pages.
    Concrete products manufacturers (A) $0.25. c. 6 pages.
    Glass and glass products manufacturers (A) $0.50. c. 8 pages.
    Lime manufacturers (A) $0.50. c. 8 pages.
    Other non-metallic mineral products industries (A) $0.25. c. 5 pages.
    Ready-mix concrete manufacturers (A) $0.25. c. 8 pages.
    Stone products manufacturers (A) $0.25. c. 6 pages.
    Clay products manufacturers (from domestic clays) (A) $0.25. c. 8 pages.
    Clay products manufacturers (from imported clays) (A) $0.25. c. 6 pages.
    Cement (M) $0.10; $1.00 yr.
    Concrete products (M) $0.10; $1.00 yr.
    Gypsum products (M) $0.10; $1.00 yr.
    Mineral wool (M) $0.10; $1.00 yr.
    Products made from Canadian clays (M) $0.10; $1.00 yr.

Petroleum and coal products:
    Refined petroleum products. Vol I & II (A) $2.50 and $5.00 respectively.
    Petroleum refineries (A) $0.50. c. 24 pages.
    Other petroleum and coal products industries (A) $0.25. c. 6 pages.
    Asphalt roofing (M) $0.10; $1.00 yr.
    Coal and coke statistics (M) $0.30; $3.00 yr.
    Refined petroleum products (M) $0.30; $3.00 yr.

Chemicals:
    Fertilizer trade (A) $0.50. c. 22 pages.
    Manufacturers of pharmaceuticals and medicines (A) $0.50. c. 9 pages.
    Paint and varnish manufacturers (A) $0.50. c. 12 pages.
    Manufacturers of plastics and synthetic resins (A) $0.25. c. 6 pages.
    Sales of pest control products by Canadian registrants (A) $0.50. c. 10 pages.
    Manufacturers of soap and cleaning compounds (A) $0.50. c. 10 pages.
    Manufacturers of toilet preparations (A) $0.50. c. 8 pages.
    Other chemical industries n.e.s. (A) $0.50. c. 14 pages.
    Manufacturers of industrial chemicals (A) $0.50. c. 12 pages.
    Manufacturers of mixed fertilizers (A) $0.25. c. 6 pages.
    Sales of toilet preparations in Canada (A) $0.25. c. 8 pages.
    Sales of paints, varnishes and lacquers (M) $0.10; $1.00 yr.
    Specified chemicals (M) $0.10; $1.00 yr.
    Soaps and synthetic detergents (M) $0.10; $1.00 yr

[continued next page

¶ B, continued

209, continued Miscellaneous manufactures:
Broom, brush and mop industry   (A) $0.25.   c. 6 pages.
Sporting goods and toy industry   (A) $0.50.   c. 14 pages.
Miscellaneous manufacturing industries   (A) $0.75.   c. 37 pages.
Scientific and professional equipment manufacturers   (A) $0.75.   c. 37 pages.
Pen and pencil and typewriter supplies manufacturers   (A) $0.50.   c. 12 pages.
Plastics fabricators   (A) $0.50.   c. 10 pages.
Signs and displays industry   (A) $0.25.   c. 6 pages.
Venetian blind manufacturers   (A) $0.25.   c. 5 pages.
Jewellery and silverware manufacturers   (A) $0.25.   c. 6 pages.
Asphalt and vinyl–asbestos floor tile   (M) $0.10; $1.00 yr.

Time factor: varies with each publication, but the data is issued as soon as it is available. Figures for earlier years or for the previous year are included for comparison.

§   En; Fr.

210   Inventories, shipments and orders in manufacturing industries. Stocks, expéditions et commandes des industries manufacturières   (Statistics Canada).

Publications Distribution, Statistics Canada, Ottawa K1A OT6.

(M).   Can$0.40; $4.00 yr.

A summary of trends, and data for individual industries.

Time factor: each issue has long runs of figures to the date of the issue and is published some three months later.

§   En; Fr (separate editions).

211   Indexes of real domestic product by industry (including the index of industrial production). Indices du produit intérieur réel par industrie (incluant l'indice de la production industrielle) (Statistics Canada).

Publications Distribution, Statistics Canada, Ottawa K1A OT6.

1971- (M).   Can$0.30; $3.00 yr.

Issued in the general series "System of national accounts".

§   En; Fr.

212   Fixed capital flows and stocks, manufacturing; Canada. Flux et stocks de capital fixe, industries manufacturières; Canada.   (Statistics Canada).

Publications Distribution, Statistics Canada, Ottawa K1A OT6.

1926/60- 1926/69.   Can$2.50.   281 pages.

Presents estimates of fixed capital flows and stocks in Canadian manufacturing industries.

Time factor: the 1926–1969 edition, with data for those years, was published in February 1972.

§   En; Fr.

¶   B,   continued

213   Census of Canada: agriculture.   Recensement du Canada: agriculture   (Statistics Canada).

Publications Distribution, Statistics Canada, Ottawa K1A OT6.

1911- 1966.   Can$3.00 per volume.   3 vols (in binders).

Volumes are numbered as part of the Census of Canada, those concerning agriculture being Vols. III, IV and V.   Volume III contains the general summary tables for Canada, showing numbers of farms, areas, tenure, crops, livestock, machinery, etc, and more detailed data for Newfoundland, Prince Edward Island, Nova Scotia and New Brunswick; Vol. IV has detailed results for Quebec and Ontario; and Vol. V has detailed results for the Western provinces of Manitoba, Saskatchewan, Alberta and British Columbia.

Time factor: the results of the 1966 census were published in 1968.

§   En.   Also available in Fr.

214   Quarterly bulletin of agricultural statistics.   Bulletin trimestriel de la statistique agricole (Statistics Canada).

Publications Distribution, Statistics Canada, Ottawa K1A OT6.

1918-.   Can$1.00; $4.00 yr.

Contains statistical data on farm finance; field crops; livestock, poultry and dairying; special crops and enterprises, meteorological records, and prices of agricultural products.

Time factor: each issue has data mainly for the period of the issue and is published some three months later.

§   En; Fr.

215   Handbook of agricultural statistics   (Statistics Canada).

Publications Distribution, Statistics Canada, Ottawa K1A OT6.

This handbook, each part of which is updated at intervals, consolidates the data already published monthly and annually for Canada and for the provinces.   It is issued in 7 parts:

Part I   Field crops, including acreage, yield, production, farm prices   (latest issue covers 1908 to 1962)
Part II   Farm income, including operating expenses   (latest issue covers 1926 to 1965)
Part III   Trends in Canadian agriculture   (latest issue covers 1926 to 1954)
Part IV   Food consumption   (latest issue covers 1926 to 1955)
Part V   Vegetables and fruits: acreage, production and value of vegetables, 1940-1966; production and value of fruits, 1926-1967.
Part VI   Livestock and animal products, 1871-1965.
Part VII Dairy statistics, 1920-68.

§   En.

216   Livestock and animal products statistics.   Statistique du bétail et des produits animaux (Statistics Canada)

Publications Distribution, Statistics Canada, Ottawa K1A OT6.

Detailed statistical coverage of livestock population, marketings, meat stocks, wool and hides, and other animal products.

1970.   Can$1.00.   84 pages.

Time factor: the 1970 edition, with data for 1970, was published in 1971.

§   En; Fr (separate editions).

¶ B, continued

217   Canadian farm economics   (Department of Agriculture. Economics Branch).

Publications Distribution, Statistics Canada, Ottawa K1A OT6
   or   Economics Branch of the Department of Agriculture, Ottawa.

(Q).   free.

Contains articles and statistical tables on current economic problems and developments of Canadian agriculture. A statistical appendix has average prices of selected farm commodities for various markets and grades, and some price and production indexes of concern to agriculture. An annual outlook issue supplements the quarterly information.

§   En; Fr.

218   Grain trade of Canada   (Statistics Canada).

Publications Distribution, Statistics Canada, Ottawa K1A OT6.

(A) 1969–70.   Can$1.00.   93 pages.

Summary of acreage, production of grains, marketing, inspections, receipts and shipments, movement in Canada, exports, and flour-milling statistics.

Time factor: the 1969–70 edition, with data for the crop year 1969–70, was published mid-1971.

§   En.

219   Fisheries statistics of Canada   (Statistics Canada).

Publications Distribution, Statistics Canada, Ottawa K1A OT6.

1969.   Can$0.50.   27 pages.

Contains data on landings, quantity, value of species; value of fishery products and by-products; sales of freshwater fish; number and value of craft employed in fishing; employment; and value of imports and exports of fish and fishery products.

Time factor: the 1969 edition, with data for that year, was published late 1971.

§   En. Available also in Fr.

220   Monthly review of Canadian fishery statistics.   La statistique mensuelle des pêches du Canada (Statistics Canada).

Publications Distribution, Statistics Canada, Ottawa K1A OT6.

Can$0.30; $3.00 yr.

Up-dates the information in the annual (219 above).

§   En; Fr (bilingual).

221   Canadian minerals yearbook   (Department of Energy, Mines and Resources: Mineral Resources Division).

Publications Distribution, Statistics Canada, Ottawa K1A OT6.

1967.   Can$7.50.   527 pages.

Contains chapters on individual minerals showing production, imports, exports, consumption, and descriptions of developments and operations in the industry.

Time factor: the 1967 edition, with data for 1967 and earlier years, was published in 1969. However, advance preprints of later volumes are available only from the Department of Energy, Mines and Resources at Ottawa, $0.25 each or $5.00 for the complete set.

§   En. Also available in Fr.

¶ B,   continued

222   Facts and figures of the automotive industry   (Motor Vehicle Manufacturers' Association).

Motor Vehicle Manufacturers' Association, 25 Adelaide Street East, Toronto 210.

(A) 1970.   not priced.   44 pages.

Includes statistical tables of the industry (production and shipments, employees, earnings of motor vehicle and allied industries), exports and imports, retail trade, registrations, revenue and tax rates, motor fuel sales, etc.

Time factor: the 1970 edition, published in 1971, has data for 1968 and 1969 and some earlier years in some tables.

§   En.

¶ C - External trade

223   Trade of Canada.   Commerce du Canada   (Statistics Canada).

Publications Distribution, Statistics Canada, Ottawa K1A OT6.

1930/31- 1968-70.   Vol I   (not yet published); Vol II   Can$6.50; Vol III   Can$10.50.   3 vols.

Volume I contains the summary and analytical tables; volume II contains detailed statistics of exports; and volume III contains detailed statistics of imports.   In both volumes II and III the main tables show the trade of Canada arranged by commodity subdivided by countries of destination and origin respectively.

Time factor: the 1968-70 edition, published in 1971, has data for 1968, 1969 and 1970.

§   En; Fr (separate editions).

Note: "Review of foreign trade" is an annual textual comment on and analysis of Canada's foreign trade.

224   Summary of exports   (Statistics Canada).

Publications Distribution, Statistics Canada, Ottawa K1A OT6.

1935- (M).   Can$0.20; $2.00 yr.

Brief statistics of exports arranged by country or trading area subdivided by main groups of products, total exports by country, total exports by commodity, etc.

Time factor: each issue has data for the month of the issue and cumulated figures for the current year to date and comparative figures for two previous years, and is published about one month later

§   En.

225   Summary of imports   (Statistics Canada).

Publications Distribution, Statistics Canada, Ottawa K1A OT6.

1947- (M).   Can$0.20; $2.00 yr.

Brief statistics of imports arranged by country or trading area subdivided by main groups of products, total imports by country, total imports by commodity, etc.

Time factor: each issue has data for the month of the issue and cumulated figures for the current year and comparative figures for two previous years, and is published about one month later.

§   En & Fr (bilingual).

¶ C, continued

226 Exports by commodities. Exportations par marchandises (Statistics Canada).

Publications Distribution, Statistics Canada, Ottawa K1A OT6.

(M). Can$0.75; $7.50 yr.

Contains detailed statistics of exports from Canada arranged by commodities subdivided by countries of destination.

Time factor: each issue has data for the date of the issue and cumulated data for the year to date, and is issued between one and two months later.

§ En; Fr (bilingual).

227 Imports by commodities. Importations par marchandises (Statistics Canada).

Publications Distribution, Statistics Canada, Ottawa K1A OT6.

(M). Can$0.75; $7.50 yr.

Contains detailed statistics of imports into Canada arranged by commodity subdivided by countries of origin.

Time factor: each issue has data for the date of the issue and cumulated totals for the year to date, and is issued between one and two months later.

§ En; Fr (bilingual).

228 Exports by countries (Statistics Canada).

Publications Distribution, Statistics Canada, Ottawa K1A OT6.

(Q). Can$1.00; $4.00 yr.

Contains detailed statistics of exports arranged by country subdivided by commodity.

Time factor: each issue has cumulated statistics for the year to date and comparative information for the preceeding year. Thus the quarterly issues cover January–March, January–June, January–September, and January–December (the full year). Publication is two or three months after the end of the period covered.

§ En.

229 Imports by countries (Statistics Canada).

Publications Distribution, Statistics Canada, Ottawa K1A OT6.

(Q). Can$1.00; $4.00 yr.

Contains detailed statistics of exports arranged by country subdivided by commodity.

Time factor: each issue has cumulated statistics for the year to date and comparative information for the previous year (see explanation in 228 above). Publication is two or three months after the end of the period covered.

§ En.

¶ C, continued

230   Chemical imports trends.   Revue des importations des produits chimiques.   (Chemicals Branch,
          Department of Industry, Trade and Commerce).

       Chemicals Branch, Department of Industry, Trade and Commerce, Ottawa 4.

       1956/64- 1965-1966-1967.   not priced.   xiii, 111 pages.

       Contains data for those chemical, petroleum, plastics and rubber commodities and other materials
          by class as reported in "Trade of Canada: imports".   Also data for those chemicals belonging
          to the 'n.e.s.' classes for which a special 4-month analysis was made.

       Time factor: the 1965-1966-1967 edition has data for those three years and was published late 1971.

       §   En; Fr (bilingual).

       Refer also to 082 and 083.

¶ D - Internal distribution

231   Retail commodity survey.   Enquête sur les marchandises vendues au détail   (Statistics Canada).

       Publications Distribution, Statistics Canada, Ottawa K1A OT6.

       1968- 1968.   Can$1.00.   87 pages.

       An enquiry into sales of approximately 150 major commodity lines in retail stores, by province and
          by kind of business.

       Time factor: the survey is to be conducted at five-yearly intervals, and the 1968 survey results
          were published in May 1971.

       §   En; Fr (separate eds).

232   Shopping centres in Canada (retail and service trade).   Les centres commerciaux au Canada
          (entreprise de détail et services).   (Statistics Canada).

       Publications Distribution, Statistics Canada, Ottawa K1A OT6.

       1956- 1969.   Can$0.50.   24 pages.

       The results of an annual survey of shopping centres and their retail and service outlets.

       Time factor: the 1969 edition, which has data for 1969, was published in March 1972.

       §   En; Fr (bilingual).

¶ D, continued

233   Wholesale trade. Commerce de gros   (Statistics Canada).

Publications Distribution, Statistics Canada, Ottawa K1A OT6.

(M). Can$0.10; $1.00 yr.

Contains data on the trade of wholesale merchants only, and includes trade in consumer goods and industrial goods. Also preliminary estimates of wholesale sales inventories.

Time factor: each issue has data for the month of the issue and cumulated figures for the year to date, and is published about one month later.

§   En; Fr (bilingual).

234   Retail trade. Commerce de détail   (Statistics Canada).

Publications Distribution, Statistics Canada, Ottawa K1A OT6.

(M). Can$0.30; $3.00 yr.

Contains data on 17 kinds of business: grocery and combination stores, other food stores, department stores, general merchandise stores, general stores, variety stores, motor vehicle dealers, service stations, men's clothing stores, women's clothing stores, family clothing stores, shoe stores, hardware stores, furniture, TV, radio and appliance stores, fuel dealers, drug stores, jewellery stores, all other stores.

§   En; Fr (bilingual).

Note: "Retail trade revisions...Commerce du détail rectification..." for 1961-1966 and 1966-1970 corrects the data published in the earlier issues of the monthly.

¶ E - Population

235   Census of Canada: population. Recensement du Canada: population   (Statistics Canada).

Publications Distribution, Statistics Canada, Ottawa K1A OT6.

1966. Can$8.00 per volume. (parts can be purchased separately - prices vary). 2 vols in binders.

Volume I and II of the Census of Canada deal with population. Volume I deals with the general characteristics of the population in 16 parts: Introduction; Electoral districts; Atlantic provinces; Quebec; Ontario; Western provinces; Incorporated cities, towns and villages; Rural and urban distribution; sex ratios; age groups (two parts); marital status; and marital status by age group and sex. Appendix A has population totals for unorganised townships; Appendix B has population totals for census tracts for 28 major cities; and Appendix C has maps.

Volume II deals with households and families in 14 parts: Introduction; dwellings by structural type and tenure; households by size; household composition; households by type; households by marital status; household characteristics by structural type and tenure of dwelling; structural type and tenure of dwellings by marital status, age, and sex of head; families by size; children in families; families by marital status, age and sex of head; family characteristics by marital status, age and sex of head; families by type; household and family status of individuals.

§   En; Fr (separate publications).

Refer also to 197 and 200.

¶ F - Standard of living

236 Income distribution by size in Canada.   Répartition du revenu au Canada selon la taille du revenu.
(Statistics Canada).

Publications Distribution, Statistics Canada, Ottawa K1A OT6.

1951/55- 1967.   Can$1.00.   83 pages.

Estimates of family and individual incomes by size of income and by major source, region, age,
sex and other characteristics.

Time factor: the 1967 edition, with data for that year, was published in December 1970.   Prior to
the publication of these final reports, preliminary information is issued - the preliminary report
for 1969 being published in 1971 (price Can$0.50).

§   En; Fr (bilingual).

237 Urban family expenditure   (Statistics Canada).

Publications Distribution, Statistics Canada, Ottawa K1A OT6.

1953- 1967.   Can$1.50.   160 pages.

A small sample survey of family expenditure in eleven major urban cities, including detailed
expenditure for families and unattached individuals, classified by city, income level, family
type, and age.

Time factor: an enquiry carried out occasionally, the results of the 1967 survey were published
in 1971.

§   En.

238 Prices and price indices.   Prix et indices des prix   (Statistics Canada).

Publications Distribution, Statistics Canada, Ottawa K1A OT6.

(M).   Can$0.40; $4.00 yr.

Contains industrial price index, consumer price indexes, and a large variety of other monthly
price indexes.

§   En; Fr (bilingual).

239 Family food expenditure in Canada.   Dépenses alimentaires des familles au Canada   (Statistics
Canada).

Publications Distribution, Statistics Canada, Ottawa K1A OT6.

1969- 1969.   Can$2.00.   208 pages.

Contains detailed information on family food purchases recorded by a sample of just over 10,000
Canadian families and individuals.

Time factor: the first of a survey to be produced occasionally, the 1969 results were published
in 1971.

§   En; Fr (separate volumes).

¶ F, continued

240
Taxation statistics: analysing the returns of individuals ... (Department of National Revenue, Taxation).

Information Canada, Publishing Division, Ottawa.

1944- 1968. Can$2.00. 184 pages.

Time factor: the 1968 edition, with data for 1968, was published in 1970.

§ En; Fr (separate editions).

There is no central statistical office on the Cayman Islands, but enquiries concerning statistical and other matters regarding the Islands may be made to the Administrator's Office, Grand Cayman. There is also a Customs Department on Grand Cayman.

Statistical publications

¶   A – General

241   Cayman Islands: colonial report   (Foreign and Commonwealth Office, London).
           H M Stationery Office, P.O.Box 569, London SE1 9NH.
           1966–70.   £0.47.   59 pages.
           The text includes a few statistical tables on population, employment, commerce, production, tourism, etc.
           Time factor: the report for the years 1966 to 1970 was published in 1972.
           §   En.

¶   E – Population

242   The West Indies population census, 1960   (Department of Statistics, Jamaica).
           Department of Statistics, 23½ Charles Street, Kingston, Jamaica.
           The census includes data for the Cayman Islands.
           §   En.

CHILE - CHILI

Central statistical office

243   Instituto Nacional de Estadísticas   [National Institute of Statistics],
Casilla 6177, Correo 5, Santiago.
t   35257.   tga Digedistica.

In 1970 a law was passed to create the National Institute of Statistics out of the 'Dirección de Estadística y Censos', the responsibilities of the Institute being to collect, analyse and publish statistical information, to organise official censuses and surveys, and to study the methodology of the collection and use of statistics.

Unpublished information can be supplied when available and the cost of extraction of the data is charged to the enquirer.

Publications other than those described in the following pages include:
Bibliografía de estudios sobre metodología estadística en Chile   [Bibliography of studies in statistical methodology in Chile]   (Published 1968).
Boletín de edificación   [Bulletin of construction]   (M).
Demografía [Demography]   (A).
Educación y justicia   [Education and justice]   (A).
Estadística de salud   [Statistics of health]   (A).
Indice de salarios y sueldos   [Index of wages and salaries]   (Q).
Turismo [Tourism]   (A).
Censo de vivienda, 1960. Resumen del país [Census of housing, 1970].
Indice de precios al por mayor   [Index of wholesale prices]   (M).

Libraries

The Instituto Nacional de Estadísticas (referred to above) has a library which is open to the public who wish to consult statistical publications.

Libraries and information services abroad

Statistical publications of Chile are available for reference in Chile's Embassies abroad, including:
United Kingdom   Embassy of Chile, 3 Hamilton Place, London W1V 0AR.   t   01-629 8382.
Canada   Embassy of Chile, 56 Sparks Street, Ottawa.   t   235-4402.

Bibliographies

244   Guia de publicaciones estadísticas, 1970   [Guide to statistical publications, 1970].
Issued by the Instituto Nacional de Estadísticas and available free on request.

Statistical publications

¶ A - General

245   Sintesis estadística   [Statistical survey]   (Instituto Nacional de Estadísticas).

           División Biblioteca y Informaciones, Av. Vicuña Mackenna 115, Casilla 6177, Correo 22, Santiago de Chile.

           1943- (M).   free.

           Contains brief statistical data on demography, culture and social conditions, fishing, agricultural production, minerals, manufacture, building, electricity, foreign trade, price indices, retail prices in Santiago, wholesale prices of agricultural products, transport, finance, money and banking.

           Time factor: each issue contains data for at least two years to about three months prior to the date of the issue.

           §   Es.

246   Boletín mensuel   [Monthly bulletin]   (Banco Central de Chile).

           Banco Central de Chile, Santiago de Chile.

           1928-.   free.

           Includes a statistical appendix with tables on money and banking, foreign trade (direction of trade), gold market, gross national product, agricultural production, mineral production, prices and price indices.

           Time factor: each issue has data for varying periods, some of which can be very up-to-date.

           §   Es.

247   Boletín   [Bulletin]   (Instituto Nacional de Estadísticas).

           División Biblioteca y Informaciones, Av. Vicuña Mackenna 115, Casilla 6177, Correo 22, Santiago de Chile.

           1928- 2 per annum.   Esc 9.00 (US$4.00).

           Contains statistical data on demography, tourism, meteorology, agriculture and livestock, fishing, mining, prices, transport, foreign trade, money and banking, public finance, labour, social assistance, police and justice.

           Time factor: the 1967 issues, with data for the period, were published in 1969.

           §   Es.

248   Boletín de estadísticas básicas regionales   [Bulletin of basic regional statistics]   (Corporación de Fomento de la Producción).

           Corporación de Fomento de la Producción, Concepción.

           1964- 3 per annum.   not priced.

           Contains data on agriculture, demography, social, industrial, construction, banking, financial and foreign trade statistics for the provinces of Concepción, Arauco, Bio-bio, Malleco and Nuble.

           §   Es.

¶ B - Production

249 Censo nacional de manufacturas [National census of manufactures] (Dirección de Estadística y Censos).

Div isión Biblioteca y Informaciones, Av. Vicuña Mackenna 115, Casilla 6177, Correo 22, Santiago de Chile.

1937- 1967. to be published in several volumes.

Volumes so far available are: a preliminary volume -
  Chile. Industria manufacturera. Número de establecimientos y ocupación en el año 1967.
    [Numbers of establishments and industries].
  Vol I. containing data on establishments with five or more employees, classified by
    occupation or industry.
  Vol II. containing data on the raw materials used by establishments with five or more employees.

Time factor: a census is taken every 10 years.

§ Es.

250 Industrias manufactureras [Manufacturing industry] (Dirección de Estadística y Censos).

División Biblioteca y Informaciones, Av. Vicuña Mackenna 115, Casilla 6177, Correo 22, Santiago de Chile.

1911- 1967. Esc 4.00 (US$1.50). 20 pages.

Contains general information on manufacturing industry, including the number of establishments and employees, power used in each industry, and indices of industrial manufacturing production.

Time factor: the 1967 edition, published in 1971, has data for 1967.

§ Es.

251 Indice de producción industrial manufacturera [Index numbers of industrial manufacturing production] (Instituto Nacional de Estadísticas).

División Biblioteca y Informaciones, Av. Vicuña Mackenna 115, Casilla 6177, Correo 22, Santiago de Chile.

1958- (M). free.

§ Es.

252 Minería [Mining] (Instituto Nacional de Estadísticas).

División Biblioteca y Informaciones, Av. Vicuña Mackenna 115, Casilla 6177, Correo 22, Santiago de Chile.

1911- 1968. Esc 5.50 (US$2.50). 89 pages.

Contains data on mining companies, production of minerals and metals, oil and gas, employment, accidents in the mines, exports, and international trade.

Time factor: the 1968 edition, published in 1971, has data generally for 1968, but only for 1966 or 1967 in some tables. Retrospective figures are also given.

§ Es.

Please insert this correction slip between pages 78 and 79.

CHILE, continued

¶ B, continued

253   Censo nacional agropecuario [National census of agriculture & stockbreeding] Dirección de
       Estadística y Censos).

       División Biblioteca y Informaciones, Av. Vicuña Mackenna 115, Casilla 6177, Correo 22,
       Santiago de Chile.

       1929/30- 1964/65.   Summary volume, Esc 15.00 (US$6.00).   25 provincial volumes,
       Esc 12.00 (US$4.00) each.

       Contains data on the area of land in use for agricultural purposes, crops, livestock, farms, &c.

       Time factor: Preliminary figures were published in 1966, but the main volumes appeared 1967 - 1969.

       §   Es.

254   Agricultura e industrias agropecuarios y pesca [Agriculture and the agricultural & fishing industries]
       (Dirección de Estadística y Censos).

       División Biblioteca y Informaciones, Av. Vicuña Mackenna 115, Casilla 6177, Correo 22,
       Santiago de Chile.

       1911/12- 1965/66.   Esc 4.00 (US$2.00).   c 100 pages.

       Contains data on the agricultural & fishing industries.

       Time factor: the 1965/66 edition, published in 1971, has data for the crop year 1965/66.

       §   Es.

255   Chile: demand & supply projections for agricultural products, 1965-1980. (Catholic University of
       Chile: Economic Research Center, under contract with the US Dept of Agriculture).

       Economic Research Center, Catholic University of Chile, La Paz.

       1969.   not priced.   xxiii, 130 pages.

       A study to present supply & demand projections for 38 Chilean agricultural products.

       §   En.

¶ C - External trade

256   Comercio exterior Chile [Chilean foreign trade] (Cámara de Comercio de Santiago de Chile /
       Santiago Chamber of Commerce).

       Cámara de Comercio de Santiago de Chile, Santa Lucia 302 - 2° piso, Casilla 1297, Santiago.

       1961- 1968.   not priced.   2 vols.

       Main tables show imports & exports arranged by commodity & subdivided by countries of origin &
       destination.   Statistics are compiled from information provided by the Instituto Nacional de
       Estadísticas.

       Time factor: the 1968 edition, containing data for that year, was published in 1970.

       §   Es.

¶   C,   continued

257   Comercio exterior   [Foreign trade]   (Instituto Nacional de Estadísticas).

Division Biblioteca y Informaciones, Av. Vicuña Mackenna 115, Casilla 6177, Correo 22,
     Santiago de Chile.

1915- 1966.   Esc 15.00 (US$6.00).

Main tables show imports and exports arranged by commodity and subdivided by countries of origin
     and destination.

Time factor: the 1966 edition, with data for 1966, was published in 1968.

§   Es.

Refer also to 082 and 083.

¶   D - Internal distribution

258   Encuesta continua de comercio interior y servicios   [Continuing survey of domestic trade and services]
     (Instituto Nacional de Estadísticas).

Division Biblioteca y Informaciones, Av. Vicuña Mackenna 115, Casilla 6177, Correo 22,
     Santiago de Chile.

1964- 1968.   Esc 5.00 (US$2.50).

A series of sample investigations into the internal trade and service industries.

Time factor: the 1968 edition, dealing with that year, was published in 1970.

§   Es.

¶   E - Population

259   Censo de población y vivienda   [Census of population and housing]   (Instituto Nacional de
     Estadísticas).

Division Biblioteca y Informaciones, Av. Vicuña Mackenna 115, Casilla 6177, Correo 22,
     Santiago de Chile.

1854- 1970.   To be published in several volumes; prices vary.

Preliminary results are being issued on the basic characteristics of the population of the country and
     of each province.   Final reports will include a general summary for the country and 25 provincial
     volumes.

§   Es.

¶   E,   continued

260   Perspectivas de crecimiento de la población Chilena, 1970–1985   [Projections of the increase in
               population, 1970–1985]   (División de Planificación Industrial, Corporación de Fomento de
               la Producción).

           División de Planificación Industrial, Corporación de Fomento de la Producción, Santiago de Chile.

           Not priced.   55 pages.

           Time factor: published 1970.

           §   Es.

           Refer also to 245 and 247.

¶   F – Standard of living

261   Encuesta nacional sobre ingresos familiares, Marzo–Junio 1968   [National survey of family incomes,
               March–June 1968]   (Instituto Nacional de Estadísticas).

           División Biblioteca y Informaciones, Av. Vicuña Mackenna 115, Casilla 6177, Correo 22,
               Santiago de Chile.

           Esc 12.00 (US$4.00).

           Time factor: published in 1970.

           §   Es.

262   Indice de precios al consumidor   [Index of consumer prices]   (Instituto Nacional de Estadísticas)

           DivisiónBiblioteca y Informaciones, Av. Vicuña Mackenna 115, Casilla 6177, Correo 22,
               Santiago de Chile.

           1958– (M).   free.

           §   Es.

263   Comercio interior y communicaciones   [Internal trade and communications]   (Instituto Nacional de
               Estadísticas).

           División Biblioteca y Informaciones, Av. Vicuña Mackenna 115, Casilla 6177, Correo 22,
               Santiago de Chile.

           1911– 1967.   Esc 8.00 (US$3.00).   204 pages.

           Contains data on prices (consumer and wholesale price indices, wholesale prices of particular
               products, and retail prices in particular areas) and on transport and communications.

           §   Es.

Central statistical office

264
Departmento Administrativo Nacional de Estadística (DANE)   [National Administrative Department
of Statistics],
Via El Dorado, Bogotá.
t   44 55 10 - 44 96 00.

The Department is, by law, the only compiler of official statistics in Colombia, and is a
department of the Centro Administrativo Nacional (CAN) [National Administration Centre].

Unpublished statistical information can be supplied if available, a charge being made based on
the amount of work to be done and the administrative costs.

Publications other than those described in the following pages are:
Anuario de fiscales y financieras   [Yearbook of public finance].
Encuesta de hogares   [Housing survey]   (A).
Educativos   [Education]   (A).
Censo de construcción, minera y energia   [Census of construction, mining and power].

Libraries

DANE has a library which is open to the public.   Some Colombian statistical publications are
also available in public libraries in Colombia.

Libraries and information services abroad

Colombian Embassies abroad have some of the official statistical publications published by
DANE, including:

United Kingdom	Colombian Embassy, 3 Hans Crescent, London SW1X 0LR.
	t 01-549 9177.
USA	Colombian Embassy, 2118 Leroy Place N W, Washington, D.C.
	t DU7-5828.
Canada	Consulate General, 1500 Stanley Street, Montreal. t 849-4852.

Bibliography

265
There is no detailed bibliography of Colombian statistical publications, but DANE issues a
sales list from time to time.

COLOMBIA, continued

Statistical publications

¶ A - General

266   Anuario general de estadística [General statistical yearbook]   (DANE).

DANE, Centro Administrativo Nacional (CAN), via El Dorado, Bogotá.

1915- 1968.   prices vary between Col$ 20.00 and 40.00.   5 vols.

Vol I   Population, social assistance, and health.
Vol II   Culture.
Vol III Transport and communications   (Col $20.00).
Vol IV   Price indices, employment and wages   (Col $40.00).
Vol V   Justice.

Time factor: the 1968 edition, the volumes of which are now being published as and when the
    information for them is available, contain statistics for 1968 and some earlier years.

§   Es.

267   Anuario estadístico de Bogotá D.E.   [Statistical yearbook of Bogota]   (DANE).

DANE, Centro Administrativo Nacional (CAN), via El Dorado, Bogotá.

1967.   Col $ 45.00.

Contains similar information to 266 above, but for Bogota only.

§   Es.

268   Boletín mensuel de estadística   [Monthly bulletin of statistics]   (DANE).

DANE, Centro Administrativo Nacional (CAN), via El Dorado, Bogotá.

1951-.   Col$ 10.00 per issue.

Contains data on socio-economic indicators, demography and social affairs, production and transport,
    money and finance, prices and wages, external economy, and the public sector.   The tables are
    followed by textual explanatory matter.

Time factor: the up-to-dateness of the tables varies considerably.

§   Es.

269   Indicadores socio-economicos [Socio-economic indicators]   (DANE).

DANE, Centro Administrativo Nacional (CAN), via El Dorado, Bogotá.

1970- (M).   not priced.

Includes data on agricultural production, industrial production, automobile production, mineral
    production, prices, etc.

§   Es.

270   Revista del Banco de la República   [Review of the Banco de la República].

Banco de la República, Bogotá.

1927- (M).   not priced.

A monthly summary of economic conditions in Colombia, covering items such as balance of payments,
    market prices for coffee, banks and banking conditions, foreign trade, prices, cost of living
    indices, etc.

§   Es.

¶ A, continued

271   Basic data on the economy   (US Department of Commerce, Bureau of International Commerce).
US Department of Commerce, Sales and Distribution Branch, Washington, D.C. 20230, USA.
US$0.15.   43 pages.

Issued as 71–048 in the series "Overseas business reports", this report presents selected basic data useful in the analysis of Colombia as a market for US exports.   Data include statistics of population, structure of the economy, agriculture, manufacturing, construction, power, etc.

Time factor: published in 1971, the report contains data for several years to 1970.

§   En.

¶ B – Production

272   Industria manufacturera nacional   [Manufacturing industry of the country]   (DANE).
DANE, Centro Administrativo Nacional (CAN), via El Dorado, Bogotá.
1966– 1969.   Col$ 40.00.   50 pages.

Contains detailed statistics of products manufactured or improved, by product.

Time Factor: the 1969 issue, with data for that year, was published in 1971.

§   Es.

Note: a separate volume of estimated figures is also issued and appears more quickly.

273   Encuesta agropecuario nacional   [National survey of agriculture and stockbreeding]   (DANE).
DANE, Centro Administrativo Nacional, via El Dorado, Bogotá.
1965– 1969.   Col$ 15.00.

An annual survey on area cultivated, crops, livestock, employees, etc.

Time factor: the 1969 edition, with data for that year, was published in 1971.

§   Es.

274   Censo agropecuario   [Census of agriculture and livestock]   (DANE).
DANE, Centro Administrativo Nacional, via El Dorado, Bogotá.
1970/71– 1970/71.

Preliminary data are now being published on the results of the census.

§   Es.

¶　C － External trade

275　　　Anuario de comercio exterior　[Yearbook of foreign trade]　(DANE).

DANE, Centro Administrativo Nacional, via El Dorado, Bogotá.

1916- 1970.　Col$ 100.00.　lxix, 653 pages.

Main tables show imports and exports arranged by commodity subdivided by countries of origin and destination.

Time factor:　the 1970 edition, with data for 1970, was published late 1971.

§　　Es.

¶　D － Internal distribution

276　　　Muestra de comercio interior　[Sample survey of internal trade]　(DANE).

DANE, Centro Administrativo Nacional, via El Dorado, Bogotá.

1967.　not priced.

Time factor:　published 1970.

§　　Es.

¶　E － Population

277　　　Censo nacional de población　[National census of population]　(DANE).

DANE, Centro Administrativo Nacional, via El Dorado, Bogotá.

1964.　Col$ 40.00 each volume.　4 vols.

One volume contains the general results of the census, and the other three contain the results for Antioquia, Cundinamarca and Boyacá respectively.　There are also volumes for each department of Colombia (Col$ 45.00 each) with population, building and housing data.

§　　Es.

Refer also to 266 and 268.

¶　F － Standard of living

Refer to 266, 268 and 270.

Central statistical office

278   Dirección General de Estadística y Censos   [General Office of Statistics and Censuses], Ministerio de Industria y Comercio [Ministry of Industry and Commerce], Apartado 10163, San José. t 21-08-83.   cables DIREGENESTAC.

The Dirección General de Estadística y Censos is responsible for the collection, co-ordination, analysis and publications of the official economic statistics of Costa Rica.

Unpublished statistical information may be provided to enquirers if it is available, and no fee is charged.

Publications other than those described in the following pages include:
Revista de estudios y estadísticas [Review of studies and statistics]   (irr).
Estadística vital [Vital statistics]   (6-monthly & annual).
Accidentes de tránsito [Traffic accidents]   (6-monthly & annual).
Población total de Costa Rica, por provincias, cantones y distrites [Total population of Costa Rica, by provinces, cantons and districts]   (Q).
Censo de vivienda, 1963 [Census of housing, 1963].

Libraries

The Dirección General de Estadística y Censos, referred to above, has a library which is open to the public for reference to statistical publications. The Instituto Centroamericano de Estadística [Central-american Statistical Institute] of the University of Costa Rica, San Pedro de Montes de Oca, San José (t 25-55-55) also has a library with similar material.

Libraries and information services abroad

Statistical publications of Costa Rica are available for reference in Costa Rican Embassies abroad, including:

United Kingdom   Costa Rican Embassy, 8 Braemar Mansions, Cornwall Gardens, London SW7 4AF. t 01-937 7883.
USA   Costa Rican Embassy, 2112 S Street N W, Washington, D.C.   t 234-2945.

Bibliographies

279   Primer inventario de las estadísticas nacionales [First inventory of national statistics] was published in 1966 by the Dirección General de Estadística y Censos. A second edition is being compiled and should be available shortly. The bibliography is a subject index to official statistics published by all Costa Rican government departments.

D

Statistical publications

¶ A - General

280   Anuario estadístico de Costa Rica   [Statistical yearbook of Costa Rica]   (Dirección General de
                  Estadística y Censos).
           Dirección General de Estadística y Censos, Ministerio de Industria y Comercio, Apartado 10163,
                  San José.
           1883- 1969.   not priced.   xxiii, 308 pages.
           Main sections:
                  Geography & climate   Industry
                  Population   Internal trade & services
                  Housing   Foreign trade
                  Health   Transport
                  Social security   Employment
                  Judicial   Price indices
                  Tourism   Money & banking
                  Agriculture & livestock
           Time factor: the 1969 edition has data for 1968, some tables having earlier figures also, and was
                  issued in 1971.
                  §   Es.

281   Boletín estadístico mensual   [Monthly statistical bulletin]   (Banco Central de Costa Rica).
           Banco Central de Costa Rica, San José.
           1950-.   not priced.
           Mainly concerned with money and banking, but also has wholesale and consumer price indices,
                  and statistics of imports and exports.
                  §   Es.

¶ B - Production

282   Censo industrias manufactureras   [Census of manufacturing industries]   (Dirección General de
                  Estadística y Censos).
           Dirección General de Estadística y Censos, Ministerio de Industria y Comercio, Apartado 10163,
                  San José.
           1950- 1964.   not priced.   xliv, 191 pages.
           Contains data on the number of establishments, number of employees, machinery, assets, electric
                  energy used, fuels used, value of sales, value of production, etc.
                  §   Es.

283   Encuesta industrial   [Industrial survey]   (Dirección General de Estadística y Censos).
           Dirección General de Estadística y Censos, Ministerio de Industria y Comercio, Apartado 10163,
                  San José.
           1959- 1965.   not priced.   20 pages.
           Contains data on the number of establishments, number of employees, wages, capital, production, etc.
           Time factor: the survey is taken occasionally and the 1965 one was published in 1967.
                  §   Es.

86

¶ B, continued

284 Encuesta agricola por muestreo: arroz, frijol, maiz [Sample enquiry into agriculture: rice, beans, maize] (Dirección General de Estadística y Censos).

Dirección General de Estadística y Censos, Ministerio de Industria y Comercio, Apartado 10163, San José.

1965- 1970. not priced. 16 pages.

§ Es.

285 Censo agropecuario [Census of agriculture & stockbreeding] (Dirección General de Estadística y Censos).

Dirección General de Estadística y Censos, Ministerio de Industria y Comercio, Apartado 10163, San José.

1950- 1963. not priced. xliii, 308 pages.

Contains data on the number and product of farms; agricultural production; use of fertilisers, pesticides and insecticides, etc; forestry exploitation; machinery used, electrical energy used, numbers of livestock, employment, etc.

§ Es.

Refer also to 280.

¶ C - External trade

286 Anuario de comercio exterior [Yearbook of foreign trade] (Dirección General de Estadística y Censos).

Dirección General de Estadística y Censos, Ministerio de Industria y Comercio, Apartado 10163, San José.

1886- 1970. not priced. xxxvii, 532 pages.

Main tables show imports and exports arranged by commodity and subdivided by countries of origin and destination.

Time factor: the 1970 edition, with data for 1970, was issued late 1971.

§ Es.

287 Estadísticas economicas: comercio exterior, movimiento marítimo internacional y construcciones [Economic statistics: foreign trade, international shipping and construction] (Dirección General de Estadística y Censos).

Dirección General de Estadística y Censos, Ministerio de Industria y Comercio, Apartado 10163, San José.

1966- 2 a yr. not priced.

Contains values of imports and exports by country and by commodity as well as shipping and construction statistics.

Time factor: each issue has data for six months (first or second half of the year) and is issued about six months later.

§ Es.

¶   C,   continued

Refer also to 082 and 083.

¶   D - Internal distribution

288   Censo de comercio y servicios   [Census of internal trade and services]   (Dirección General de
           Estadística y Censos).

           Dirección General de Estadística y Censos, Ministerio de Industria y Comercio, Apartado 10163,
           San José.

           1950/51- 1964.   not priced.   xli, 74 pages.

           Contains the number of establishments by activity, province, value of trade, employees and
           wages, etc.

           Time factor: taken every five years, the 1964 census report was published in 1967.

           §   Es.

           Refer also to 280.

¶   E - Population

289   Censo de población   [Census of population]   (Dirección General de Estadística y Censos).

           Dirección General de Estadística y Censos, Ministerio de Industria y Comercio, Apartado 10163,
           San José.

           1963.   not priced.   xliv, 633 pages.

           This final report of the census includes general information on the population, occupations,
           educational attainments, families and migration.

           §   Es.

290   El area metropolitana de San José según los censos de 1963 y 1964   [The metropolitan area of San
           José in the census of 1963 and 1964]   (Dirección General de Estadística y Censos).

           Dirección General de Estadística y Censos, Ministerio de Industria y Comercio, Apartado 10163,
           San José.

           Not priced.   xxxv, 256 pages.

           Contains data on the population, housing, industry and commerce of San José.

           §   Es.

           Refer also to 280.

¶ F – Standard of living

291   Indice de precios al por menor   [Index of wholesale prices]   (Dirección General de Estadística y Censos).

Dirección General de Estadística y Censos, Ministerio de Industria y Comercio, Apartado 10163, San José.

1960–   6 a yr.   not priced.

Wholesale price indices for the metropolitan area of San José, Valle Central, Golfito, Quepos and Limon.

Time factor: each issue has data for the two months of the issue and is published about five months later.

§   Es.

Refer also to 280 and 281.

Central statistical office

292   Dirección Central de Estadística   [Central Office of Statistics],
       Junta Central de Planificación [Central Council for Planning], Plaza de la Revolución, La Habana.
       † 79 7610.

       The Dirección Central de Estadística was set up in 1965 under the present political regime, and,
at present, issues two publications of a statistical nature which are described in the following pages.
Unpublished statistical information will be provided to enquirers if the information is available.

Libraries

       The Dirección Central de Estadística has a library but it is not open to the public.   Cuban statistical
publications are, however, available for reference in the Biblioteca Nacional 'José Marti' [the national
library] in La Habana.

Libraries and information services abroad

       Copies of the publications of the Dirección Central de Estadística are available for reference in
Cuban Embassies abroad, including:

       United Kingdom   Cuban Embassy, 57 Kensington Court, London W8 5DQ.   † 01-937 8226
       Canada   Cuban Embassy, 330 Chapel Street, Ottawa.   † 233-1497.

Statistical publications

¶ A - General

293   Compendio estadístico de Cuba   [Statistical compendium of Cuba]   (Dirección Central de
          Estadística).
       Dirección Central de Estadística, Plaza de la Revolución, La Habana.
       1965- 1968.   free, exchange of publications preferred.   viii, 53 pages.
       Main sections:
            Geography & climate   Transport & communication
            Population   Foreign trade
            World indicators   Education
            Agriculture   Culture
            Industry   Public health
            Construction   Recreation
       Time factor: the 1968 edition has data for five to ten years to 1968 or 1968/69 and was published
          in 1969.
       §   Es.

¶ A, continued

294   Cuba 1968: a supplement to the Statistical abstract of Latin America   (University of California. Latin American Center).

University of California, Latin American Center, Los Angeles, California, USA.

Time factor: published 1970.

§   En.

295   Boletín estadístico [Statistical bulletin]   (Dirección Central de Estadística).

Dirección Central de Estadística, Plaza de la Revolución, La Habana.

1965- 1967.   free, exchange of publications preferred.   xv, 189 pages.

Contents include statistical data on geography and climate, population, world indicators, employment and wages, agriculture, industry, construction, transport, communications, internal trade, foreign trade, education, cultural activities, public health, sport and recreation, and traffic accidents.

Time factor: the 1967 edition has long runs of annual figures to 1967 and also monthly figures for 1967 in some tables. The 1967 edition was published in 1969.

§   Es.

296   Economía y desarrollo [Economy and planning]   (Instituto de Economía de la Universidad de La Habana).

Instituto de Economía, Universidad de La Habana, La Habana.

1970- (Q).   Can$7.00 (Can$10.00 in Europe).

Includes an economic section with a very few statistics in the text.

§   Es.

297   Cuba economic news   (Cámara de Comercio de la República de Cuba [Chamber of Commerce of Cuba]).

Departamento de Información, Cámara de Comercio de la República de Cuba, Apartado 370, La Habana.

1965- (M).   not priced.

A news bulletin which includes a few statistics on industry, agriculture and fishing, livestock, aviculture, construction, transport and communication, foreign commerce, science and technology, fairs, congresses and exhibitions.

§   En.   There is also a Spanish version.

¶ B - Production

Refer to 293 and 295.

¶ C - External trade

298   Cuba foreign trade   (Cámara de Comercio de la República de Cuba).

Departamento de Información, Cámara de Comercio de la República de Cuba, Apartado 370, La Habana.

1964- bi-monthly. not priced.

Discusses aspects of Cuban imports, exports, foreign exchange, etc., under the present political regime.

§   En. There is also a Spanish edition.

¶ D - Internal distribution

Refer to 295.

¶ E - Population

299   Resumen de estadísticas de población   [Summary of population statistics]   (Dirección Central de Estadística).

Dirección Central de Estadística, Plaza de la Revolución, La Habana.

No.1, 1965- No.5, 1965-70.   not priced.

Time factor: the 1965-1970 edition was published in 1971.

§   Es.

Refer also to 293 and 295.

Central statistical office

300   Statistical Department,
Ministry of Finance, Trade and Industry, Government Headquarters, Kennedy Avenue, Roseau.
t   2401-9.

       The Statistical Department of the Ministry of Finance, Trade and Industry collects, analyses and publishes statistics for Dominica. Unpublished statistical information can be supplied if available, and a fee is not usually charged.

Statistical publications

¶   A - General

301   Annual statistical digest   (Statistical Department).

Statistical Department, Government Headquarters, Kennedy Avenue, Roseau.

1963- 1969.   EC$2.00.   95 pages.

Main sections:

Climate	Transport & communications
Population & vital statistics	Industrial production
Migration & tourism	Land, agriculture, forestry & fishing
Labour & employment	Public finance
Justice & crime	National accounts
Social conditions (health, educat-ion, electorate, social assistance, housing)	External trade
	Miscellaneous (co-operative societies, credit unions, post office savings, government savings bank, public library).

Time factor: published every three years, the 1969 edition has data for a number of years to 1967 or 1968.

§   En.

302   Basic data on the economy   (US Department of Commerce, Bureau of International Commerce).

US Department of Commerce, Sales and Distribution Branch, Washington, D.C. 20230, USA.

US$0.15.   8 pages.

Issued as 70-86 in the series "Overseas business reports", this report presents selected basic data useful in the analysis of the Windward Islands (of which Dominica is one) as a market for US exports. Data include statistics of population, structure of the economy, agriculture, manufacturing, construction, power, etc.

Time factor: published in December 1970, the report contains data for several years to 1969.

§   En.

¶   B - Production

Refer to 301.

¶   C – External trade.

303   Annual overseas trade report   (Statistical Department).
            Statistical Department, Government Headquarters, Kennedy Avenue, Roseau.
            1920– 1969.   EC$4.00.   122 pages.
            Main tables show imports, exports and re-exports arranged by commodity and subdivided by
               countries of origin and destination.
            Time factor: the 1969 edition, published in 1970, has data for 1969.
            §   En.

            Refer also to 301.

¶   E – Population

304   West Indies population census, 1960   (Department of Statistics, Jamaica).
            Department of Statistics, 23½ Charles Street, Kingston, Jamaica.
            Includes data on the population of Dominica.
            §   En.

304a   Eastern Caribbean population census, 1960   (Central Statistical Office, Trinidad & Tobago).
            Government Printer, 2 Victoria Avenue, Port of Spain, Trinidad.
            Volume, part D contains a comprehensive description of each enumerative district of the Windward
               Islands, including Dominica; Vol II has summary tables for the Windward Islands.
            §   En.

            Refer also to 301.

Central statistical office

305   Oficina Nacional de Estadística   [National Statistical Office],
           Calle Mercedes no.27, Santo Domingo.
           t   689 7586.

           The Oficina Nacional de Estadística is responsible for the collection, analysis and publication of
the official statistics of the Dominican Republic.

           Unpublished statistical information may be supplied to enquirers if it is available, and no charge
is made.

           Publications other than those described in the following pages include:

           Estadística demográfica de la República Dominicana   [Demographic statistics of the Dominican
                Republic]   (A).
           Finanzas municipales (estadística de ingresos y egresos)   [Local government finance (statistics
                of income and expenditure)]   (A).
           Movimiento marítimo y aéreo   [Shipping and air transport]   (A).
           Movimiento postal, telefónico y radiotelegráfico   [Postal, telephone and radiotelephone
                service]   (A).

Libraries

           The Oficina Nacional de Estadística has a library which is open to the public for reference during
ordinary office hours (7.30a.m. to 1.30p.m.).

Libraries and information services abroad

           Embassies abroad of the Dominican Republic have available for consultation the statistical publications
of the country, including:

           United Kingdom   Dominican Republic Embassy, 4 Braemar Mansions, Cornwall Gardens,
                                    London SW7 4AG.   t   01-937 1921.
           USA   Dominican Republic Embassy, 1715 22nd Street N W, Washington, D.C.
                                    t   DE2-6280.
           Canada   Dominican Republic Embassy, 200 Ridean Terrace, Ottawa.
                                    t   745-6545.

Statistical publications

¶   A - General

306   República Dominicana en cifras   [The Dominican Republic in figures]   (Oficina Nacional de
                Estadística).

           Oficina Nacional de Estadística, Calle Mercedes no.27, Santo Domingo.

           1964- 1970.   not priced.   xv, 157 pages.

[continued next page

¶   A,   continued

306,   continued

Main sections:

Meteorology	Transport & communications
Population	Other economic aspects
Education	National finance
Agriculture	Money & banking
Fishing	National income & product
Minerals	Prices
Manufactures	Wages
Electricity	Social situation
Internal trade	Co-operatives
Foreign trade	Consumption.

Time factor: the 1970 edition covers various years to 1968, 1969 and estimated figures for 1970, and was published in December 1970.

§   Es.

307   Boletín mensual   [Monthly bulletin]   (Banco Central de la República Dominicana).

Banco Central de la República Dominicana, Santo Domingo.

1948-.   not priced.

Contains statistical data on banking, money, government finance, foreign trade, prices and price indices, sales, and production.

§   Es.

308   Cuentas nacionales de la República Dominicana: producto nacional bruto, 1960-1968
             [National accounts of the Dominican Republic: gross national product, 1960-1968]
             (Banco Central de la República Dominicana).

Banco Central de la República Dominicana, Santo Domingo.

1963/67- 1960/68.   not priced.   approx 70 pages.

Contains data for the country as a whole and for each industrial sector on national income and product, gross domestic product by sector (agriculture, livestock, industry, construction, and finance), physical volume of production by sector, prices, etc.

Time factor: the 1960/68 edition, published in 1970, has data for each year from 1960 to 1968.

§   Es.

¶   B - Production

309   Estadística industrial de la República Dominicana   [Industrial statistics of the Dominican Republic]
             (Oficina Nacional de Estadística).

Oficina Nacional de Estadística, Calle Mercedes no.27, Santo Domingo.

1950- 1968.   not priced.   xiv, 77 pages.

Contains data on industrial production, including the use of raw materials; number of factories by groups; electric power production; the sugar industry; and rural industries.

Time factor: the 1968 edition, with data for 1968, was published in January 1971.

§   Es.

¶ B,   continued

310

Indice de la producción industrial manufacturera   [Index of industrial manufacturing production] (Oficina Nacional de Estadística).

Oficina Nacional de Estadística, Calle Mercedes no.27, Santo Domingo.

1966- 1970.   not priced.   xi, 18 pages.

Time factor: the 1970 edition has data for the period 1960 to 1968 and was published in 1970.

§   Es.

311

Censo nacional agropecuario   [National census of agriculture & stockbreeding]   (Oficina Nacional de Estadística).

Oficina Nacional de Estadística, Calle Mercedes no.27, Santo Domingo.

1960.   not priced.   xiii, 338 pages.

Contains the final results of the fifth agricultural and livestock census, including the area cultivated, crops, numbers of livestock, employees, farms, etc.

Time factor: the results of the 5th, 1960 census were published in 1969 (the 6th census was taken in 1971).

§   Es.

¶ C – External trade

312

Comercio exterior de la República Dominicana   [Foreign trade of the Dominican Republic] (Oficina Nacional de Estadística).

Oficina Nacional de Estadística, Calle Mercedes no.27, Santo Domingo.

1953- 1968.   not priced.   xviii, 324 pages.

Main tables show detailed statistics of imports and exports by commodity subdivided by countries of origin and destination, and also arranged first by country and subdivided by commodities.

Time factor: the 1968 edition has data for 1968 and 1967 for comparison, and was published early in 1971.

§   Es.

Refer also to 306 and 307.

¶ D – Internal distribution

Refer to 306 and 307.

DOMINICAN REPUBLIC, continued

¶ E - Population

313 Censo nacional de población y habitación [National census of population and housing] (Oficina Nacional de Estadística).

Oficina Nacional de Estadística, Calle Mercedes no.27, Santo Domingo.

1960. not priced.

Time factor: the final results of the 1960 census were published in 1966. Another census was taken in 1970 and the preliminary results are now about to be published.

§ Es.

Refer also to 306.

¶ F - Standard of living

314 Encuesta de ingresos y gastos de los familias en la ciudad de Santo Domingo, 1969 [Survey of income and the expenses of families in the city of Santo Domingo, 1969] (Oficina Nacional de Estadística).

Oficina Nacional de Estadística, Calle Mercedes no.27, Santo Domingo.

§ Es.

Refer also to 306.

Central statistical office

315
Instituto Nacional de Estadística   [National Institute of Statistics],
Edificio Seminario Menor, Quito.
t   211-126 and 212-402.   Cables   INE QUITO-ECUADOR.

The Institute, previously titled "Dirección General de Estadística y Censos", is attached to the Junta Nacional de Planificación y Coordinación Económica   [National Council of Economic Planning and Co-ordination].   It is responsible for the collection, analysis and publication of economic statistics of Ecuador and for the taking of various censuses.

Unpublished statistical information may be supplied to enquirers when it is available.

Publications other than those described in the following pages include:
Anuario de estadísticas vitales   [Yearbook of vital statistics].
Anuario de estadísticas hospitalarias   [Yearbook of hospital statistics].
Anuario estadísticas de transportes   [Statistical yearbook of transport].
Encuesta de edificaciones (permisos de construcción)   [Survey of buildings (construction
permits)]   (A).

Libraries

The Junta Nacional de Planificación y Coordinación, referred to above, has a library which is open to the public for reference to statistical publications.   Banco Central del Ecuador, Departamento de Investigaciones Económicas, in Quito (t 510-400) also has a similar library which is also open to the public for reference.

Libraries and information services abroad

Statistical publications of the Institute and the Bank are available for reference at Ecuadorian Embassies and Consulates abroad, including:

United Kingdom	Ecuadorian Embassy, 3 Hans Crescent, London SW1X 0LS. t 01-584 1367.
	Ecuadorian Consulate, Tower Buildings, Water Street, Liverpool 3. t 051-236 1554.
USA	Ecuadorian Embassy, 2535 15th Street N W, Washington, D.C. t 234-7200.
Canada	Ecuadorian Consulate, 2150 St Luke Street, Montreal. t 931-1215.

Statistical publications

¶   A - General

316
Boletín del Banco Central del Ecuador   [Bulletin of the Central Bank of Ecuador].

Banco Central del Ecuador, Secretaría General, Quito.

1928- (Q).   free distribution.

Includes a statistical section with tables of foreign trade, production, and price indices as well as
[continued next page

¶   A,   continued

316,   continued   banking and finance.

§ Es.

Note: the bulletin is updated by a weekly 'Información estadística' solely concerned with banking information.

317   Memoria del gerente general del Banco Central del Ecuador   [Report of the general management of the Central Bank of Ecuador].

Banco Central del Ecuador, Secretaría General, Quito.

1928- 1969.   free distribution.   226 + 139 pages.

Includes a statistical annex with data on foreign trade, balance of payments, foreign exchange, price indices, etc.

Time factor: the 1969 edition, published late 1970, has data for 1969 and some earlier years.

§   Es.

318   Anuario de estadística, 1963-68   [Statistical yearbook, 1963-68]   (Instituto Nacional de Estadística).

Instituto Nacional de Estadística, Edificio Seminario Menor, Quito.

Includes data on population, vital statistics, industry, external trade, social statistics, etc.

Time factor: covers the years 1963 to 1968.

§   Es.

319   Quito y sus estadísticas, 1965   [Quito and its statistics, 1965]   (Universidad Central del Ecuador, Facultad de Ciencias Económicas y Administrativas, Instituto de Investigaciones Económicas y Financieras).

Universidad Central del Ecuador, Quito.

1965 is No.1.   not priced.   168 pages.

Contains general information and illustrations of Quito, statistical data including geography & climate, demography, social services, education & culture, economic information (agriculture, industry, trade, production, transport, communications, money, prices, finance, services: telephone, water, electricity, and administration).

Time factor: published early 1967.

§   Es.

320   Basic data on the economy   (US Department of Commerce, Bureau of International Commerce).

US Department of Commerce, Sales and Distribution Branch, Washington, D.C. 20230, USA.

US$0.15.   11 pages.

Issued as 71-056 in the series "Overseas business reports", this report presents selected basic data useful in the analysis of Ecuador as a market for US exports.   Data include statistics of population, structure of the economy, agriculture, manufacturing, construction, power, etc.

Time factor; published late in 1971, the report contains data for several years to 1970.

§   En.

¶ B - Production

321   Encuesta de manufactura y minería   [Survey of the manufacturing and minerals industries] (Instituto Nacional de Estadística).

Instituto Nacional de Estadística, Quito.

1964- 1969.   not priced.   135 pages.

Contains data on employment, wages, raw materials used, power used, value and depreciation, production in the manufacturing and mineral industries.

Time factor: the 1969 report has data for 1969 and was published in 1971.

§   Es.

322   Producción estimativa de los principales cultivos agrícoles del Ecuador   [Estimated production of the principal agricultural products of Ecuador]   (Ministerio de Agricultura y Ganadería).

Ministerio de Agricultura y Ganadería, Quito.

1962- 1966.   not priced.   20 pages.

Time factor: the 1966 edition, with data for that year, was published in 1968.

§   Es.

Refer also to 316.

¶ C - External trade

323   Anuario de comercio exterior   [External trade yearbook]   (Instituto Nacional de Estadística).

Instituto Nacional de Estadística, Edificio Seminario Menor, Quito.

1957- 1967.   not priced.   611 pages.

Includes detailed statistics of imports and exports arranged by commodity and subdivided by countries of origin and destination.

Time factor: the 1967 edition, with data for 1967, was published in 1970.

§   Es.

324   Comercio exterior Ecuatoriano   [Foreign trade of Ecuador]   (Banco Central del Ecuador).

1947- (M).   not priced.

Contains data on licences granted to export and import certain commodities, and movement at the ports.

§   Es.

¶ E – Population

325   Censo de población y vivienda   [Census of population and housing]   (Junta Nacional de
         Planificación y Coordinación Económica.   Division de Estadística y Censos).

     Instituto Nacional de Estadística, Edificio Seminario Menor, Quito.

     1950- 1962.   4 vols.   not priced.

     Contains characteristics of the population and of the housing in Ecuador as a whole and for Bolivar,
         Azuay, El Oro, Región Oriental, Los Ríos, Loja and Imbabura.

     §   Es.

¶ F – Standard of living

326   Indice de precios al consumidor: Quito, Guayaquil y Cuenca   [Consumer price indices: Quito,
         Guayaquil and Cuenca]   (Instituto Nacional de Estadística).

     Instituto Nacional de Estadística, Edificio Seminario Menor, Quito.

     (M).   not priced.

     §   Es.

Refer also to 316 and 317.

327   Falkland Islands and dependencies: report for the year   (Foreign and Commonwealth Office).
H M Stationery Office, P.O.Box 569, London SE1 9NH.
1968 and 1969.   £0.55.   84 pages.
Mainly textual, but includes some statistics of population, employment, etc.
Time factor: the 1968 and 1969 edition, with data for those years, was published in March 1971.
§   En.

Central statistical office

328   Institut National de la Statistique et des Etudes Economiques   [National Institute for Statistics and
        Economic Research],
        29 Quai Branly, 75 Paris 7, France.
        t   468 96 00 and 468 98 10.

        INSEE is the central organisation for economic information on France and it also collects and
publishes information on French overseas territories.   It is concerned with social and economic demography,
consumption, prices, income, national accounts, and national and regional economic planning.   There is
a departmental service in Cayenne, Guyane Française (Boîte Postale 757-97-3).

Statistical publications

¶   A – General

329   La zone franc   [The franc area]   (Comité Monétaire de la Zone Franc).

        Comité Monétaire de la Zone Franc, 39 rue Croix des Petits Champs, 75 Paris 1, France.

        1969.   not priced.   343 pages.

        Contains data on trends in production, and on foreign trade, finance and investment, money and
            credit, balance of payments, currency reserves, etc in the French-speaking and franc CFA
            countries, including Guyane Française.   Tables are included in the text.

        Time factor: the 1969 edition, published early 1971, contains data for two to three years to 1969.

        §   Fr.

¶   C – External trade

330   Statistiques du commerce extérieur des départements d'outre-mer: importations - exportations (en
            N.D.B.)   [Statistics of the foreign trade of the overseas departments: imports - exports (by the
            Brussels Nomenclature)]   (Direction Général des Douanes et des Droits Indirects, Paris).

        Imprimerie Nationale, 39 rue de la Convention, 75 Paris 15, France.

        1966- 1968.   Fr 90.00 (Fr 104.00 abroad).   xiii, 758 pages.

        Contains detailed statistics of imports and exports arranged by commodity subdivided by countries
            of origin and destination for each of the overseas departments of France (Guadeloupe, Martinique,
            Guyane and Réunion).

        Time factor: the 1968 edition, with data for 1968, was published in 1969.

        §   Fr.

        Refer also to 082 and 083.

¶ E - Population

331
Résultats statistiques du recensement général de la population de 1967: Guyane. 1ère partie:
    tableaux statistiques [Statistical results of the general census of the population of Guyane,
    1967. statistical tables]   (Institut National de la Statistique et des Etudes Economiques).

Institut National de la Statistique et des Etudes Economiques, 29 Quai Branly, 75 Paris 7, France.

1961- 1967.   not priced.   172 pages.

Time factor: published in 1971.

§   Fr.

¶ F - Standard of living

332
Enquête sur les dépenses des ménages: Guyane   [Survey of the expenditure of households: Guyana]
    (Institut National de la Statistique et des Etudes Economiques).

Institut National de la Statistique et des Etudes Economiques, 29 Quai Branly, 75 Paris 7, France.

1967.   Fr 4.00.

Time factor: published 1968.

§   Fr.

Grenada is self-governed in association with Britain, which retains powers and responsibilities for defense and external affairs. Enquiries concerning statistics for the island could be made to the Minister of Finance, Trade and Production, at St George's, or to the Grenada Chamber of Commerce Inc, P.O.Box 129, St George's.

Statistical publications

¶   A - General

333   Grenada: report for the year   (Foreign and Commonwealth Office).

H M Stationery Office, P.O.Box 569, London SE1 9NH.

1955/56- 1965 & 1966.   £0.50.   64 pages.

Mainly textual, but contains some statistics on population, employment, commerce, tourism, production, finance, etc.

Time factor: published in 1969.

§   En.

334   Economic survey and projections (British Development Division in the Caribbean).

Not priced.   xiv, 31 pages.

Deals with the economy of Grenada and has a statistical appendix showing projections for exports, construction and engineering, hotels, government and other sectors.

Time factor: published in 1967.

§   En.

335   Basic data on the economy   (US Department of Commerce, Bureau of International Commerce).

US Department of Commerce, Sales and Distribution Branch, Washington, D.C. 20230, USA.

US$0.15.   8 pages.

Issued as 70-86 in the series "Overseas business reports", this report presents selected basic data useful in the analysis of the Windward Islands (of which Grenada is one) as a market for US exports. Data include statistics of population, structure of the economy, agriculture, manufacturing, construction, power, etc.

Time factor: published in December 1970, the report contains data for several years to 1969.

§   En.

¶   C - External trade

336   Annual overseas trade report   (Government of Grenada, W.I.).

Government Printer, St George's, Grenada.

1921- 1967.   not priced.   154 pages.

Main tables show statistics of imports and exports arranged by commodity and subdivided by countries of origin and destination.

Time factor: the 1967 edition, with data for 1967, was published in 1970.

§   En.

¶   C,   continued

337   Quarterly overseas trade report   (Government of Grenada, W.I.).
            Government Printer, St George's, Grenada.
            (Q).   not priced.
            Main tables show statistics of imports and exports arranged by commodity and subdivided by countries
                of origin and destination.
            Time factor: each issue has data for that quarter and cumulated figures for the year to date.
            §   En.

¶   E – Population

338   West Indies population census, 1960   (Department of Statistics, Jamaica).
            Department of Statistics, $23\frac{1}{2}$ Charles Street, Kingston, Jamaica.
            Includes data on the population of Grenada.
            §   En.

339   Eastern Caribbean population census, 1960   (Central Statistical Office, Trinidad & Tobago).
            Government Printer, 2 Victoria Avenue, Port of Spain, Trinidad.
            Volume I, part D contains a comprehensive description of each enumerative district of the Windward
                Islands, including Grenada; Volume II has summary tables for the Windward Islands.
            §   En.

Central statistical office

340   Institut National de la Statistique et des Etudes Economiques [National Institute for Statistics and
           Economic Research],
        29 Quai Branly, 75 Paris 7, France.
        t 468 96 00 and 468 98 10.

        INSEE is the central organisation for economic information on France and it also collects and publishes information on French overseas territories. It is concerned with social and economic demography, consumption prices, income, national accounts, and national and regional economic planning. There is a departmental service in the Préfecture, Basse-Terre, Guadeloupe.

Statistical publications

¶ A - General

341   Annuaire statistique de la Guadeloupe [Statistical yearbook of Guadeloupe]   (Institut National
           de la Statistique et des Etudes Economiques).

        Institut National de la Statistique et des Etudes Economiques, 29 quai Branly, 75 Paris 7, France
          or   Service Départemental de Statistique d'Outre-Mer, Préfecture, Basse-Terre, Guadeloupe.

        1949/53- 1963/67. Fr 25.00. xi, 111 pages.

        Main sections:

Geography & administration, agriculture	Elections
Climate	Production
Population	Transport & communications
Health & social aid	Foreign trade
Education	Prices, wages, social security
Housing	Money, credit
Justice	Public finance
	Economic accounts

        Time factor: the 1963/67 edition has data for 1963, 1964, 1965, 1966 and 1967 for most tables, and was published in 1969.

        §   Fr.

342   La zone franc [The franc zone] (Comité Monétaire de la Zone Franc).

        Comité Monétaire de la Zone Franc, 39 rue Croix des Petits Champs, 75 Paris 1, France.

        1969. not priced. 343 pages.

        Contains data on trends in production, and on foreign trade, finance and investment, money and credit, balance of payments, currency reserves, etc in the French-speaking and franc CFA countries, including Guadeloupe. Tables are included in the text.

        Time factor: the 1969 edition, published early 1971, contains data for two or three years to 1969.

        §   Fr.

¶   A,   continued

343   Basic data on the economy   (US Department of Commerce, Bureau of International Commerce).
           US Department of Commerce, Sales and Distribution Branch, Washington, D.C. 20230, USA.
           US$0.15.   8 pages.

           Issued as 69-50 in the series "Overseas business reports", this report presents selected basic data
               useful in the analysis of Guadeloupe as a market for US exports.   Data include statistics of
               population, structure of the economy, agriculture, manufacturing, construction, power, etc.

           Time factor: published in October 1969, the report contains data for several years to 1968.

           §   En.

344   Comptes économiques de la Guadeloupe   [Economic accounts of Guadeloupe]   (Institut National
               de la Statistique et des Etudes Economique).

           Institut National de la Statistique et des Etudes Economiques, 29 quai Branly, 75 Paris 7, France
               or   Service Départemental de Statistique d'Outre-Mer, Préfecture, Basse-Terre, Guadeloupe.

           1965/67- 1969.   not priced.   33 pages.

           Contains textual data on the economy of Guadeloupe and statistical tables of resources and the use of
               goods and services; analysis of production by industry; statistical data on enterprises, administration
               and houses; and foreign trade.

           Time factor: the 1969 edition, with data for 1969, was published in 1971.

           §   Fr.

345   Comptes économiques des départements d'outre-mer (sauf la Guyane)   [Economic accounts for the
               overseas departments (except Guyana)]   (Institut National de la Statistique et des Etudes
               Economiques).

           Institut National de la Statistique et des Etudes Economiques, 29 quai Branly, 75 Paris 7, France.

           1968- 1968.   not priced.   19 pages.

           Contains information for Guadeloupe, Martinique and Réunion, but is much briefer than 338 above.

           Time factor: the 1968 edition, with data for 1968, was published in 1971.

           §   Fr.

¶   B - Production

           Refer to 341.

¶   C - External trade

346   Statistiques du commerce extérieur des départements d'outre-mer: importations - exportations
        (en N.D.B.) [Statistics of the foreign trade of the overseas departments: imports - exports
        (by the Brussels Nomenclature)]   (Direction Général des Douanes et des Droits Indirects, Paris).

        Imprimerie Nationale, 39 rue de la Convention, 75 Paris 15, France.

        1966- 1968.   Fr 90.00 (Fr 104.00 abroad).   xiii, 758 pages.

        Contains detailed statistics of imports and exports arranged by commodity and subdivided by countries
        of origin and destination for each of the overseas departments of France (Guadeloupe, Martinique,
        Guyane and Réunion).

        Time factor: the 1968 edition, with data for 1968, was published in 1969.

        §   Fr.

        Refer also to 082, 083 and 341.

¶   E - Population

347   Recensement démographique de la Guadeloupe   [Demographic census of Guadeloupe]
        (Institut National de la Statistique et des Etudes Economiques).

        Institut National de la Statistique et des Etudes Economiques, 29 quai Branly, 75 Paris 7, France
        or   Service Départemental de Statistique d'Outre-Mer, Préfecture, Basse-Terre, Guadeloupe.

        1961- 1967.   not priced.

        Time factor: the provisional principal results were published in 1970.

        §   Fr.

        Refer also to 341.

¶   F - Standard of living

        Refer to 341.

Central statistical office

348   Dirección General de Estadística   [General Statistical Office],
10a Calle 7–69, Zona 1, Guatemala City.
t 22808.

A statistical section of the Ministry of Public Works was formed in 1879 and elevated to "Dirección General de Estadística" in 1886. It was transferred to the Ministry of the Economy in 1944. The functions of the Office are to collect, analyse and publish official statistics which may be required, including the taking of censuses of population, industry, agriculture, etc.

Unpublished statistical information can be provided to enquirers if it is available.

Publications other than those described in the following pages include:
Estadísticas de vehicules en circulación   [Motor vehicle registration statistics]   (A).
Censo de transportes 1952   [Census of transport 1952].
Finanzas municipales   [Local government finance]   (A).
Algunas cifras acerca de Guatemala (Folleto de Bolsillo)   [Some figures relating to Guatemala (pocketbook)]   (A).

Libraries

The Dirección General de Estadística, referred to above, has a library which is open to the public for reference to statistical publications.

Libraries and information services abroad

Guatemalan Embassies abroad receive copies of Guatemalan statistical publications, including:
USA   Guatemalan Embassy, 2220 R Street N W, Washington, D.C.   t DE2–2865.

Statistical publications

¶ A – General

349   Guatemala en cifras   [Guatemala in figures]   (Dirección General de Estadística).

Dirección General de Estadística, 10a, Calle 7–69, Zona 1, Guatemala City.

1955– 1969.   not priced.   160 pages.

Main sections:

Geography	Finance
Demography	Money & banking
Agriculture	Balance of payments & national income
Livestock	Insurance
Industrial production & consumption	Social, cultural & judicial
Transport	Hospital
Foreign trade	Employment & social security
Price indices	

[continued next page

¶   A,   continued

349,   continued

Time factor: the 1969 edition, with tables usually covering 10 years to 1969, was published in
April 1971.

§   Es.

350   Trimestro estadístico   [Quarterly statistics]   (Dirección General de Estadística).

Dirección General de Estadística, 10a Calle 7–69, Zona 1, Guatemala City.

1946–.   not priced.

Includes statistical data on income and expenditure, industrial activity, cost of living, etc.

Time factor: recent issues have been published annually and contain only annual figures.   The 1968
edition, with long runs of figures to 1968, was published early in 1971.

§   Es.

351   El informador estadístico   [Statistical information]   (Dirección General de Estadística).

Dirección General de Estadística, 10a Calle 7–69, Zona 1, Guatemala City.

1962– bi-monthly.   not priced.

§   Es.

352   Estudio económico y memoria de labores   [Economic study and report of activities]
(Banco de Guatemala).

Banco de Guatemala, 7a Avenida 22–01, Zona 1, Guatemala City.

1946– 1970.   not priced.   xxxii, 262 pages.

Statistical tables follow the text of each section of the report, which are: national economic
situation (production, power, transport & communications, foreign trade, etc); balance of
payments; monetary situation; banking situation; public finance; and operations and account
of the Bank.

Time factor: the 1970 edition, published mid–1971, has data for 1969 and 1970.

§   Es.

353   Boletín estadístico   [Statistical bulletin]   (Banco de Guatemala).

Banco de Guatemala, 7a Avenida 22–01, Zona 1, Guatemala City.

1948– (Q).   not priced.

Contains statistical tables and charts on money and banking, public finance, prices, foreign trade,
and other economic indicators.

§   Es.

GUATEMALA,   continued

¶   A,   continued

354   Informe económico   [Economic report]   (Banco de Guatemala).
           Banco de Guatemala, 7a Avenida 22-01, Zona 1, Guatemala City.
           1953-   (Q).   not priced.
           An economic survey, with data on foreign trade, balance of payments, prices of raw materials on
               the international market.   Also information on markets for cotton, sugar and vanilla.   Some
               statistics are included in the text.
           §   Es.

¶   B - Production

355   Censo de industria   [Census of industry]   (Dirección General de Estadística).
           Dirección General de Estadística, 10a Calle 7-69, Zona 1, Guatemala City.
           1946- 1965.   not priced.   2 vols.
           The report of the 4th census of industry is to be published as Volumes V and VI of the "Censos
               económicos"   [Economic censuses].
           §   Es.

356   Censo agropecuario   [Census of agriculture and stockbreeding]   (Dirección General de Estadística).
           Dirección General de Estadística, 10a Calle 7-69, Zona 1, Guatemala City.
           1950- 1964.   not priced.   2 vols.
           Contains data on area cultivated, crops, livestock, employment, etc.
           §   Es.

357   Encuesta agropecuario   [Survey of agriculture and stockbreeding]   (Dirección General de
               Estadística).
           Dirección General de Estadística, 10a Calle 7-69, Zona 1, Guatemala City.
           1967/68- 1967/68.   not priced.   24 pages.
           The results of a survey on the production of crops and numbers of livestock.
           Time factor: the survey was undertaken in May 1968 and published in 1970.
           §   Es.

           Refer also to 349.

¶   C – External trade

358   Anuario de comercio exterior   [Yearbook of foreign trade]   (Dirección General de Estadística).
            Dirección General de Estadística, 10a Calle 7–69, Zona 1, Guatemala City.
            1952– 1967–68.   not priced.   lxiii, 517 pages.
            Main tables show imports and exports arranged by commodity and subdivided by country of origin
                and destination.
            Time factor: the 1967–68 edition has data for both 1967 and 1968, and was published mid–1971.
            §   Es.

            Refer also to 082, 083 and 349.

¶   D – Internal distribution

359   Censo de comercios   [Commercial census]   (Dirección General de Estadística).
            Dirección General de Estadística, 10a Calle 7–69, Zona 1, Guatemala City.
            1959– 1965.   not priced.   2 vols.
            The report of the second census of commerce of Guatemala is published as Volumes II and IV of the
                "Censos económicos"   [Economic censuses].
            §   Es.

360   Censo de servicios   [Census of services]   (Dirección General de Estadística).
            Dirección General de Estadística, 10a Calle 7–69, Zona 1, Guatemala City.
            1965– 1965.   not priced.   2 vols.
            The report of the first census of services in Guatemala is published as Volumes I and III of the
                "Censos económicos"   [Economic censuses].
            §   Es.

¶   E – Population

361   Censo de población   [Census of population]   (Dirección General de Estadística).
            Dirección General de Estadística, 10a Calle 7–69, Zona 1, Guatemala City.
            1824– 1964.   not priced.
            A sample census was taken in 1964 and several volumes of results have been published, including
                a general volume, one on the population of the City of Guatemala, and one on housing.
            §   Es.

            Refer also to 349.

¶ F - Standard of living

362 Indices de precios en la Ciudad de Guatemala [Index of prices in the City of Guatemala]
  (Dirección General de Estadística).

  Dirección General de Estadística, 10a Calle 7-69, Zona 1, Guatemala City.

  (A) 1969. not priced.

  Time factor; the 1969 edition, with data for several years up to that date was published in 1970.

  § Es.

363 Número índices de precios: República de Guatemala [Price index numbers: Guatemala]
  (Dirección General de Estadística).

  Dirección General de Estadística, 10a Calle 7-69, Zona 1, Guatemala City.

  (M). not priced.

  § Es.

Central statistical office

364   Statistical Bureau,
           Ministry of Economic Development, Avenue of the Republic, Georgetown.
           t 4764.

           The Statistical Bureau of the Ministry of Economic Development is the organisation responsible for the collection, analysis and publication of statistics of Guyana (ex-British Guiana).

           Publications of the Bureau, other than those described in the following pages, include:
               Quarterly bulletin of financial statistics.

Statistical publications

¶   A – General

365   Economic survey of Guyana   (Statistical Bureau, Ministry of Economic Development).

           Statistical Bureau, Ministry of Economic Development, Avenue of the Republic, Georgetown.

           (A) 1969.   G$2.00.   92 pages.

           Main sections, each of which has tables interspersed within the text:

General review	Investment
National income & product	Construction
Agriculture (sugar, rice, livestock)	Banking & finance
Mining	Retail sales & prices
Manufacturing	Public finance
Electricity production	Population & migration
External trade	Prospect for [the future].
Balance of payments	

           Time factor: the 1969 edition, published in 1971, has data for 1969.

           §   En.

366   Quarterly statistical digest   (Statistical Bureau, Ministry of Economic Development).

           Statistical Bureau, Ministry of Economic Development, Avenue of the Republic, Georgetown.

           1960-.   G$1.50 per copy.

           Includes statistical data on the weather, population and vital statistics, migration, consumer prices, overseas trade, internal trade, building, transport & communications, industrial production, and labour.   Crime statistics and balance of payments and national income appear only in the December issues.

           Time factor: each issue has data for the period of the issue and various runs of retrospective annual and quarterly figures, and is issued about six months later.

           §   En.

¶ A, continued

367   Bank of Guyana economic bulletin.
           Bank of Guyana, P.O.Box 658, Georgetown.
           1967- (M).   not priced.
           Includes a statistical annex with data on production, consumption, investment, exports and imports,
               balance of payments, public finance, and monetary developments.
           §   En.

¶ B – Production

           Refer to 365, 366 and 367.

¶ C – External trade

368   Annual account relating to external trade   (Statistical Bureau, Ministry of Economic Development).
           Statistical Bureau, Ministry of Economic Development, Avenue of the Republic, Georgetown.
           1879- 1968.   G$3.00.   208 pages.
           Main tables show imports, exports and re-exports arranged by commodity and subdivided by countries
               of origin and destination.
           Time factor: the 1968 edition, published in 1970, has data for 1968.
           §   En.

369   Monthly account relating to external trade   (Statistical Bureau, Ministry of Economic Development).
           Statistical Bureau, Ministry of Economic Development, Avenue of the Republic, Georgetown.
           1955-.   G$1.00 per copy.
           Main tables show imports, exports and re-exports arranged by commodity and subdivided by countries
               of origin and destination.
           Time factor: each issue has data for the month of the issue and cumulated figures for the year to
               date, and is published three or four months later.
           §   En.

370   External trade with CARIFTA territories   (Statistical Bureau, Ministry of Finance).
           Statistical Bureau, Ministry of Finance, Avenue of the Republic, Georgetown.
           1968- (Q).   not priced.
           Contains cumulative statistics of the trade of Guyana with the other Caribbean Free Trade Area
               territories.
           §   En.

           Refer also to 365, 366 and 367.

E

¶   D – Internal distribution

Refer to 365 and 366.

¶   E – Population

371   British Guiana population census   (Central Statistical Office, Port of Spain, Trinidad).
Central Statistical Office, 2 Victoria Avenue, Port of Spain, Trinidad.
1960.   3 vols.
The census covered the whole of the Eastern Caribbean within the British Commonwealth.
   Vol I Part A is a description of the census and methods used; Vol I Part C contains a
   comprehensive description of each enumerative district of what was then British Guiana;
   Vol II contains summary tables including British Guiana; Vol III contains the major
   tabulations of the whole census with less geographical detail.
§   En.

Refer also to 365 and 366.

¶   F – Standard of living

Refer to 365 and 366.

Central statistical office

372   Institut Haitien de Statistique   [Haitian Institute of Statistics],
Cité de l'Exposition, Boulevard Harry Truman, Port-au-Prince.

The Institute compiles a quarterly statistical bulletin (see 373) and, occasionally, some special publications.

In principle, the Institute will provide available unpublished statistical data on request.

Libraries

The Institut Haitien de Statistique has a library which is open to the public.

Libraries and information centres overseas

Copies of the Institute's quarterly bulletin are sent to embassies overseas, including:
   USA   Haitian Embassy, 4400 17th Street N W, Washington, D.C.   t RA3-7000.
   Canada   Haitian Embassy, 150 Driveway, Ottawa.   t 232-2855.

Statistical publications

¶   A - General

373   Bulletin trimestriel de statistique   [Quarterly bulletin of statistics]   (Institut Haitien de Statistique).
Institut Haitien de Statistique, Cité de l'Exposition, Boulevard Harry Truman, Port-au-Prince.
1951-.   not priced.
   Main sections:

Climate	Foreign trade
Demography	Transport & communications
Population & demographic indices	Finance
Housing	Prices & cost of living
Energy	Social security
Agriculture & fisheries	Accidents at work
Industrial production	Police & justice
Industrial & commercial	Social & cultural affairs
establishments	Miscellaneous.

   Time factor: each issue has data for the period of the issue and some earlier figures, and may be
      published up to two years later.
   §   Fr.

¶ A, continued

374   Recensement général de la République d'Haiti   [General census of the Republic of Haiti]
            (Institut Haitien de Statistique).
        Institut Haitien de Statistique, Port-au-Prince.
        1950.   not priced.   5 vols.
        Contains data on demography, economy, family and housing, agriculture and livestock.
            §   Fr.

375   Basic data on the economy   (US Department of Commerce, Bureau of International Commerce).
        US Department of Commerce, Sales and Distribution Branch, Washington, D.C. 20230, USA.
        US$0.15.   8 pages.
        Issued as 70-24 in the series "Overseas business reports", this report presents selected basic data
            useful in the analysis of Haiti as a market for US exports.   Data include statistics of population,
            structure of the economy, agriculture, manufacturing, construction, power, etc.
        Time factor: published in June 1970, the report contains data for several years to 1969.
            §   En.

¶   B - Production

        Refer to 373.

¶   C - External trade

376   Rapport annuel   [Annual report]   (Administration Générale des Douanes).
        Administration Générale des Douanes, Port-au-Prince.
        1955- 1967/68.   not priced.   145 pages.
        Main tables show imports and exports arranged by commodity and subdivided by countries of origin
            and destination.
        Time factor: the 1967/68 edition, covering the fiscal year 1967/68, was published early 1971.
            §   Fr.

        Refer also to 373.

¶   D - Internal distribution

        Refer to 373.

¶ E – Population

Refer to 373

¶ F – Standard of living

Refer to 373

Central statistical office

377   Dirección General de Estadística y Censos [General Office of Statistics and Censuses],
6a Avenida 8a Calle no.718, Comayaguela, Tegucigalpa D.C.
t 2-8450 and 2-8448.

    The Dirección General de Estadística y Censos is responsible for the collection, analysis and publication of the statistics of Honduras, and in connection with this work the Office has also published some directories (of primary schools, industrial and commercial organisations). With the 1969 edition of "Anuario estadístico" (see 378) the data previously published in individual subject volumes have been brought together within the one overall title.

Libraries

    The Dirección General de Estadística y Censos (see above) has a library which is open to the public for reference to statistical publications.

Libraries and information services abroad

    The publications of the Dirección General de Estadística y Censos are sent to Honduras embassies abroad, including:
    United Kingdom   Honduran Embassy, 48 George Street, London W1H 5RF. t 01-486 4880.
    USA   Honduran Embassy, 4715 16th Street N W, Washington, D.C. 20011.
            t 723 4923.

Bibliographies

377a   Inventario estadístico nacional al 31 diciembre de 1969 [National inventory of statistics as at 31 December 1969].

    Dirección General de Estadística y Censos, 6a Avenida 8a Calle no.718, Comayaguela D.C.

    Published in June 1970, this detailed publication includes a list of organisations producing statistics and a list of statistics produced, arranged by general subject subdivided by the organisation responsible, details of tables, and title of publication.

Statistical publications

¶   A - General

378   Anuario estadístico   [Statistical yearbook]   (Dirección General de Estadística y Censos).

Dirección General de Estadística y Censos, 6a Avenida 8a Calle no.718, Comayaguela D.C.

1952- 1969.   not priced.   5 volumes in 10.

Contents:
    Tomo I   Climate, population, vital statistics, public health, and social assistance.
    Tomo II   Education.
    Tomo III   Foreign trade
                 Vol I   Exports, main tables showing exports arranged by commodity,
                         subdivided by countries of origin and destination.
                 Vols II, III & IV   Imports, main tables showing imports arranged by
                         commodity, subdivided by countries of origin and destination.
                 Vol V   Trade with Central America.
    Tomo IV   Indices of foreign trade, prices, banking and monetary statistics, income and
                 expenditure of central government.
    Tomo V   Agricultural statistics, production of electric energy, construction, and
                 transport.

Time factor: the 1969 edition commenced publication in 1970, and refers to 1969 and earlier
    years in some cases.

§   Es.

379   Compendio estadístico   [Statistical compendium]   (Dirección General de Estadística y Censos in
       collaboration with Consejo Superior de Planificacion Económica).

Dirección General de Estadística y Censos, 6a Avenida 8a Calle no.718, Comayaguela D.C.

1966- 1967/68.   not priced.   266 pages.

Main sections:
    Demography   Public sector
    Housing   External trade
    Public health & social assistance   Agriculture
    Education   Industry
    National accounts   Electricity
    Banking & money   Transport

Time factor: the 1967/68 edition, published in 1970, has long runs of figures to 1967.

§   Es.

¶   B - Production

380   Censo: la industria en Honduras   [Census of industry in Honduras]   (Dirección General de
       Estadística y Censos).

Dirección General de Estadística y Censos, 6a Avenida 8a Calle no.718, Comayaguela D.C.

1966- 1966.   not priced.   188 pages.

Contains data on manufacturing establishments, including the number of establishments, number of
    employees, occupations of employees, wages and salaries, the value of materials used, power
    used, production and sales, etc.

Time factor: the 1966 edition, with data for 1966, was issued in 1969.

§   Es.

¶   B,   continued

381   Censo nacional agropecuario   [National census of agriculture & stockbreeding]   (Dirección General
           de Estadística y Censos).
         Dirección General de Estadística y Censos, 6a Avenida 8a Calle no.718, Comayaguela D.C.
         1952- 1965/66.   not priced.
         A preliminary volume (111 pages) has been published including data on the number and size of
           holdings, numbers of livestock, etc.
         Time factor: the 1965/66 census refers to the crop year 1965/66, and the preliminary volume
           was published in 1967.
             §   Es.

         Refer also to 378 and 379.

¶   C – External trade

         Refer to 378 and 379; but there is also "Comercio exterior" [Foreign trade] which is sometimes
           issued on a cumulative quarterly basis for the periods January to March, January to June,
           and January to September.   All three issues seldom appear for each year, and they are
           published about 18 months after the end of the period covered.

¶   E – Population

382   Censo nacional de población y vivienda   [National census of population and housing]
           (Dirección General de Estadística y Censos).
         Dirección General de Estadística y Censos, 6a Avenida 8a Calle no.718, Comayaguela D.C.
         1881- 1961.   not priced.   3 vols.
         Volume I contains data on the general and educational characteristics of the population;
           Volume II contains data on the economic characteristics of the population; and Volume III
           deals with housing.
             §   Es.

         Refer also to 378 and 379.

¶   F – Standard of living

         Refer to 378.

Central statistical office

383   Department of Statistics,
           23½ Charles Street, Kingston.
           t   929-2330.

The Department of Statistics is the organisation responsible for the collection, analysis and publication of most of the economic statistics of Jamaica.

Available but unpublished statistical information can be supplied and there is no charge involved except in cases where the volume of the data requested cannot be handled by the staff in their regular working hours.   A fee would then be charged for overtime work.

Publications other than those described in the following pages include:
        Monetary statistics   (Q).
        Wage rates and hours in selected industries   (A).

Libraries

The Department of Statistics, referred to above, has a library which is open to the public wishing to consult statistical publications.

Libraries and information services abroad

Publications of the Department of Statistics are available for reference in the offices of the Jamaican information services in various countries, including those at the following addresses:

United Kingdom   Office of the High Commissioner for Jamaica, 48 Grosvenor Street, London W1X 0BJ.   t 01-499 3871.

Canada   Office of the High Commissioner for Jamaica, 85 Range Road, Ottawa. t 233-9311.

Statistical publications

¶ A - General

384   Annual abstract of statistics   (Department of Statistics).

Department of Statistics, 23½ Charles Street, Kingston.

1947- 1968.   not priced.   approx. 120 pages.

Main sections:

Area: population-density & climate	Economic accounts
Population & vital statistics	Prices & wages
Travel & migration	Transport & communications
Production	Government
External trade	Social statistics (education, health, crime, employment & earnings, accidents, and industrial disputes).
Financial accounts	

[continued next page

¶ A, continued

384, continued

Time factor: the 1968 edition, published mid-1969, has data for several years to 1967 and 1968.

§ En.

385   Quarterly abstract of statistics (Jamaica)   (Department of Statistics).

Department of Statistics, 23½ Charles Street, Kingston.

1947-. not priced.

Up-dates much of the information given in the annual abstract (378 above).

§ En.

386   Economic survey   (Central Planning Unit).

Central Planning Unit, Ministry of Finance, Kingston.

1957- 1970. not priced.   151 pages.

Statistical tables are included in the text, which is divided into chapters on a summary of economic activities, national accounts, balance of payments, external trade, population and migration, agriculture, construction and installation, tourism, banking and finance, consumer prices, employment and industrial relations, mineral industry, manufacturing and processing, electricity and telephones, central government expenditure and receipts, legislation.

Time factor: the 1970 edition, published mid-1971, has data for five or six years to 1970.

§ En.

387   Bank of Jamaica bulletin.

Research Department, Bank of Jamaica, P.O.Box 621, Kingston.

1962- (Q). not priced.

Contains a review of financial and economic conditions and statistical tables. Apart from financial and banking statistics, the tables include data on production of selected commodities, external trade, and consumer price index.

Time factor: each issue has long runs of monthly figures to the date of the issue and is published about three months later.

§ En.

388   National income and product: preliminary estimates   (Department of Statistics).

Department of Statistics, 23½ Charles Street, Kingston.

1958- 1970. J$0.30.   33 pages.

Contains data on gross domestic product at factor cost by industrial origin, expenditure on gross national product, net national product (national income), personal consumption expenditure, per capita indicators, fixed capital formation by industrial sectors, fixed capital formation by type of capital goods, and national income by industry.

Time factor: the 1970 edition, published mid-1971, has data for 1961 to 1970.

§ En.

¶   B – Production

389   Cost output and investment survey programme   (Department of Statistics).

              Department of Statistics, 23½ Charles Street, Kingston.

              This survey data is still being analysed; volumes produced so far are:
                   Vol 1   Sources and uses of funds in corporate establishments (flow of funds account)
                                1962–1966   (J$1.00)
                   Vol 2.1   Production costs and output in large establishments manufacturing (provisional
                                report), 1964   (J$1.50)
                   Vol 2.2   Production cost and output in large and small agriculture (provisional report),
                                1964   (J$1.00).
              and there are to be other reports covering mining, small manufacture, large and small construction,
              real estate, investment in non-corporate establishments, and a general report.

                 §   En.

390   Census of agriculture   (Department of Statistics and the former Ministry of Agriculture and Lands).

              Department of Statistics, 23½ Charles Street, Kingston.

              1943– 1968/69.

              Part of the FAO-sponsored World Agricultural Census Programme, the census includes data on
                   climate, area and number of farms, employment, land tenure and ownership, land utilisation,
                   agricultural techniques, and production.

              Time factor: Vol I. Preliminary report was published at the end of 1970 (price J$0.60, 40 pages).

                 §   En.

              Refer also to 384, 385 and 386.

¶   C – External trade

391   External trade of Jamaica   (Department of Statistics. Trade Statistics Unit).

              Department of Statistics, 23½ Charles Street, Kingston.

              1947– 1968.   J$1.30.   xvi, 330 pages.

              Main tables show imports, exports and re-exports arranged by commodity and subdivided by countries
                   of origin and destination.

              Time factor: the 1968 edition, published in 1969, has data for 1968.

                 §   En.

              Note: Provisional data is published in "External trade: annual bulletin"   (J$0.30).

392   External trade bulletin   (Department of Statistics. Trade Statistics Unit).

              Department of Statistics, 23½ Charles Street, Kingston.

              1947– (M).   not priced.

              Main tables show imports, exports and re-exports arranged by commodity and subdivided by countries
                   of origin and destination.

              Time factor: each issue has data for that month and cumulated figures for the year to date and is
                   published 9 to 12 months later.

                 §   En.

¶ C, continued

Refer also to 384 and 385.

¶ E - Population

393   Commonwealth Caribbean population census: Jamaica   (Division of Censuses and Surveys, Department of Statistics).

Department of Statistics, $23\frac{1}{2}$ Charles Street, Kingston.

1970.   not priced.

The reports of the census are now being published, and include a general preliminary report and a preliminary report with the data classified by constituencies and type of household.

Time factor: the preliminary bulletins are being published from 1971-. For detailed statistics not yet published for 1970, reference should be made to the "West Indies population census, 1960", which included data for Jamaica.

§   En.

Refer also to 384 and 385.

¶ F - Standard of living

394   Monthly consumer price indices: urban and rural   (Department of Statistics).

Department of Statistics, $23\frac{1}{2}$ Charles Street, Kingston.

J$0.10 per copy.

The data is based on the household budget survey carried out during 1964 and 1965 regarding expenditure patterns for 1963 and 1964, which was published as "Expenditure patterns of working class households" in 1967.

§   En.

Refer also to 384, 385, 386 and 387.

Central statistical office

395   Institut National de la Statistique et des Etudes Economiques [National Institute for Statistics
           & Economic Research],
       29 Quai Branly, 75 Paris 7, France.
       t   468 96 00 and 468 98 10.

       INSEE is the central organisation for economic information on France and it also collects and
publishes information on French overseas territories.   It is concerned with social and economic demography,
consumption, prices, income, national accounts, and national and regional economic planning.   There is
a departmental service in Fort-de-France, Martinique (Boîte postale 605).

Statistical publications

¶   A - General

396   Annuaire statistique de la Martinique   [Statistical yearbook of Martinique]   (Institut National
           de la Statistique et des Etudes Économiques).

       Institut National de la Statistique et des Etudes Economiques, 29 Quai Branly, 75 Paris 7, France
           or   Service Départemental de Statistique d'Outre-Mer, B.P. 605, Fort-de-France, Martinique.

       1952/56- 1966/69.   Fr 20.00.   148 pages.

       Main sections:
               Geography   Fisheries
               Climate   Industry
               Demography   Transport & communications
               Population   Foreign trade
               Health & social aid   Prices, wages & social security
               Education   Money, credit
               Justice   Public finance
               Elections   Economic accounts
               Agriculture

       Time factor: the 1966/69 edition has data for 1966, 1967, 1968 and 1969 for most tables, and was
           published in 1971.

       §   Fr.

397   Comptes économiques de la Martinique   [Economic accounts of Martinique]   (Institut National de
           la Statistique et des Etudes Economiques).

       Institut National de la Statistique et des Etudes Economiques, 29 Quai Branly, 75 Paris 7, France
           or   Service Départemental de Statistique d'Outre-Mer, B.P. 605, Fort-de-France, Martinique.

       1965/67- 1968.   not priced.   20 pages.

       Contains textual data on the economy of Martinique and statistical tables of resources and the use of
           goods and services; analysis of production by industry; statistical data on enterprises, administration
           and houses; and foreign trade.

       Time factor: the 1968 edition, with data for 1968, was published mid-1970.

       §   Fr.

¶ A, continued

398   Comptes économiques des départements d'outre-mer (sauf la Guyane)   [Economic accounts for the overseas departments (except Guiana)]   (Institut National de la Statistique et des Etudes Economiques).
       Institut National de la Statistique et des Etudes Economiques, 29 Quai Branly, 75 Paris 7, France.
       1968- 1968.   not priced.   19 pages.
       Contains information for Guadeloupe, Martinique and Réunion, but is much briefer than 397 above.
       Time factor: the 1968 edition, with data for 1968, was published in 1971.
       §   Fr.

399   La zone franc   [The franc area]   (Comité Monétaire de la Zone Franc).
       Comité Monétaire de la Zone Franc, 39 rue Croix des Petits Champs, 75 Paris 1, France.
       1969.   not priced.   343 pages.
       Contains data on trends in production, and on foreign trade, finance and investment, money and credit, balance of payments, currency reserves, etc in the French-speaking and franc CFA countries, including Martinique.   Tables are included in the text.
       Time factor: the 1969 edition, published early 1971, contains data for 2 or 3 years to 1969.
       §   Fr.

400   Basic data on the economy   (US Department of Commerce, Bureau of International Commerce).
       US Department of Commerce, Sales and Distribution Branch, Washington, D.C. 20230, USA.
       US$0.15.   8 pages.
       Issued as 69-26 in the series "Overseas business reports", this report presents selected basic data useful in the analysis of Martinique as a market for US exports.   Data include statistics of population, structure of the economy, agriculture, manufacturing, construction, power, etc.
       Time factor: published in June 1969, the report contains data for several years to 1968.
       §   En.

¶ B - Production

       Refer to 396.

130

¶ C - External trade

401   Statistiques du commerce extérieur des départements d'outre-mer: importations - exportations
(en N.D.B.) [Statistics of the foreign trade of the overseas departments: imports - exports
(by the Brussels Nomenclature)] (Direction Général des Douanes et des Droits Indirects, Paris).

Imprimerie Nationale, 39 rue de la Convention, 75 Paris 15, France.

1966- 1968.   Fr 90.00 (Fr 104.00 abroad).   xiii, 758 pages.

Contains detailed statistics of imports and exports arranged by commodity subdivided by countries of
origin and destination for each of the overseas departments of France (Guadeloupe, Martinique,
Guyane, and Réunion).

Time factor: the 1968 edition, with data for 1968, was published in 1969.

§   Fr.

Refer also to 082, 083 and 396.

¶ E - Population

402   Résultats statistiques du recensement général de la population des départements d'outre-mer:
tableaux statistiques: Martinique [Statistical results of the census of population of the
French overseas departments: statistical tables: Martinique] (Institut National de la
Statistique et des Etudes Economiques).

Institut National de la Statistique et des Etudes Economiques, 29 Quai Branly, 75 Paris 7, France
or   Service Départemental de Statistique d'Outre-Mer, B.P. 605, Fort-de-France, Martinique.

1954- 1967.   not priced.   134 pages.

Contains detailed statistics of the population of Martinique.

§   Fr.

Refer also to 396.

Central statistical office

403
Dirección General de Estadística   [Central statistical office],
Secretaria de Industria y Comercio   [Secretariat of Industry and Commerce], Balderas 71,
    Mexico 1 D.F.
t   5-21-12-74.

The Secretariat of Industry and Commerce is in charge of official statistics of Mexico, under which there are two statistical offices, one to collect the statistical data and the other to evaluate it.

Unpublished statistical information can be consulted, free of charge, at the central statistical office at the address given above.   Photocopies are made only in special cases.

Publications other than those described in the following pages include:
Censo de transportes, 1966   [Census of transport, 1966].

Libraries

The Dirección General de Estadística y Censos has a library at Balderas 71, Mexico City, which is open to the public.

Libraries and information services overseas

Mexican embassies abroad are provided with the more important statistical publications of the Dirección General de Estadística y Censos, including:

United Kingdom   Mexican Embassy, 48 Belgrave Square, London SW1X 8QY.
                      t 01-235 6393.
USA   Mexican Embassy, 2829 16th Avenue N W, Washington, D.C.
                      t AD4-6000.
Canada   Mexican Embassy, 88 Metcalfe Street, Cttawa.   t 233-8988.

Bibliographies

404
The Bibliographical and publications department of the Dirección General de Estadística y Censos issues a 'Catalogo de publicaciones' from time to time.   The 1970 edition is the latest issue of this sales list.

405
More comprehensive bibliographies were issued in 1942 and 1966 (Inventario de estadística nacionales, 1966) by the Dirección General de Estadística y Censos.

Statistical publications

¶ A – General

406   Anuario estadístico de los Estados Unidos Mexicanos   [Statistical yearbook of the United States of Mexico]   (Dirección General de Estadística y Censos).

Dirección General de Estadística y Censos, Balderas 71, Mexico 1 D.F.

1893–   1968–1969.   Mex$100.00 ($130.00 abroad).   approx. 350 pages.

Main sections:

Physical characteristics	Agriculture, livestock, forestry,
Population	fishing
Vital statistics	Irrigation
Migration	Industry (minerals, petrol, electricity,
Tourism	construction, processing)
Housing	Communications & transport
Assistance, health & social	Internal trade
security	Foreign trade
Education & culture	Finance
Justice	National product & balance of payments.

Time factor: the 1968/69 edition, published 1971, has data for 1968 and 1969, and earlier years for some tables.

§   Es.

407   Anuario estadístico compendiado de los Estados Unidos Mexicanos   [Annual statistical compendium of the United States of Mexico]   (Dirección General de Estadística y Censos).

Dirección General de Estadística y Censos, Balderas 71, Mexico 1 D.F.

1941–   1968.   Mex$45.00 (Mex$50.00 abroad).   350 pages.

Main sections:

Geography	Agriculture, livestock, forestry & fisheries
Population	Irrigation
Demography, migration, tourism	Industry
Housing	Communications & transport
Social assistance, health, security	Internal trade
Education & culture	Foreign trade
Justice	Finance
Employment	National product & balance of payments,

Time factor: the 1968 edition, published 1969, has data mainly for 1967 but some 1968 figures and retrospective runs are included.

§   Es.

408   Revista de estadística   [Review of statistics]   (Dirección General de Estadística y Censos).

Dirección General de Estadística y Censos, Balderas 71, Mexico 1 D.F.

1933– (M).   Mex$17.50 ($20.00 abroad); Mex$175.00 yr ($200.00 abroad).

Contains data on production (agriculture, minerals, metallurgy, electrical energy, industry), prices and cost of living indices, domestic trade, foreign trade, balance of payments of Mexico, communications & transport, and finance.

Time factor: each issue has data to the months of the issue and is published some six months later.

§   Es.

¶ A, continued

409   Mexico: facts, figures, trends   (Banco Nacional de Comercio Exterior SA).

Banco Nacional de Comercio Exterior SA, Mexico 1 D.F.

1960- 1970.   not priced.   253 pages.

A liberally-illustrated introduction to Mexico for the Mexican or foreign reader, covering the Mexican and his homeland, the national economy, society and culture. Statistical tables are interspersed in the text.

Time factor: the 1970 edition of this biennial was published in the Autumn of 1970 and has statistical data for the years 1965 to 1969.

§   En.

410   Informe anual   [Annual report]   (Banco de Mexico SA).

Banco de Mexico SA, Mexico 1 D.F.

1922- 1970.   not priced.   144 pages.

Includes a statistical section with data on wholesale prices and price indices, industrial production, foreign trade, etc, as well as banking statistics.

Time factor: the 1970 edition, published late 1971, has data for several years to 1970.

§   Es.

411   Review of the economic situation   (Banco Nacional de Mexico SA).

Banco Nacional de Mexico SA, Isabel la Católica 44, Mexico 1 D.F.

1926- (M).   not priced.

Reviews the economy in each area of Latin America and in the USA. There is a statistical section with tables on monetary circulation, Mexico City price indices, commercial balance, volume of industrial production, and price trends.

Time factor: although announced as a monthly, it appears less regularly, about quarterly, and each issue has long runs of figures to about three months prior to the date of the issue.

§   En.

412   Basic data on the economy   (US Department of Commerce, Bureau of International Commerce).

US Department of Commerce, Sales and Distribution Branch, Washington, D.C. 20230, USA.

US$0.15.   24 pages.

Issued as 70-90 in the series "Overseas business reports", this report presents selected basic data useful in the analysis of Mexico as a market for US exports. Data include statistics of population, structure of the economy, agriculture, manufacturing, construction, power, etc.

Time factor: published December 1970, the report contains data for several years to 1969.

§   En.

¶ A, continued

413   Principales indicadores economicos de México   [Principal economic indicators of Mexico] (Dirección General de Estadística y Censos).

Dirección General de Estadística y Censos, Balderas 71, Mexico 1 D.F.

(M). not priced.

Contains index numbers of agricultural production, fisheries, mineral and metal production, oil and petro-chemical production, industrial production, electric energy, tourism, foreign trade.

§   Es.

414   Comercio exterior de México   [Foreign trade of Mexico]   (Banco Nacional de Comercio Exterior SA).

Banco Nacional de Comercio Exterior SA, Venustiano Carranza 32, Mexico D.F.

1951- (M). not priced.

Devoted to Mexican business conditions and economy, including a few statistical tables.

§   Es, Fr and En editions, all with Spanish title.

¶ B – Production

415   Censo industrial de los Estados Unidos Mexicanos: resumen general   [Industrial census of Mexico: general results]   (Dirección General de Estadística y Censos).

Dirección General de Estadística y Censos, Balderas 71, Mexico 1 D.F.

1930- 1965. Mex$65.00 (Mex$80.00 abroad). lxii, 872 pages.

Contains the general results of the census of industry, including number of establishments, number of employees by occupation and by industry, raw materials and power used, etc.

§   Es.

416   Censo agricola, ganadero y ejidal de los Estados Unidos Mexicanos: resumen general [Census of agriculture, stockbreeding and land of Mexico: general results] (Dirección General de Estadística y Censos).

Dirección General de Estadística y Censos, Balderas 71, Mexico 1 D.F.

1930- 1960. Mex$45.00 (Mex$52.00 abroad).

§   Es.

417   Boletín mensuel de la Dirección General de Economía Agricola   [Monthly bulletin of the General Office of Agricultural Economics].

Dirección General de Economía Agricola, Balderas 71, Mexico 1 D.F.

(M). not priced.

Contains preliminary data on agricultural production and internal trade.

§   Es.

Refer also to 406, 407 and 408.

¶ C – External trade

418   Anuario estadístico del comercio exterior de los Estados Unidos Mexicanos   [Statistical yearbook
            of the foreign trade of Mexico]   (Dirección General de Estadística y Censos).

    Dirección General de Estadística y Censos, Balderas 71, Mexico 1 D.F.

    1896/97– 1969.   Mex$100.00 (Mex$125.00 abroad).   xv, 824 pages.

    Main tables show imports and exports arranged by commodity and subdivided by countries of origin
            and destination.

    Time factor: the 1969 edition, with data for 1969, was published late 1970.

        §   Es.

419   Anuario estadístico del comercio exterior de los Estados Unidos Mexicanos con los paises de la ALALC
            [Statistical yearbook of the foreign trade of Mexico with the countries of the Latin American
            Common Market]   (Dirección General de Estadística y Censos).

    1964– 1969.   Mex$50.00 (Mex$55.00 abroad).

        §   Es.

420   Boletín estadístico de comercio exterior   [Statistical bulletin of foreign trade]
            (Dirección General de Estadística y Censos).

    Dirección General de Estadística y Censos, Balderas 71, Mexico 1 D.F.

    1967– (M).   not priced.

    Contains tables showing imports and exports arranged by commodity and tables showing imports and
            exports arranged by country.

    Time factor: each issue has data for the previous month and the cumulated figures for the year to
            date, and also the same periods for the previous year, and is published a few months later.

        §   Es.

    Refer also to 082 and 083.

¶ D – Internal distribution

421   Censo comercial de los Estados Unidos Mexicanos: resumen general   [Commercial census of Mexico:
            general results]   (Dirección General de Estadística y Censos).

    Dirección General de Estadística y Censos, Balderas 71, Mexico 1 D.F.

    1939– 1965.   Mex$43.00 (Mex$53.00 abroad).   liv, 400 pages.

    Contains data on the principal characteristics of the commerce of Mexico by various groupings,
            employment, income from sales,etc.

    Time factor: published 1968, having been taken in 1966 on 1965 data.

        §   Es.

¶ D, continued

422   Censo de servicios de los Estados Unidos Mexicanos: resumen general   [Census of service industry
           in Mexico: general results]   (Dirección General de Estadística y Censos).

       Dirección General de Estadística y Censos, Balderas 71, Mexico 1 D.F.

       1939– 1965.   Mex$28.00 (Mex$35.00 abroad).   liv, 229 pages.

       Includes data on services connected with recreation, hotels and motels, education, finance,
           medicine, hairdressers, laundries, restaurants and bars, law, garages, agents (commission,
           travel, etc), undertakers, photographers, etc.

       Time factor: the data for 1965 was collected in 1966 and published in 1967.

       §   Es.

       Refer also to 406, 407 and 408.

¶ E – Population

423   Censo de población de los Estados Unidos Mexicanos   [Population census of Mexico]
           (Dirección General de Estadística y Censos).

       Dirección General de Estadística y Censos, Balderas 71, Mexico 1 D.F.

       1960.   General volume: Mex$35.00 (Mex$50.00 abroad).   32 regional volumes at various prices.

       Contains data on the principal characteristics of the population, in various groupings.

       §   Es.

424   Proyecciones de la población de México, 1960–1980   [Projections of the population of Mexico,
           1960–1980]   (Banco de Mexico SA).

       Banco de Mexico SA, Mexico 1 D.F.

       Not priced.   246 pages.

       Time factor: published in 1966.

       §   Es.

       Refer also to 406 and 407.

¶ F – Standard of living

       Refer to 408.

Montserrat has been governed by an Administrator since 1960. Enquiries concerning statistical data for the territory could be made to him, or to Montserrat Chamber of Commerce, Plymouth, Montserrat.

Statistical publications

¶   A – General

425   Montserrat: report for the year   (Foreign and Commonwealth Office).

H M Stationery Office, P.O.Box 569, London SE1 9NH.

1955/56– 1965 & 1966.   £0.25.   40 pages.

Mainly textual, but includes some statistics on population, employment, commerce, tourism, production, finance, etc.

Time factor: published 1968.

§   En.

¶   E – Population

426   West Indies population census, 1960   (Department of Statistics, Jamaica).

Department of Statistics, $23\frac{1}{2}$ Charles Street, Kingston, Jamaica.

Includes data on the population of Montserrat.

§   En.

Central statistical office

427   Bureau voor de Statistiek   [Bureau of Statistics],
Departement van Sociale en Economische Zaken [Department of Social and Economic Affairs],
Fort Amsterdam, Curaçao.

The Bureau is responsible for the collection, analysis and publication of the official economic statistics for Curaçao and Aruba.

Publications other than those described in the following pages include:
Statistiek van de meteorologische waarnemingen in de Nederlandse Antillen [Statistics of meteorological observations in the Netherlands Antilles]   (A).
Criminele politiële statistiek [Criminal and police statistics]   (A).

Statistical publications

¶ A – General

428   Statistisch jaarboek: Nederlandse Antillen [Statistical yearbook: Netherlands Antilles] (Bureau voor de Statistiek).

Bureau voor de Statistiek, Departement van Sociale en Economische Zaken, Fort Amsterdam, Curaçao.

1956– 1970.   Ant Fl 6.–.   142 pages.

Main sections:

Area & climate	Transport & communications
Population	Money & banking
Public health	National accounts
Housing	Balance of payments
Religion & politics	Public finance
Education	Income
Economically active population, employment & unemployment	Prices
	Social affairs
Agriculture	Justice & prisons
Manufacture	International data
Foreign trade	

Time factor: the 1970 edition, published early 1971, has data for 1969 and five earlier years for many tables.

§   En, Nl, Es.

429   Statistische mededelingen: Nederlandse Antillen [Statistical information: Netherlands Antilles] (Bureau voor de Statistiek).

Bureau voor de Statistiek, Departement van Sociale en Economische Zaken, Fort Amsterdam, Curaçao.

1954– (M).   Ant Fl 18.– yr.

Contents include data on climate, population, public health, housing, agriculture, industry, foreign trade, traffic and transport, banking, public finance, prices, social affairs, justice and prisons, and international data.

Time factor: each issue is published during the month of the issue and contains data for varying periods up to three or four months earlier.

§   Nl. Contents list also in En.

¶ A, continued

430   Basic data on the economy   (US Department of Commerce, Bureau of International Commerce).

US Department of Commerce, Sales and Distribution Branch, Washington, D.C. 20230.

US$0.15.   20 pages.

Issued as 69-73 in the series "Overseas business reports", this report presents selected basic data useful in the analysis of the Netherlands Antilles as a market for US exports. Data include statistics of population, structure of the economy, agriculture, manufacturing, construction, power, etc.

Time factor: published in May 1970, the report contains data for several years to 1969.

§   En.

¶ B - Production

Refer to 428 and 429.

¶ C - External trade

431   Kwartaalstatistiek van de in- en uitvoer per goederensoort van Curaçao en Aruba
         [Quarterly statistics of imports and exports by commodity of Curaçao and Aruba]
         (Bureau voor de Statistiek).

Bureau voor de Statistiek, Departement van Sociale en Economische Zaken, Fort Amsterdam, Curaçao.

Ant Fl 30.- yr; annual issue only Ant Fl 20.-.

Contains detailed statistics of imports and exports arranged by commodity and subdivided by countries of origin and destination. Separate figures are given for Curaçao and Aruba. The figures cumulate in each subsequent issue each year, and the final issue for the year is titled "Jaarstatistiek ..."

Time factor: each issue has data for the quarter and cumulated figures for the year to date and appears some considerable time later.

§   Nl. Tables of contents also in En.

432   Kwartaalstatistiek van de in- en uitvoer per land van Curaçao en Aruba   [Quarterly statistics of imports and exports by country of Curaçao and Aruba]   (Bureau voor de Statistiek).

Bureau voor de Statistiek, Departement van Sociale en Economische Zaken, Fort Amsterdam, Curaçao.

Ant Fl 30.- yr; annual issue only Ant Fl 20.-.

Contains detailed statistics of imports and exports arranged by countries of origin and destination, subdivided by commodities. Separate figures are given for Curaçao and Aruba. The figures cumulate in each subsequent issue each year and the final issue for the year is titled "Jaarstatistiek ..."

Time factor: each issue has data for the quarter and cumulated figures for the year to date and appears some considerable time later.

§   Nl. Tables of contents also in En.

¶ C, continued

433 Bonaire: in- en uitvoer statistiek per goederensoort [Bonaire: imports and exports statistics by commodity] (Bureau voor de Statistiek).

Bureau voor de Statistiek, Departement van Sociale en Economische Zaken, Fort Amsterdam, Curaçao.

(A) 1970. not priced. 64 pages.

Statistics of foreign trade arranged by commodity and subdivided by countries of origin and destination.

Time factor: the 1970 edition has data for 1970, and was published in 1971.

§ Nl.

Refer also to 082 and 083.

¶ E - Population

434 Volkstelling [Population census] (Statistiek- en Planbureau).

Statistiek- en Planbureau, Fort Amsterdam, Curaçao.

1960. Ant Fl 10.-. 236 pages.

The report of the census covers Curaçao, Bonaire, and Bovenwindse Eilanden (St Maarten, St Eustatius and Saba).

§ Nl. English summary.

Refer also to 428 and 429.

¶ F - Standard of living

Refer to 428 and 429.

Central statistical office

435   Dirección General de Estadística y Censos   [General Office of Statistics and Censuses],
Ministerio de Economía   [Ministry of Economics], Managua D.N.
t   21-701.

The Dirección General de Estadística y Censos works with the Banco Central de Nicaragua to collect, analyse and publish economic statistics of Nicaragua, other than foreign trade statistics. Some of these statistical publications are described in the following pages.

Other important organisations publishing statistics

436   Banco Central de Nicaragua   [Central Bank of Nicaragua],
Apartado 2252, Managua D.N.
t   21-801.

The Departamento de Estudios Económicos [Department of Economic Studies] of the Bank assists the Dirección General de Estadística y Censos, referred to above, in the collection, analysis and publication of economic statistics.

     Other publications of the Bank not described in the following pages include:
       Boletín trimestral del Banco Central   [Quarterly bulletin].

437   Dirección General de Aduanas   [General Office of Customs],
21 Avenida N E y 3a Calle, Chico Pelon, Apartado 47, Managua D.N.
t   40-801 and 40-261.

The Dirección General de Aduanas is the official source of statistics of foreign trade of Nicaragua.

Libraries

The Banco Central de Nicaragua (see above) has a library which includes statistical publications of Nicaragua.

Statistical publications

¶   A - General

438   Anuario estadístico   [Statistical yearbook]   (Dirección General de Estadística y Censos and
       Banco Central de Nicaragua).
Dirección General de Estadística y Censos, Ministerio de Economía, Managua D.N.
1942- 1968.   not priced.   138 pages.
Main sections:

Meteorology	Education
Demography	Building activity
Health & social assistance	Public services (water, electric energy)

[continued next page

¶ A, continued

438, continued Transport & communications   Industrial production (extractive &
                Employment & wages   manufacturing)
                Agricultural production   Banking & finance.

   Time factor: the 1968 edition, published 1970, has data for varying periods to 1968.

   §   Es.

439   Boletín estadístico   [Statistical bulletin]   (Dirección General de Estadística y Censos <u>and</u>
             Banco Central de Nicaragua).

          Dirección General de Estadística y Censos, Ministerio de Economía, Managua D.N.

          1944- (A).   not priced.

          Main sections:
                Population & climate   Transport & communications
                Agriculture   Wages & prices
                Extractive industry   Banking & finance
                Electric energy   Education
                Buildings authorised

          Time factor: issued in advance of the statistical yearbook (438) each issue has data for a full
             year and the first six months of the following year, being published about six months later.

          §   Es.

440   Informe anual   [Annual report]   (Banco Central de Nicaragua).

          Banco Central de Nicaragua, Managua D.N.

          1961- 1970.   not priced.   387 pages.

          Contains chapters, interspersed with tables, on the national economy, (gross domestic product,
             balance of payments, foreign trade, public sector, central government, agriculture, fisheries,
             hunting, manufacturing industry, construction, housing, agrarian reform, etc) and on the
             Central American Common Market as well as banking and financial matters.

          §   Es.

          Note: some of the information in the annual is up-dated by the Bank's "Boletín trimestral
             [Quarterly bulletin]".

¶ B - Production

          Refer to 438 and 439 for statistics of industrial production.

441   Censo agropecuario   [Census of agriculture & stockbreeding]   (Dirección General de Estadística
             y Censos).

          Dirección General de Estadística y Censos, Ministerio de Economía, Managua D.N.

          1963.   not priced.   1 vol.

          §   Es.

          Refer also to 438 and 439 for agricultural production.

¶ C – External trade

442   Memoria de la Dirección General de Aduanas   [Report of the Customs Office].

Dirección General de Aduanas, 21 Avenida N E 3a Calle, Chico Pelon, Apartado 47, Managua D.N.

1911/13- 1970.   not priced.   lxvii, 265 pages.

Main tables show imports and exports arranged by commodity and subdivided by countries of origin and destination.

Time factor: the 1970 issue, with data for 1970, was published late 1971.

§   Es.

443   Nicaragua: comercio exterior   [Nicaragua: foreign trade]   (Ministerio de Economía and Banco Central de Nicaragua).

Ministerio de Economía, Nicaragua or Banco Central de Nicaragua.

1970.   not priced.   2 vols.

Volume I contains data on foreign trade arranged by commodities and subdivided by countries of origin and destination.   Volume II contains data on foreign trade arranged by countries of origin and destination subdivided by commodities.

Time factor: the 1970 issue has data for 1970 and was published late 1971.

§   Es.

Note: a similar publication "Nicaragua: comercio con Centroamerica" has data for Nicaragua's trade with other Central American countries.

Refer also to 082 and 083.

¶ E – Population

444   Censo de población   [Census of population]   (Dirección General de Estadística y Censos).

Dirección General de Estadística y Censos, Ministerio de Economía, Managua D.N.

1963.   not priced.   5 vols.

Volume I   General characteristics of the population by departments and towns
     Volume II   Educational characteristics of the population by departments and towns
     Volume III   Economic characteristics of the population by departments, and principal cities
     Volume IV   Dempgraphic characterisitcs of the population by departments and principal cities
     Volume V   Economic characteristics of the population by principal cities.

§   Es.

Refer also to 438 and 439.

¶ F – Standard of living

Refer to 439

Central statistical office

445   Dirección de Estadística y Censo   [Office of Statistics and Census],
          Calle 36 y Avenia 6a, Apartado 5213, Panamá 5.
          † 23 7619.

       The Dirección de Estadística y Censo is a part of the Departamento de la Contraloría General de la República and is responsible for the collection, analysis and publication of the official statistics of the country, many of which are issued within a series "Estadística Panameña".

       Unpublished statistical information may be supplied to enquirers if it is available and usually free of charge, although a charge is made for special work, the cost being determined by the time taken by the employees and the cost of materials.

       Publications other than those described in the following pages include:
          Población y asistencia social   [Population and social assistance]   (A).
          Estadísticas vitales   [Vital statistics]   (A).
          Balanza de pagos   [Balance of payments]   (A).
          Transportes y comunicaciones   [Transport and communications]   (A).
          Educación   [Education]   (A).
          Estadísticas del trabajo   [Employment statistics]   (A).
          Precios recibidos por el agricultor   [Prices received for agricultural products]   (M).
          Actividades estadísticas de la República de Panamá, 1967-1970   [Statistical activities of the Republic of Panama, 1967-1970].

Libraries

       The Dirección de Estadística y Censo, referred to above, has a library which is open to the public who wish to refer to the statistical publications of Panama and other countries. Some university and public libraries also take the statistical bulletins, etc.

Libraries and information services abroad

       Panama's statistical publications are sent to Panamanian Embassies abroad, including:
       United Kingdom   Panamanian Embassy, 16 The Boltons, London SW10 9TA.
                         † 01-373 2198.
          USA   Panamanian Embassy, 2601 29th Street N W, Washington, D.C.
                         † 387-7400.

Bibliographies

446   The Dirección de Estadística y Censo issues a sales list of its publications at intervals.

447   A new bibliography, "Inventario estadístico nacional", is being compiled by the Dirección de Estadística y Censo, and is due for publication in 1972.

Statistical publications

¶　A - General

448　Panamá en cifras: compendio estadístico　[Panama in figures: statistical compendium]
　　　(Dirección de Estadística y Censo).
　　　Dirección de Estadística y Censo, Contraloría General de la República, Apartado 5213, Panamá 5.
　　　1958/62- 1966-70.　Free.　xiii, 229 pages.
　　　Main sections:
　　　　　　Population　　　　　　　　　Companies
　　　　　　Vital statistics　　　　　　Industry
　　　　　　Social assistance　　　　　Agriculture, livestock, fishing
　　　　　　Social security　　　　　　Prices
　　　　　　Education　　　　　　　　Employment
　　　　　　Justice　　　　　　　　　Transport & communications
　　　　　　National income　　　　　Foreign trade
　　　　　　Balance of payments　　　Accidents in transit
　　　　　　Public finance　　　　　　Meteorology
　　　　　　Banking
　　　Time factor:　the 1966-1970 edition, published late 1971, has data for the years 1966 to 1970.
　　　§　Es.

449　Indicadores económicos　[Economic indicators]　(Dirección de Estadística y Censo).
　　　Dirección de Estadística y Censo, Contraloría General de la República, Apartado 5213, Panamá 5.
　　　1971- (Q).　B/0.10　(B/0.20 abroad).
　　　Contains tables showing trends in the economic situation of Panama.
　　　§　Es.

450　Ingreso nacional　[National income]　(Dirección de Estadística y Censo).
　　　Dirección de Estadística y Censo, Contraloría General de la República, Apartado 5213, Panamá 5.
　　　1950/58- 1968 & 1969.　B/0.10　(B/0.20 abroad).　41 pages.
　　　Contains data relative to the income and product, both national and per capita of Panama, together
　　　　with statistical tables on the economy of Panama in general.
　　　Time factor:　the 1968 and 1969 edition, published in 1971, contains data for 1968 and 1969.
　　　§　Es.

¶　B - Production

451　Índustrias (encuesta)　[Industry (survey)]　(Dirección de Estadística y Censo).
　　　Dirección de Estadística y Censo, Contraloría General de la República, Apartado 5213, Panamá 5.
　　　1957- 1970.　B/0.10　(B/0.20 abroad).　70 pages.
　　　Contains data on manufacturing industry, trade, services, construction and electricity.
　　　Time factor:　the 1970 edition, with data for several years to 1970, was published in mid-1971.
　　　§　Es.

¶ B, continued

452   Industrias [Industry] (Dirección de Estadística y Censo).

Dirección de Estadística y Censo, Contraloría General de la República, Apartado 5213, Panamá 5.
1940- (Q). B/0.10 (B/0.20 abroad).

Contains data on the production of important manufactures, production and consumption of electricity and gas, consumption of water, and construction within the private sector.

Time factor: each issue has data for the period of the issue and is published about six months later.

§   Es.

453   Información agropecuaria encuestas [Survey of agriculture and stockbreeding] (Dirección de Estadística y Censo).

Dirección de Estadística y Censo, Contraloría General de la Republica, Apartado 5213, Panamá 5.
1941- 3 a year. B/0.10 (B/0.20 abroad).

Contains results of studies of crops, livestock and fisheries.

§   Es.

454   Censo agropecuario [Census of agriculture and stockbreeding] (Dirección de Estadística y Censo).

Dirección de Estadística y Censo, Contraloría General de la República, Apartado 5213, Panamá 5.
1971. available free.

The census was taken in May 1971 and preliminary reports are planned for publication in five volumes on the characteristics of agriculture, production of crops, production of livestock, a general compendium, and regional data.

§   Es.

¶ C - External trade

455   Anuario de comercio exterior [Yearbook of foreign trade] (Dirección de Estadística y Censo).

Dirección de Estadística y Censo, Contraloría General de la República, Apartado 5213, Panamá 5.
1958- 1968. B/2.00 (B/2.50 abroad). 889 pages.

Main tables show detailed statistics of imports and exports arranged by commodity and subdivided by countries of origin and destination. Data on the trade of the Free Zone of Colon (the Canal Zone) are also included.

Time factor: the 1968 edition, with data for that year, was published late 1970.

§   Es.

456   Comercio exterior [Foreign trade] (Dirección de Estadística y Censo).

Dirección de Estadística y Censo, Contraloría General de la República, Apartado 5213, Panamá 5.
1941- 1970. B/0.50 (B/0.75 abroad). xii, 132 pages.

Contains preliminary figures of imports, exports and re-exports arranged by commodity and subdivided by countries of origin and destination; and arranged by country and subdivided by very broad subject groups. Data on the trade of the Canal Zone are also included.

Time factor: the 1970 edition, with data for 1970, was published in 1971.

§   Es.

¶ C, continued

Refer also to 448

¶ E - Population

457   Censos nacionales   [National census]   (Dirección de Estadística y Censo).

Dirección de Estadística y Censo, Contraloría General de la República, Apartado 5213, Panamá 5.

1960.   available free.   9 vols and a supplement.

Contents:
Vol I	Population by geographical location
Vol II	Agricultural census (in 3 parts)
Vol III	Population and housing
Vol IV	General characteristics of the population
Vol V	Economic characteristics of the population
Vol VI	Educational attainments of the population
Vol VII	Family characteristics of the population
Vol VIII	Internal migration
Vol IX	Indigenous population

Supplement: General compendium of the population.

The preliminary results of the 7th census of population taken in 1970 are due to be published shortly. There is to be a volume for each province; a general volume containing data on general characteristics, education, economic position, families and internal migration; and a volume on housing.

§   Es.

Refer also to 448.

¶ F - Standard of living

458   Indice de precios al por major y al consumidor   [Wholesale and consumer price indices] ·
       (Dirección de Estadística y Censo).

Dirección de Estadística y Censo, Contraloría General de la República, Apartado 5213, Panamá 5.

1941-   (Q).   B/0.10 (B/0.20 abroad).

§   Es.

Refer also to 448 and 450.

There is no central statistical office, but statistical information can be obtained from the Panama Canal Information Office, Balboa Heights, Canal Zone.

Statistical publications

¶ A - General

459   Panama Canal Company [and] Canal Zone Government: annual report.

The Panama Information Office, Balboa Heights, Canal Zone.

1970/71.   not priced.   vii, 147 pages.

The two separate reports are published in one volume, the Governor of the Canal Zone also being the President of the Panama Canal Company.   The Panama Canal Company report includes statistical data on finance, shipping, water supply, dredging operations, electrical power generated, cargo handled across piers, vessels serviced, marine bunkering, and railroad operations.   The Canal Zone Government report includes statistics of hospital occupancy, school enrollment, police statistics, fire service statistics, postal service statistics, and customs activities.

Time factor: in the 1970/71 edition, the data for the Canal Company cover the period 1968 to 1971, and the data for the Government cover 1970 and 1971.

§   En.

¶ B - Production

460   Industrias [Industry]   (Dirección de Estadística y Censo, República de Panamá).

Dirección de Estadística y Censo, Contraloría General de la República, Apartado 5213, Panamá 5.

1940- (Q).   B/0.10 (B.0.20 abroad).

Includes data on the production of important manufactures, production and consumption of electricity and gas, consumption of water, and construction within the private sector for the Panama Canal Zone, as well as for the Republic of Panama.

Time factor: each issue has data for the period of the issue and is published about six months later.

§   Es.

¶ C - External trade

461   Anuario de comercio exterior [Yearbook of foreign trade]   (Dirección de Estadística y Censo, República de Panamá).

Dirección de Estadística y Censo, Contraloría General de la República, Apartado 5213, Panamá 5.

1958- 1968.   B/2.00 (B/2.50 abroad).   889 pages.

Includes imports and exports statistics for the Free Zone of Colon (the Canal Zone).

Time factor: the 1968 edition, with data for that year, was published late 1970.

§   Es.

F

¶ C, continued

462   Comercio exterior [Foreign trade]   (Dirección de Estadística y Censo, República de Panamá).
        Dirección de Estadística y Censo, Contraloría General de la República, Apartado 5213, Panamá 5.
        1941- 1970.   B/0.50 (B/0.75 abroad).   xii, 132 pages.
        Includes preliminary figures of imports, exports and re-exports statistics for the Free Zone of Colon
            (the Canal Zone).
        Time factor: the 1970 edition, with data for 1970, was published in 1971.
        §   Es.

¶ E - Population

463   Censos nacionales [National census]   (Dirección de Estadística y Censo, República de Panamá)
        Dirección de Estadística y Censo, Contraloría General de la República, Apartado 5213, Panamá 5.
        1960.   available free.   9 vols and a supplement.
        Includes data for the Free Zone of Colon (the Canal Zone).   See 457 for details of content of
            volumes.
        §   Es.

        Refer also to 674.

Central statistical office

464   Dirección General de Estadística y Censos   [General Office of Statistics and Censuses], Humaitá entre Alberdi y 14 de Mayo, Asunción.
t   47900.

The Dirección General de Estadística y Censos has, as one of its duties, the compilation and publication of national statistics, and the organisation of the censuses of population and housing; but other government departments also collect and publish statistics, e.g., the Ministry of Agriculture.

Unpublished statistical information can be provided for enquirers in certain cases, when available.

Publications other than those described in the following pages include:
Demografía (hechos vitales)   [Vital statistics]   (2 per annum).

Libraries

The Dirección General de Estadística y Censos has a library which is open to the public for reference to statistical publications.

Libraries and information services abroad

Paraguayan Embassies abroad have statistical publications of Paraguay, including:
United Kingdom   Paraguayan Embassy, Braemar Lodge, Cornwall Gardens, London SW7 4AQ.   t 01-937 1253.
USA   Paraguayan Embassy, Connecticut Avenue N W, Washington, D.C.   t   HU3-6960.

Statistical publications

¶   A - General

465   Anuario estadístico del Paraguay   [Statistical yearbook of Paraguay]   (Dirección General de Estadística y Censos).

Dirección General de Estadística y Censos, Humaitá entre Alberdi y 14 de Mayo, Asunción.

1886- 1969.   not priced.   122 pages.

Main sections:
Climate	Agriculture, livestock & industry
Demography	Transport & communications
Education	Foreign trade
Health & social aid	Miscellaneous.
Banking & finance	

Time factor: the 1969 edition has data for 1969 or, in some tables, 1968 and several earlier years. It was published in 1970.

§   Es.

¶ A, continued

466   Boletín estadística del Paraguay   [Statistical bulletin of Paraguay]   (Dirección General de
             Estadística y Censos).

        Dirección General de Estadística y Censos, Humaitá entre Alberdi y 14 de Mayo, Asunción.

        1957- 2 per annum.   not priced.

        Contains statistical data on the climate, demography, tourism, immigration, transport and
             communications, finance and banking, local government, and consumer price indices.

        Time factor: each issue has data for the six months previous to that of the date of the issue.

        §   Es.

467   Boletín estadístico mensual   [Monthly statistical bulletin]   (Banco Central del Paraguay).

        Banco Central del Paraguay, Asunción.

        1948-.   not priced.

        A statistical survey of Paraguayan banks, currency and exchange, foreign trade, production,
             balance of payments, and consumer price indices.

        Time factor: the currency of the data varies and can be up to 12 months prior to the date of
             the issue.

        §   Es.

¶ B - Production

468   Censos económicos   [Economic census]   (Ministerio de Industria y Comercio).

        Ministerio de Industria y Comercio, Asunción.

        1963- 1963.   not priced.   298 pages.

        This volume contains the final results of an industrial census, including general aspects, employment,
             wages, machinery, value of raw materials and power consumed, value of production, etc.
             It also contains the final report of a commercial census, with details of commercial activity;
             a census of service industries; and a directory of industrial and commercial establishments.

        Time factor: the results of the censuses were published in 1966.

        §   Es.

469   Censo agropecuario   [Census of agriculture and stockbreeding]   (Ministerio de Agricultura y
             Ganadería).

        Ministerio de Agricultura y Ganadería, Asunción.

        1956.   not priced.   1 vol.

        A sample census was taken in 1961, also.

        §   Es.

470   Boletín estadístico   [Statistical bulletin]   (Ministerio de Agricultura y Ganadería, Dirección de
             Mercadeo y Economía Agrícola).

        Ministerio de Agricultura y Ganadería, Asunción.

        1965- (M).   not priced.

        §   Es.

¶ C – External trade

471   Boletín estadístico de comercio exterior   [Statistical bulletin of foreign trade]   (Dirección
         General de Estadística y Censos).

         Dirección General de Estadística y Censos, Humaitá entre Alberdi y 14 de Mayo, Asunción.
         1963/64– 1966.   not priced.   253 pages.

         The main tables show detailed statistics of imports and exports arranged by commodity subdivided
         by countries of origin and destination.   There are also less-detailed tables showing the trade
         by countries subdivided by broad commodity groupings.

         Time factor: the 1966 edition, with data for 1966, was published in 1968.

         §   Es.

         Refer also to 465 and 467.

¶   D – Internal distribution

         Refer to 468.

¶   E – Population

472   Censo de población y vivienda   [Census of population and housing]   (Dirección General de
         Estadística y Censos).

         Dirección General de Estadística y Censos, Humaitá entre Alberdi y 14 Mayo, Asunción.
         1962.   not priced.   59 pages.

         Time factor: this final report was published in 1966.

         §   Es.

         Refer also to 465 and 466.

¶   F – Standard of living

         Refer to 466 and 467.

Central statistical office

473   Oficina Nacional de Estadística y Censos   [National Office of Statistics and Censuses],
        Ministerio de Economía y Finanzas   [Ministry of Economy and Finance], Avenida Abancay,
           6 piso, Lima.
        t   27 9552.

        The Oficina Nacional de Estadística y Censos is responsible for the collection, analysis and publication of economic statistics of Peru.   Unpublished statistical information may be supplied to enquirers if available, and no charge is made for this service.

Libraries

        The Oficina Nacional de Estadística y Censos has a library which is open to the public for reference to statistical publications.   Such material is also available for reference in the libraries of the national universities and in the National Library of Peru.

Libraries and information services abroad

        Peruvian Embassies abroad have some statistical material, particularly the statistical yearbook and the monthly statistical bulletin, and the embassies include:
        United Kingdom   Peruvian Embassy, 52 Sloane Street, London SW1X 9SP. t 01-235 8975.
        USA   Peruvian Embassy, 1320 16th Street N W, Washington, D.C.
                    t   DU7-5150.
        Canada   Peruvian Embassy, 539 Island Park Drive, Ottawa.   t 722-7186.

Bibliographies

        It is understood that a bibliography of both official and non-official statistical publications of Peru is being compiled, by the Oficina de Estadística y Censos.

Statistical publications

¶ A - General

474   Anuario estadístico del Perú   [Statistical yearbook of Peru]   (Dirección General de Estadística y
           Censos).
        Oficina Nacional de Estadística y Censos, Ministerio de Economía y Finanzas, Avenida Abancay,
           6 piso, Lima.
        1919- 1966.   S/.400.00.   1605 pages.

[continued next page

¶ A, continued

474, continued

Main sections:

Geography, climate, etc.   Construction and housing
Demography   Transport
Tourism   Internal trade
Social security, defence and   Foreign trade
    services   Prices and salaries
Education and culture   Consumption
Agriculture, livestock, forestry,   Money, banking and insurance
    fishing   Public finance
Mining   National accounts
Manufacturing   Balance of payments
Petroleum   International statistics.
Electricity

Time factor: the 1966 edition, with data for the years 1958 to 1966, was published in 1969.

§   Es.

475   Reseña económica y financiera   [Economic and financial review]   (Banco Central de Reserva
              del Perú).

          Banco Central de Reserva del Perú, Lima.

          1944- 1970 & Jan-June 1971.   not priced.

          Includes statistics in the text and also contains a statistical annex, with data on production,
              monetary developments, balance of payments, principal exports, imports, public finance,
              and economic indicators.

          §   Es.

476   Boletín del Banco Central de Reserva del Perú   [Bulletin of the Central Reserve Bank of Peru].

          Banco Central de Reserva del Perú, Lima.

          1931- (M).   not priced.

          Includes statistics on the economic situation, banking, exchange, foreign trade, wholesale prices,
              and public finance.

          §   Es.

477   Boletín estadístico de industria y comercio   [Statistical bulletin of industry and commerce]
              (Ministerio de Industria y Comercio).

          Ministerio de Industria y Comercio, Lima.

          1970- (irr).   not priced.

          Presents brief statistical picture of principal activities, including data such as indices of industrial
              manufacturing production, exports, tourism, etc.

          §   Es.

¶   A,   continued

478   Basic data on the economy   (US Department of Commerce, Bureau of International Commerce).
           US Department of Commerce, Sales and Distribution Branch, Washington, D.C. 20230.
           US$0.15.   24 pages.
           Issued as 69–65 in the series "Overseas business reports", this report presents selected basic data
               useful in the analysis of Peru as a market for US exports.   Data include statistics of population,
               structure of the economy, agriculture, manufacturing, construction, power, etc.
           Time factor: published in December 1969, the report contains data for several years to 1968.
           §   En.

¶   B – Production

479   Censo nacional económico   [National economic census]   (Dirección Nacional de Estadística y
               Censos).
           Oficina Nacional de Estadística y Censos, Ministerio de Economía y Finanzas, Avenida Abancay,
               piso 6, Lima.
           1963– 1963.   not priced.
           The census covered both industry and commerce.   The volumes concerned with production are:
               'Industria manufacturera' and 'Industria manufacturera: suplemento' which include data on
                   the number of establishments, employees, wages, raw materials consumed, production, etc.
               'Directorio de la industria manufacturera con 5 o mas persones ocupados', a directory of
                   manufacturing firms with 5 or more employees.
               'Resultados del censo de mineria y directorio', with similar information for the mining industry.
           Time factor: the data in the 1963 census relates to that year, and was published in 1967 and 1968.
           §   Es.

480   Estadística industrial (manufactura)   [Industrial statistics (manufacturing)]   (Ministerio de
               Industria y Comercio).
           Ministerio de Industria y Comercio, Lima.
           1965– 1970.   not priced.   2 vols.
           Volume 1 contains the results of activities in the manufacturing sector, including gross value of
               production, number of establishments, number of employees, wages, by type of product and
               by industry group; and gross value of production by industry and industry groups, power used,
               etc.
           Volume 2 contains detailed information on national production and consumption of primary materials,
               etc, utilised by the industrial sector.
           Time factor: the 1970 edition, published in 1971, covers the period 1965 to 1968.
           §   Es.

¶ B, continued

481   Anuario de la mineria del Perú   [Yearbook of mining in Peru]   (Ministerio de Energia y Minas.
              Dirección General de Mineria).

           Ministerio de Energia y Minas, Dirección General de Mineria, Lima.

           1969.   not priced.   142 pages.

           Contains a general review of the situation in the industry, statistics of production subdivided by
              destinations, numbers of employees, etc.

           Time factor: the 1969 edition has data for 1969 and some earlier years in some tables, and was
              published in 1971.

           §   Es.

482   Estadística petrolera del Perú   [Petroleum statistics of Peru]   (Ministerio de Energia y Minas,
              Dirección General de Hidrocarburos).

           Ministerio de Energia y Minas, Dirección General de Hidrocarburos, Lima.

           1950- 1969.   not priced.   144 pages.

           Contains statistics of production, refining, manufacture, sales, and employment in the petroleum
              industry.

           Time factor: the 1969 edition, published late 1971, has data for both 1969 and 1968.

           §   Es.

483   Censo nacional agropecuario   [National census of agriculture and stockbreeding]   (Dirección
              Nacional de Estadística y Censos).

           Oficina Nacional de Estadística y Censos, Avenida Abancay, piso 6, Lima.

           1961- 1961.   not priced.   xxvii, 146 pages.

           Contains data on the area cultivated, crops, livestock, employees, etc.

           Time factor: published in 1966.

           §   Es.

484   Estadística agraria: Perú [Agricultural statistics: Peru]   (Ministerio de Agricultura, Oficina
              de Estadística).

           Ministerio de Agricultura, Oficina de Estadística, Camilo Carrillo no.315, Lima.

           1963- 1967.   not priced.   2 vols.

           Volume 1 contains general information and data on cultivation and its production. Volume 2
              contains data on land, population and production of fish and poultry, a summary of production,
              foreign trade, value of production, internal demand generally and per capita, production
              from forestry, fisheries, and a general summary.

           Time factor: the 1967 edition has data for 1967 and was published in 1970.

           §   Es.

¶   C - External trade

485   Estadístico del comercio exterior   [Statistics of foreign trade]   (Dirección de Aduanas).
         Dirección de Aduanas, Ministerio de Economía y Finanzas, Avenida Abancay, piso 7, Lima.
         1891- 1969.   not priced.   lxi, 519 pages.
         Tables include detailed statistics of imports and exports by commodity subdivided by countries of
              origin and destination, and trade by country subdivided by commodity classification numbers.
         Time factor: the 1969 edition, with data for 1969, was published late 1970.
         §   Es.

486   Perú: estadísticas de exportación   [Peru: export statistics]   (Banco Industrial del Perú.
              Division de Comercio Exterior).
         Banco Industrial del Perú, Avenida Abancay 491, piso 6, Casilla Postal 1230, Lima.
         1968- 1969.   not priced.   205 pages.
         Contains detailed statistics of exports arranged by commodity and subdivided by country of
              destination.
         Time factor: the 1969 edition, published in 1971, has data for the period 1965 to 1969.
         §   Es.

487   Estadística de comercio exterior 1965-1970   [Statistics of foreign trade 1965-1970]
              (Ministerio de Industria y Comercio).
         Ministerio de Industria y Comercio, Lima.
         Not priced.   2 vols.
         Produced by the Planning Office of the Ministry, volume I has data on exports and volume II on
              imports.   Statistical tables include balance of payments, and detailed trade by country
              subdivided by commodities.
         Time factor: published mid-1971.
         §   Es.

         Refer also to 475 and 476.

¶ D - Internal distribution

488

Censo nacional económico [National economic census] (Dirección Nacional de Estadística y Censos).

Oficina Nacional de Estadística y Censos, Ministerio de Economía y Finanzas, Avenida Abancay, piso 6, Lima.

1963- 1963. not priced.

The census covered both industry and commerce. The volumes concerning internal distribution are:
'Censo de comercio y de servicios', which includes data on the number of establishments in the various retail and service trades, employees, wages, sales figures, etc.
'Directorio de comercio al por mayor', a directory of firms with 5 or more employees.
'Directorio de comercio al por menor', a directory of firms with less than 5 employees.
(The two directories are published in one volume).

Time factor: the data in the 1963 census relates to that year, and was published in 1968.

§ Es.

Refer also to 474.

¶ E - Population

489

Censo nacional de población [National census of population] (Dirección Nacional de Estadística).

Oficina Nacional de Estadística y Censos, Ministerio de Economía y Finanzas, Avenida Abancay, piso 6, Lima.

1836- 1961. not priced. 6 vols in 11.

Contents:
Vol 1   Tomo 1   contains comparative statistics, geographical distribution, age and sex, place of birth of the population
         Tomo 2   contains data on migration, nationality, conjugal state, religion, fecundity
         Tomo 3   deals with educational attainments of the population
         Tomo 4   deals with the economic characteristics of the population
         Tomo 5   has information on local usages and customs.
Vol 2   is in two parts (tomos) and contains the results of the first national census of housing.
Vol 3   has the results of the first national census of agriculture.
Vol 4   contains results for each department of Peru.
Vol 5   analyses the census results.
Vol 6   contains data on the methodology used for the census.

§ Es.

490

Population of Peru, estimates and projections, 1962-2002 (Bureau of the Census, US Department of Commerce).

Superintendent of Documents, US Government Printing Office, Washington, D.C. 20402, USA.

US$1.00. 100 pages.

Published in the series "Current population reports: P-96", in September 1971.

§ En.

Refer also to 474.

¶ F – Standard of living

491 Indices de precios al consumidor: de la ciudades de Lima y Callao [Consumer price indices in the cities of Lima and Callao] (Oficina Nacional de Estadística y Censos).

Oficina Nacional de Estadística y Censos, Ministerio de Economía y Finanzas, Avenida Abancay, piso 6, Lima.

1962- (M). not priced.

§ Es.

Refer also to 474.

Central statistical office

492   Junta de Planificación   [Planning Board],
           Negociado de Analysis Económico y Social   [Bureau of Economic and Social Analysis],
              Apartado 9447, Santurce 00908.
           t   723 4600, ext 105.

           The Puerto Rico Planning Board is the main source of economic statistics on Puerto Rico,   other than
       those published by the United States Department of Commerce, Bureau of the Census.

           Publications of the Planning Board other than those described in the following pages include:
              Balanza de pagos   [Balance of payments]   (A).

Statistical publications

¶   A - General

493   Anuario estadístico.   Statistical yearbook: Puerto Rico   (Bureau of Economic and Social
              Analysis, Puerto Rico Planning Board).

           Bureau of Economic and Social Analysis, Puerto Rico Planning Board, Apartado 9447, Santurce 00908.

           1965- 1967.   not priced.   x, 234 pages.

           A summary of economic and social statistics of general interest, with sections on:

Population	Agricultural production & related
Demographic statistics	subjects
Climate & other physical	Industry
characteristics	Prices, distribution of products &
Public health & welfare	services
Crime & delinquency	Construction & housing
Education	Transportation & communications
Labour force, employment &	Passenger movement & tourism
payroll	Banking, finance & insurance
National accounts & related	Public finance
economic statistics	External trade.

           Time factor: the 1967 edition, published in 1969, has data for 1966 and 1967 and for some
              earlier years.

           §   Es & En.

494   Indicadores económicos de Puerto Rico.   Economic indicators of Puerto Rico   (Negociado de
              Analysis Económico y Social, Junta de Planificación).

           Negociado de Analysis Económico y Social, Junta de Planificación, Apartado 9447, Santurce 00908.

           (M).   not priced.

           Contains the latest available monthly data on production, employment, manufactures, construction,
              tourism, passenger movement, transport, external trade, banking, public treasury, and
              personal consumption.

           §   Es & En.

¶ A,   continued

495   Ingreso y producto: Puerto Rico (tablas seleccionadas)   [Income and product: Puerto Rico
       (selected tables)]   (Negociado de Analysis Económico y Social, Junta de Planificación).

       Negociado de Analysis Económico y Social, Junta de Planificación, Apartado 9447, Santurce 00908.

       1956- 1969.   not priced.   iv, 26 pages.

       Contains data on gross national product, national income by industry, personal income, price
       indices, and cost of personal consumption of certain commodities, etc.

       Time factor: the 1969 edition, published in 1970, has data for 1950 and 1960 to 1969.

       §   Es.

496   Economy and finances of Puerto Rico   (Department of the Treasury, Puerto Rico).

       Department of the Treasury, San Juan.

       1970.   not priced.   36 pages.

       Contains brief data on economic activity, including production and sales, investment expenditure,
       net income, employment, world trade, cargo, passenger movement and tourism, private and
       public financial activity.

       §   En.

¶ B - Production

497   Censo de industrias manufactureras de Puerto Rico.   Census of manufacturing industries of Puerto Rico.
       (Negociado de Estadísticas del Trabajo [Bureau of Labour Statistics]).

       Negociado de Estadísticas del Trabajo, San Juan.

       1946- 1970.   not priced.   xiii, 31 pages.

       Actually a census of employment in the manufacturing industries, including number of establishments
       and employees by major industry groups, as well as hours of work, earnings, etc.

       Time factor: published in 1971, the census has data for 1969 and 1970.

       §   Es & En.

       Refer also to 493 and 494; to 637 for the census of agriculture, and to 640 for fishery statistics.

¶ C - External trade

498   External trade statistics   (US Department of Commerce. Bureau of the Census).

       Bureau of the Census, Department of Commerce, Suitland, Md. 20233, USA   or
       Puerto Rico Planning Board, Apartado 9447, Santurce 28, Puerto Rico.

       1969.   not priced.   562 pages.

       Contains data on United States trade with Puerto Rico, imports and exports of Puerto Rico generally
       arranged by commodity subdivided by countries of origin and destination, and Puerto Rican trade
       with the Virgin Islands of the United States.

       Time factor: the 1969 edition, published in 1971, has data for 1969.

       §   En.

¶   C,   continued

499   U.S. foreign trade. FT 800: US trade with Puerto Rico and the United States Possessions
                  (Bureau of the Census).

                  Superintendent of Documents, US Government Printing Office, Washington, D.C. 20402, USA.

                  (M) & (A).   Monthly US$0.20; $2.50 yr ($3.25 abroad); annual US$0.25.

                  For Puerto Rico and for each Possession (Virgin Islands of the US, Guam, American Samoa) the data
                  is arranged by commodity subdivided by method of transport.

                  Time factor: data is not cumulative, and the monthly and annual figures appear about three months
                  after the period covered.

                  §   En.

¶   D – Internal distribution

500   Census of business, Puerto Rico   (Bureau of the Census, US Department of Commerce).

                  Superintendent of Documents, US Government Printing Office, Washington, D.C. 20402
                       or   Puerto Rico Planning Board, Apartado 9447, Santurce 00908, Puerto Rico.

                  1963.   US$2.00.   298 pages.

                  Contains data on wholesale trade, retail trade and selected service trades, by kind of business,
                  size of business by receipts and by employees, etc.   Includes data on a regional basis.

                  Time factor: the 1963 census was published in 1965.

                  §   En.

                  Refer also to 673.

¶   E – Population

                  Refer to 493 and 674.

There is no central statistical office on the islands, but enquiries for statistical information could be put to the Minister of Finance, Trade, Development and Tourism at Basseterre, St Kitts, or to St Kitts-Nevis Chamber of Commerce, Basseterre, St Kitts.

Statistical publications

¶ A - General

501   St Kitts-Nevis-Anguilla: report   (Foreign and Commonwealth Office).

            H M Stationery Office, P.O.Box 569, London SE1 9NH.

            1955/56- 1959/62.   o.p.   80 pages.

            Mainly textual, but includes some statistics on population, employment, commerce, tourism, production, finance, etc.

            Time factor: published in 1966.

            §   En.

¶   C - External trade

502   External trade of St Kitts-Nevis-Anguilla   (Ministry for Finance, Trade, Development & Tourism).

            Ministry for Finance, Trade, Development & Tourism, Basseterre, St Kitts.

            (A) 1967.   not priced.   iii, 163 pages.

            Main tables show imports and exports arranged by commodity subdivided by countries of origin and destination.

            Time factor: the 1967 edition, with data for 1967, was published in 1969.

            §   En.

¶   E - Population

503   West Indies population census, 1960   (Department of Statistics, Jamaica).

            Department of Statistics, 23½ Charles Street, Kingston, Jamaica.

            Includes data on the population of St Kitts, Nevis and Anguilla.

            §   En.

Central statistical office

504   Government Statistical Office,
           Government Buildings, Castries.
           t   2487-8.

     This statistical office has only recently been set up, and it intends to collect and disseminate
statistics of population, manpower, agriculture, forestry, fishing, manufacturing industries, distribution
(urban and rural administration area), transport and foreign trade.

     Unpublished information is supplied on request when available, and no fee is charged.

Statistical publications

¶   A - General

505   Annual statistical digest   (Development, Planning and Statistics).

           Development, Planning and Statistics, Premier's Office, Castries.

           1966- 1968.   not priced.   65 pages.

           Main sections:
                Climate   Banking
                Population & vital statistics   Overseas trade
                Transport & passenger movement   Prices
                Labour & employment   Social conditions
                Industrial production   Education
                Agriculture & forestry   Health
                Public finance   Crime.
                Remittances

           Time factor: the 1968 edition contains data from 1961 to 1968, with quarterly figures for 1968
                also, and was published in 1970.

           §   En.

506   Basic data on the economy   (US Department of Commerce, Bureau of International Commerce).

           US Department of Commerce, Sales and Distribution Branch, Washington, D.C. 20230, USA.

           Issued as 70-86 in the series "Overseas business reports", this report presents selected basic data
                useful in the analysis of the Windward Islands (of which St Lucia is one) as a market for US
                exports. Data include statistics of population, structure of the economy, agriculture,
                manufacturing, construction, power, etc.

           Time factor: published in December 1970, the report contains data for several years to 1969.

           §   En.

¶   B - Production

           Refer to 505.

¶   C - External trade

507   Overseas trade of St Lucia   (Statistical Office).
              Government Statistical Office, Government Buildings, Castries.
              1951- 1967.   EC$ 2.00.   xx, 195 pages.
              Main tables show imports and exports arranged by commodity and subdivided by countries of
                  origin and destination.
              Time factor: the 1967 edition, published in 1971, has data for 1967.
              §   En.

508   Quarterly overseas trade report   (Statistical Office).
              Government Statistical Office, Government Buildings, Castries.
              1960-.   not priced.
              Main tables show imports and exports arranged by commodity and subdivided by countries of
                  origin and destination.
              §   En.

              Refer also to 505.

¶   E - Population

509   West Indies population census, 1960   (Department of Statistics, Jamaica).
              Department of Statistics, 23½ Charles Street, Kingston, Jamaica.
              Includes data on the population of St Lucia.
              §   En.

510   Eastern Caribbean population census, 1960   (Central Statistical Office, Trinidad and Tobago).
              Government Printer, 2 Victoria Avenue, Port of Spain, Trinidad.
              Volume I, part D contains a comprehensive description of each enumerative district of the Windward
                  Islands, including St Lucia; Volume II has summary tables for the Windward Islands.
              §   En.

              Refer also to 505.

¶   F - Standard of living

              Refer to 505.

Central statistical office

511   Institut National de la Statistique et des Etudes Economiques   [National Institute for Statistics and Economic Research],
         29 Quai Branly, 75 Paris 7, France.
         t   468 96 00 and 468 98 10.

       INSEE is the central organisation for economic information on France and it also collects and publishes information on French overseas territories. It is concerned with social and economic demography, consumption, prices, income, national accounts, and national and regional economic planning.

Statistical publications

¶   A - General

512   Annuaire statistique des territoires d'outre mer   [Statistical yearbook for the overseas territories] (Institut National de la Statistique et des Etudes Economiques).

       Imprimerie Nationale, 39 rue de la Convention, 75 Paris 15, France.

       1959- 1967/68.   not priced.   255 pages.

       Main sections:

Geography	Prices & wages
Climate	Transport & communication
Demography	Foreign trade
Active population	Money, credit
Health	Public finance
Education	Economic accounts.
Production	

       St Pierre et Miquelon is one of the territories for which data is included.

       Time factor: the 1967/68 edition, with data for 1967 and 1968, was published in 1970.

       §   Fr.

513   La zone franc   [The franc area]   (Comité Monétaire de la Zone Franc).

       Comité Monétaire de la Zone Franc, 39 rue Croix des Petits Champs, 75 Paris 1, France.

       1969.   not priced.   343 pages.

       Contains data on trends in production, and on foreign trade, finance and investment, money and credit, balance of payments, currency reserves, etc, in the French-speaking and franc CFA countries, including St Pierre et Miquelon.   Tables are included in the text.

       Time factor: the 1969 edition, published early 1971, contains data for two or three years to 1969.

       §   Fr.

¶   B - Production

       Refer to 512.

¶   C – External trade

514   Statistiques du commerce et de la navigation de Saint Pierre et Miquelon   [Foreign trade statistics
             of St Pierre and Miquelon]   (Direction des Douanes de St Pierre et Miquelon).

          Direction des Douanes, St Pierre et Miquelon   or   INSEE, 29 Quai Branly, 75 Paris 7, France.

          1964- 1970.   Fr 4.00.   26 pages.

          Main tables show detailed statistics of imports and exports by commodity subdivided by countries
             of origin and destination.

          Time factor: the 1970 edition, with data for 1970, was published in 1971.

          §   Fr.

          Refer also to 512.

¶   E – Population

515   Recensement de la population du territoire de Saint-Pierre et Miquelon   [Census of population for
             the territory of St Pierre and Miquelon]   (Institut National de la Statistique et des Etudes
             Economiques, Paris).

          Institut National de la Statistique et des Etudes Economiques, 29 Quai Branly, 75 Paris 7, France.

          1962- 1967.   Fr 5.00.   36 pages.

          Contains data on the population of the territory by sex, age, matrimonial conditions, nationality,
             families, and housing.

          Time factor: published 1970.

          §   Fr.

          Refer also to 512.

Central statistical office

516   Statistical Office,
Kingstown, St Vincent.
t 2111.

The Statistical Office is responsible for the collection, analysis and publication of statistical information concerning St Vincent.

Statistical publications

¶   A - General

517   Digest of statistics   (Statistical Office).

Government Printing Office, Kingstown, St Vincent, W.I.

1959- (Q).   not priced.

Main sections:

Overseas trade	Prices
Finance & banking	Population & vital statistics
Transport	Climate
Production	Education & social services.

Time factor: each issue has data for the period of the issue and some earlier figures, and is published several months later.

§   En.

518   Basic data on the economy   (US Department of Commerce, Bureau of International Commerce).

US Department of Commerce, Sales and Distribution Branch, Washington, D.C. 20230.

US$0.15.   8 pages.

Issued as 70-86 in the series "Overseas business reports", this report presents selected basic data useful in the analysis of the Windward Islands (of which St Vincent is one) as a market for US exports. Data include statistics of population, structure of the economy, agriculture, manufacturing, construction, power, etc.

Time factor: published in December 1970, the report contains data for several years to 1969.

§   En.

¶   B - Production

Refer to 517.

¶ C – External trade

519   Annual trade report   (Customs Department).

Government Printing Office, Kingstown, St Vincent, W.I.

1954– 1967.   EC $2.00.   144, xxii pages.

Main tables show detailed statistics of imports and exports arranged by commodity, subdivided by countries of origin or destination.

Time factor: the 1967 edition, Published 1969, contains data for 1967.

§   En.

520   Quarterly overseas trade report   (Customs Department).

Government Printing Office, Kingstown, St Vincent, W.I.

1965–.   not priced.

Main tables show statistics of imports and exports arranged by commodity subdivided by countries of origin and destination.

Time factor: each issue has data for that quarter and cumulated totals for the year to date, being issued some months after the end of the period covered.

§   En.

¶ E – Population

521   Population census   (Central Statistical Office, Port of Spain).

Government Printer, 2 Victoria Avenue, Port of Spain, Trinidad.

1960.   TT $1.50 each volume.

The census covered the whole of the Eastern Caribbean within the British Commonwealth. Vol I Part A is a description of the census and methods used; Vol I Part D contains a comprehensive description of each enumerative district in each of the Windward Islands; Vol II contains summary tables including the Windward Islands; Vol III contains the major tabulations of the whole census with less geographical detail.

§   En.

Refer also to 517.

¶ F – Standard of living

Refer to 517.

Central statistical office

522   Dirección General de Estadística y Censos   [General Office of Statistics and Censuses],
           Ministerio de Economía   [Ministry of the Economy], Calle Arca no.953, San Salvador.
           † 21-9920, 21-9921 and 21-3782.

           A National Department of the Censuses was created in 1948, but in 1955 a law was passed
           organising a national statistical service which made obligatory the taking of 10-yearly censuses of
           population and housing, and 5-yearly censuses of agriculture, industry and commerce, as well as
           the collection, analysis and publication of statistics on a monthly, quarterly or annual basis.

           Unpublished information is supplied on request if available, and is usually in the form of
           computer printout.

Libraries

           The Dirección General de Estadística y Censos (see above) has a library which is open to the
           public; the more important statistical publications are also available in the national library and the
           university library in San Salvador.

Statistical publications

¶   A - General

523   Anuario estadístico   [Statistical yearbook]   (Dirección General de Estadística y Censos).
           Dirección General de Estadística y Censos, Ministerio de Economía, Calle Arca no.953,
               San Salvador.
           1911- 1970.   free distribution.   5 vols.
           Contents of the volumes are:
                 Vol I   Part I   Imports
                            Part II   Exports
                            Part III   Free trade of the Central American countries.
                        (In each case the main tables are arranged by commodity, subdivided by countries of
                            origin or destination).
                 Vol II   Demography and health.
                 Vol III   Industry, commerce and service trades.
                 Vol IV   Meteorology, agriculture and livestock, cost of living and internal trade,
                                transport and communications, construction, finance and banking.
                 Vol V   Education, culture and justice.
           Time factor: the 1970 edition, with data for that year, was published from October 1971 onwards.
           §   Es.

¶ A, continued

524   Boletín estadístico [Statistical bulletin] (Dirección General de Estadística y Censos).

Dirección General de Estadística y Censos, Ministerio de Economía, Calle Arca no.953, San Salvador.

1935- (Q). free distribution.

Up-dates the annual issue (517 above), with mainly provisional data for demography, education and culture, justice, industry, livestock slaughter, external trade, internal trade, transport and communications, construction and finance.

Time factor: each issue carries data for the period of the issue and some earlier figures, and is published about six months after the end of the period covered.

§ Es.

525   Revista mensual [Monthly review] (Banco Central de Reserva).

Banco Central de Reserva, San Salvador.

Not priced.

A monthly statistical survey of money and banking, foreign trade, public finance, production and prices, which also contains information on government economic agreements and decrees.

§ Es.

526   El Salvador en graficas [El Salvador in figures] (Dirección General de Estadística y Censos).

Dirección General de Estadística y Censos, Ministerio de Economía, Calle Arca no.953, San Salvador.

1956- 1970. free distribution. vii, 89 pages.

Main sections:

Population	Industry
Demography	Prices
Health	Construction
Transport	Electricity
Communications	Social affairs
Education	Finance
Culture	Banking
Justice	External trade
Agriculture	Meteorology.
Livestock	

Time factor: the charts, histograms and a few tables cover the period 1961 to 1970 in most cases in the 1970 edition, which was issued in Autumn 1971.

§ Es.

527   Indicadores económicos y sociales [Economic and social indicators] (Consejo Nacional de Planificación y Coordinación Económica [National Council for Planning and Economic Co-ordination]).

Consejo Nacional de Planificación y Coordinación Económica, San Salvador.

(Q). not priced.

§ Es.

¶   B - Production

528   Censo industrial   [Industrial census]   (Dirección General de Estadística y Censos).

Dirección General de Estadística y Censos, Ministerio de Economía, Calle Arca no.953,
San Salvador.

1951- 1961.   not priced.   xx, 314 pages.

Contains data on industrial establishments with five or more employees and with four or less
employees.   There is also data on the construction industry and the electricity industry.

§   Es.

Refer also to 523 and 524 for data on industrial production.

529   Censo agropecuario   [Census of agriculture and stockbreeding]   (Dirección General de
Estadística y Censos).

Dirección General de Estadística y Censos, Ministerio de Economía, Calle Arca no.953,
San Salvador.

1950- 1961.   free distribution.   xxv, 433 pages.

A ten-yearly census of farms, employees on the land, acreages of land, crops and livestock.

Time factor: the report on the 1961 census was published in 1967; a third census was taken in 1971.

§   Es.

530   Estadísticas agropecuarias continuas   [Continuing statistics of agriculture and stockbreeding]
(Ministerio de Agricultura y Ganadería).

Ministerio de Agricultura y Ganadería, San Salvador.

1960- 1966/67.   not priced.

§   Es.

¶   C - External trade

Refer to 082, 083, 523 and 524.

¶   D - Internal distribution

Refer to 523 and 524.

¶   E - Population

531   Censo nacional de población   [National census of population]   (Dirección General de Estadística
             y Censos).

           Dirección General de Estadística y Censos, Ministerio de Economía, Calle Arca no.953,
             San Salvador.

           1930- 1961.   free distribution.   xxxiii, 834 pages.

           Time factor: the results of the 1961 census were published in 1965.   A fourth census was taken in
             1971, and preliminary figures were published in November 1971 ("Cifras preliminares").

           §   Es.

           Refer also to 523, 524 and 526.

¶   F - Standard of living

532   Indice de precios al consumidor obrero   [Consumer price indices]   (Dirección General de
             Estadística y Censos).

           Dirección General de Estadística y Censos, Ministerio de Economía, Calle Arca no.953,
             San Salvador.

           (M).   free distribution.

           §   Es.

           Refer also to 523 and 526.

Central statistical office

533   Algemeen Bureau voor de Statistiek   [General Bureau of Statistics],
Ministerie van Algemene Zaken, Paramaribo.

The Bureau is responsible for the collection, analysis and publication of the official economic statistics for Surinam, many of which are issued in the series "Suriname in cijfers" [Surinam in figures].

Publications other than those described in the following pages include:
Bouwactiviteiten [Building activity] (A).
Statistiek van het onderwijs [Education statistics] (A).
Statistiek der motorrijtuigen [Motor vehicle statistics] (A).

Statistical publications

¶ A - General

534   Jaarcijfers voor Suriname. Statistical yearbook of Surinam   (Algemeen Bureau voor de Statistiek).

Algemeen Bureau voor de Statistiek, Paramaribo.

1956/60- 1958/62. not priced.

Contains statistical data on the economy, industrial production, agriculture, fishing, building, education, trade, finance, tourism, etc.

Time factor: the 1956/62 edition was published in 1965.

§   Nl, En.

535   Basic data on the economy   (US Department of Commerce, Bureau of International Commerce).

US Department of Commerce, Sales and Distribution Branch, Washington, D.C. 20230, USA.

US$0.15.   12 pages.

Issued as 67-51 in the series "Overseas business reports", this report presents selected basic data useful in the analysis of Surinam as a market for US exports. Data include statistics of population, structure of the economy, agriculture, manufacturing, construction, power, etc.

Time factor: published in August 1967, the report contains data for several years to 1966.

§   En.

536   Statistische berichten [Statistical bulletin] (Algemeen Bureau voor de Statistiek).

Algemeen Bureau voor de Statistiek, Paramaribo.

1956- (M). not priced.

Each issue is devoted to a different subject: prices, balance of payments, shipping, finance, money, etc.

§   Nl, En.

¶ A,   continued

537   Verslag   [Report]   (Centrale Bank van Suriname).

Centrale Bank van Suriname, Paramaribo.

(A) 1965.   not priced.   c. 150 pages.

Contains text and tables on the economy, agriculture, fish, forestry, minerals, industrial
    production, building activity, trade and tourism.

Time factor: the 1965 edition has data for 1963, 1964 and 1965, and was published in 1966.

§   NI.

¶ B - Production

538   Bedrijfs- en beroepstelling.   Census of industries and occupations.   (Algemeen Bureau voor de
    Statistiek).

Algemeen Bureau voor de Statistiek, Paramaribo.

1961.   not priced.   10 vols.

The reports include volumes for each of the districts, for Paramaribo, for Suriname, and a
    summary volume.   Data include the number of persons employed and wages by major industry
    group; occupations and wages; number of establishments, by size; number of persons
    employed, by district, etc.

Time factor: published in 1962.

§   NI, En.

539   Statistiek van de industriële produktie.   Statistics of industrial production   (Algemeen Bureau
    voor de Statistiek).

Algemeen Bureau voor de Statistiek, Paramaribo.

1965- 1965.   not priced.   20 pages.

Contains data similar to that included in 538 above.

Time factor: the 1965 edition, published in May 1966, up-dates the information in 538 above.

§   NI, En.

¶ C - External trade

540   In- en uitvoer.   Imports and exports   (Algemeen Bureau voor de Statistiek).

Algemeen Bureau voor de Statistiek, Paramaribo.

1953- 1964.   not priced.

Contains data on imports and exports arranged by commodity subdivided by countries of origin
    and destination,

Time factor: the 1964 edition, with data for 1964, was published in 1966.

§   NI, En.

¶   C,   continued

541   Maandstatistiek van de in- en uitvoer per goederensoort en per land   [Monthly statistics of
            imports and exports by commodity and by country]   (Algemeen Bureau voor de Statistiek).

         Algemeen Bureau voor de Statistiek, Paramaribo.

         Time factor: contains data for the month of the issue, and cumulative totals for the year to date.

         §   Nl.

¶   E - Population

542   Volkstelling.   Population census   (Algemeen Bureau voor de Statistiek).

         Algemeen Bureau voor de Statistiek, Paramaribo.

         1964.   not priced.   8 vols.

         Each volume is devoted to a separate district.

         Time factor: published in 1964 and 1965.

         §   Nl, En.

¶   F - Standard of living

543   Prijsontwikkeling   [Price development]   (Algemeen Bureau voor de Statistiek).

         Algemeen Bureau voor de Statistiek, Paramaribo.

         Not priced.   27 pages.

         Text and statistics on $12\frac{1}{2}$ years of price development.

         Time factor: published June 1966.

         §   Nl.

Central statistical office

544   Central Statistical Office,
           2 Edward Street, Port of Spain, Trinidad.
           t   54970 or 53733.

The Central Statistical Office collects, analyses and publishes all the official statistics of Trinidad and Tobago, and has also, in the past, been involved in carrying out censuses of population for Trinidad, Tobago and some other parts of the West Indies.

Publications other than those described in the following pages include:
Monthly travel.
Population and vital statistics   (A).
International travel report   (A).
Education digest   (A).
Financial statistics   (A).

Libraries

The Central Statistical Office, referred to above, has a library which is open to the public for reference to statistical publications.   Other libraries where statistical publications may be consulted are those of the Central Bank of Trinidad and Tobago, the Industrial Development Corporation, and the University of the West Indies, as well as the public library in Port of Spain.

Libraries and information services abroad

The statistical publications of Trinidad and Tobago are sent to Embassies abroad, including:
United Kingdom   High Commission, 42 Belgrave Square, London SW1.   t 01-245 9351.
USA   Embassy of Trinidad and Tobago, 2209 Massachusetts Avenue N W,
                    Washington, D.C.   t 232-3134.
Canada   High Commission for Trinidad and Tobago, 75 Albert Street, Ottawa.
                    t 232-2418.

Bibliographies

545   The Central Statistical Office issues a sales list of its publications at intervals. The 1967 edition
           is the latest.

Statistical publications

¶   A – General

546   Annual statistical digest   (Central Statistical Office).

           Government Printer, 2 Victoria Avenue, Port of Spain.

           1935/51– 1969.   TT$ 1.50.   xvi, 168 pages.

           Main sections:

Labour & employment	Mining & refining
Justice & crime	National income & expenditure
Social conditions	Overseas trade
Transport & communications	Prices
Industrial production	Banking.
Agriculture	

           Time factor: the 1969 edition, published early 1971, contains data for 1969 and earlier years
               from about 1960.

           §   En.

547   Quarterly economic report   (Central Statistical Office).

           Government Printer, 2 Victoria Avenue, Port of Spain.

           1950–.   TT$ 1.25 per copy.

           Contains data on overseas trade, prices, agriculture and fishing, industrial production, employment,
               transport and communications, finance and banking, population and vital statistics, and
               Tobago trade.

           Time factor: each issue contains data for that quarter and some retrospective annual and quarterly
               figures, and is issued about four months after the end of the period covered.

           §   En.

¶ B – Production

548   Monthly bulletin: petroleum industry   (Ministry of Petroleum and Mines).

           Government Printer, 2 Victoria Avenue, Port of Spain.

           Not priced.

           Includes statistics on drilling, crude oil production, refinery throughput, natural gas production,
               crude oil imports, etc.

           Time factor: each issue has data for the month of issue or the previous month, and is issued three
               or four months later.

           §   En.

¶   B,   continued

549   Agricultural census   (Central Statistical Office).

Government Printer, 2 Victoria Avenue, Port of Spain.

1946- 1963.   TT$ 1.00 each part.   2 vols in 3.

Vol I is a report on procedure and methodology, together with summary tables.
Vol II is in two parts. Part A has data on the holder and his holdings, numbers of acres and holdings; Part B is on land utilisation.

§   En.

Refer also to 546 and 547.

¶   C - External trade

550   Overseas trade   (Central Statistical Office).

Government Printer, 2 Victoria Avenue, Port of Spain.

1951- 1969.   Part A TT$ 3.50; Part B TT$ 1.50.   2 vols.

Part A contains a detailed analysis of the year's trade arranged by commodity and subdivided by countries of origin and destination; Part B combines a review with summary tables.

Time factor: the 1969 edition has data for 1969, Part A having been published early 1971 and Part B later that year.

§   En.

551   Overseas trade: monthly report - revised series   (Central Statistical Office).

Government Printer, 2 Victoria Avenue, Port of Spain.

1951-.   TT$ 2.00 per copy; TT$ 20.00 yr.

Contains provisional data on monthly overseas trade. The main table has statistics of imports and exports arranged by SITC commodity classifications, and there is also a table showing direction of trade.

Time factor: each issue has data for the month of the issue and cumulated figures for the year to date, and is published about four months later.

§   En.

Refer also to 082, 083, 546 and 547.

¶ E – Population

552   Population census of Trinidad and Tobago   (Central Statistical Office).

Government Printer, 2 Victoria Avenue, Port of Spain.

1960.   3 vols in 10 parts.

Volume I, Part A describes the methodology of the census (TT$ 7.50), and there is a supplementary volume showing the boundaries of enumeration districts (TT$ 5.00), and a volume of maps (TT$ 20.00).

Volume II, Part A has detailed tables of households and families, etc (TT$ 25.00), and Part B has detailed tables on the labour force (TT$ 12.00).

Volume III, Part A has data on population by type of household, type of institution, internal migration, foreign-born population, educational attainment, and ethnic origin (TT$ 1.50); Part B has data by marital status (TT$ 2.00); Part D has data by age group (TT$ 2.50); Part E has data by household (TT$ 3.00); and Part G has data of the labour force (TT$ 10.00).

§   En.

Refer also to 546 and 547.

¶ F – Standard of living

Refer to 546 and 547.

G

The Governor of the Bahamas is also the Governor of the Turks and Caicos Islands but there are no other links. From 1969, an Administrator was appointed, and enquiries regarding statistical data for the Turks & Caicos Islands could be addressed to him.

Statistical publications

¶   A – General

553   Turks and Caicos Islands: report for the year   (Foreign and Commonwealth Office).
           H M Stationery Office, P.O.Box 569, London SE1 9NH.
           1965 & 1966.   £0.30.   64 pages.
           Mainly textual, but contains some statistics on population, employment and wages, public
                finance and taxation, commerce, production, etc.
           Time factor: published 1968.
           §   En.

¶   E – Population

554   West Indies population census, 1960   (Department of Statistics, Jamaica).
           Department of Statistics, 23½ Charles Street, Kingston, Jamaica.
           Includes data on the population of the Turks & Caicos Islands.
           §   En.

Central statistical office

555
Bureau of the Census,
Department of Commerce, Washington, D.C. 20230.
t (202)735 2000.

The Bureau of the Census is responsible for arranging periodical censuses of population, housing, agriculture, irrigation, mineral industries, transport and government for which it collects, analyses and publishes the statistical data. It is also responsible for current population reports and projections, distribution of consumer income statistics and buying intentions, wholesale and retail trade statistics, construction statistics, manufacturing activity data, foreign trade statistics, etc.

The Bureau also provides special services whereby users of statistics may obtain information at an earlier date than the release of published reports, or may obtain data in greater detail than that available in the statistics regularly released. The entire cost of extra work or duplication of data is charged to the subscriber.

Publications other than those described in the following pages include:
Census of housing, 1970.
Construction statistics.
Census of transportation, 1967.
Current population reports P-20: population characteristics   (irr).
Census of construction industries, 1967.

Some other important organisations publishing statistics

Other bureaux or offices of the Department of Commerce which publish statistics include:

556
Bureau of International Commerce, Washington, D.C. 20230
(concerned with foreign economic trends and their implications for the United States);

557
Business Economics Office, Washington, D.C. 20230
(responsible for the 'Survey of current business', and concerned with business generally);

558
Bureau of Domestic Commerce, Washington, D.C. 20230
(until 1970 the Business and Defence Services Administration);

559
National Technical Information Service, Springfield, Virginia 22151
(responsible for the data processing of statistical information).

560
Economic Research Service,
Department of Agriculture, Washington, D.C. 20250.
This organisation is responsible for research into agricultural economics.

561
Bureau of Labor Statistics,
Department of Labor, 415 5th Street N W, Washington, D.C. 20212.
t (202) 961-3152.

The Bureau is the principal data-gathering agency of the Federal Government in the field of labour economics. Since 1884, the Bureau has collected, interpreted and presented data relating

[continued next page

Some other important organisations publishing statistics,   continued

561,   continued

to employment and unemployment, productivity, prices, wages, industrial relations, and industrial safety.   It is responsible for the wholesale price index and the consumer price index, frequently called the 'cost of living' index, as well as for may other series of statistics, including:

Estimated retail food prices by cities   (M).
Employment and earnings   (M).
Employment and earnings for United States, 1909-1970.
Wholesale prices and price indexes   (M).

Libraries

The Library of the Bureau of the Census, Room 2455, Federal Office Building No.3, Washington, D.C., may be consulted for research purposes during office hours.   Other government departments in Washington also have libraries.   In New York, there is the New York Public Library and the Statistics Library in the United Nations main building.   Other university and public libraries throughout the country have selected items of United States statistical publications.

Libraries and information services overseas

A selection of United States statistical publications are available for reference in US Embassies abroad, including:

United Kingdom	United States Embassy, Grosvenor Square, London W1A 1AE. t 01-499 9000.
Canada	United States Embassy, 100 Wellington Street, Ottawa. t CE6-2341.
Australia	United States Embassy, State Circle, Canberra. t 7 1351.

Bibliographies

562

Statistical services of the United States government   (US Office of Management and Budget).

The revised edition of this useful work was issued in 1968.   Designed to serve as a basic reference document on the statistical programme of the US government, it describes the system of Federal government, gives brief descriptions of the principal economic and social statistical series collected by government agencies, and contains a brief statement of the statistical responsibilities of each agency and a list of its principal statistical publications.

563

Bureau of the Census catalog   (Bureau of the Census).

Superintendent of Documents, US Government Printing Office, Washington, D.C. 20402.

Quarterly, cumulating to an annual volume, and with 12 monthly supplements.   US$3.00 (US$3.75 abroad) yr.

Bibliographies,   continued

564   Guide to foreign trade statistics   (Bureau of the Census).

Superintendent of Documents, US Government Printing Office, Washington, D.C. 20402.
1967- 1971.   US$1.50.   ix, 182 pages.

Contains a description of the foreign trade statistics programme, published foreign trade reports, foreign trade reference material, list of classification schedules, and availability of special services.

Time factor: published annually, the 1971 edition was issued in June 1971.

565   Business service checklist   (Department of Commerce).

Superintendent of Documents, US Government Printing Office, Washington, D.C. 20402.
Weekly.   US$2.50 (US$4.00 abroad) yr.

A weekly guide to new Department of Commerce publications.

566   Publications of the Bureau of Labor Statistics, 1886-1967   (Bureau of Labor Statistics).

Bureau of Labor Statistics, 415 5th Street N W, Washington, D.C. 20212.

Issued as Bulletin 1567 in 1968 (price US$1.00) it is kept up-to-date by 6-monthly supplements, which are available free.

567   Statistical reporter: current developments in Federal statistics   (Office of Management and Budget).

Superintendent of Documents, US Government Printing Office, Washington, D.C. 20402.
(M).   US$0.20; US$2.00 (US$2.50 abroad) yr.

Gives advance information on new statistical works, surveys and publications.

Statistical publications

¶   A - General

568   Statistical abstract of the United States   (Bureau of the Census).

Superintendent of Documents, US Government Printing Office, Washington, D.C. 20402.

1878- 1971.   US$5.50.   xxiv, 1008 pages.

Main sections:

Population	State & local government finances
Vital statistics, health &	& employment
nutrition	Banking, finance & insurance
Immigration & naturalization	Business enterprise
Education	Communications
Law enforcement, federal courts	Power
& prisons	Science
Geography & environment	Transportation - land
Public lands, parks, recreation	Transportation - air & water
& travel	Agriculture
Labour force, employment &	Forests & forest products
earnings	Fisheries
National defence & veterans'	Mining & mineral products
affairs	Construction & housing
Social insurance & welfare	Manufactures
services	Distribution & services
Income, expenditure & wealth	Foreign commerce & aid
Prices	Outlying areas under the jurisdiction
Elections	of the United States
Federal government finances &	Comparative international statistics
employment	Metropolitan area statistics.

Time factor: the 1971 edition has data for several years to 1970 and was published in November 1971.

§   En.

Note: the abstract also includes a guide to recent statistical abstracts for individual States.

Supplements to the "Statistical abstract" include:
"County and city data book, 1967" which contains statistical data for each county in the US, for 224 standard metropolitan statistical areas, and for incorporated cities having 25,000 inhabitants or more.   Information included is based largely on the results of the censuses of governments, business, manufactures and mineral industries, agriculture, and population and housing.
"Historical statistics...to 1957".
"Historical statistics...continuation to 1962 and revisions".
"Congressional district data".

569   Pocket data book, USA   (Bureau of the Census).

Superintendent of Documents, US Government Printing Office, Washington, D.C. 20402.

1967- 1971.   US$1.75.   352 pages.

Contains graphic and tabular statistics on population, vital statistics, immigration, area and climate, government, elections, national defence and veterans, law enforcement, health, education, science, labour, agriculture, forests, fisheries, business enterprise, manufactures, mining, construction, housing, transportation, communications, power, finance and insurance, distribution and services, foreign commerce, welfare, income, prices, parks and recreation.

Time factor: published every two years as a supplement to the 'Statistical abstract', the 1971 edition contains data for 1970 and some earlier years, having been published late 1971.

§   En.

¶   A,   continued

570   Economic almanac   (National Industrial Conference Board).

      National Industrial Conference Board, 845 Third Avenue, New York, N.Y. 10022.

      1940-   1967/68.   £4.20; US$12.00.   655 pages.

      Contains much the same data as the United States Statistical Abstract (see 568 above) but there
      is much reworking of data to make it easier to use and more to the point.

      Time factor: published every two years, the 1967/68 edition was issued in 1969 and contains
      data for various years, mainly up to 1965 or 1966.

      §   En.

Statistical yearbooks or abstracts are also available for individual States:

571   Economic abstract of Alabama, 1966   (University of Alabama, Center for Business and Economic
      Research).

572   Alaska statistical review, 1970   (Department of Economic Development, Juneau).

573   Arizona statistical review, 27th ed., 1971   (Valley National Bank, Phoenix).

574   Arkansas almanac, 12th ed., 1971/72   (Arkansas Almanac Inc, Little Rock).

575   California statistical abstract, 11th ed., 1970   (Department of Finance, Sacramento).

576   Colorado yearbook, 26th ed., 1962-64   (State Planning Division, Denver).

577   Connecticut market data, 1971   (Connecticut Development Commission, Hartford).

578   A statistical profile of the State of Delaware, 1968   (Delaware State Planning Office, Dover).

579   Florida statistical abstract, 5th ed., 1971   (University of Florida, Gainsville).

580   Georgia statistical abstract, 1970   (University of Georgia, Athens).

581   The State of Hawaii data book: a statistical abstract, 5th ed., 1971   (Department of Planning
      and Economic Development, Honululu).

582   Idaho statistical abstract, 1971   (University of Idaho, Moscow).

583   Illinois regional economic data-book, 1971   (Department of Business and Economic Development,
      Springfield).

584   Statistical abstract of Indiana counties, 1963   (Indiana State Chamber of Commerce, Indianapolis).

585   1970 statistical profile of Iowa   (Iowa Development Commission, Des Moines).

586   Kansas statistical abstract, 6th ed., 1970   (University of Kansas, Lawrence).

587   Deskbook of Kentucky economic statistics, 8th ed., 1970   (Department of Commerce, Frankfurt).

588   Statistical abstract of Louisiana, 4th ed., 1971   (Louisiana State University, New Orleans).

589   Maine pocket data book - a statistical abstract, 3rd ed., 1971   (Department of Economic
      Development, Augusta).

590   Statistical abstract [of Maryland], 1970   (Department of Economic Development, Annapolis).

591   Fact book [of Massachussetts] 1970   (Department of Commerce and Development, Boston).

592   Michigan statistical abstract, 8th ed., 1970   (Michigan State University, East Lansing).

¶ A,   continued

Statistical yearbooks for individual States, continued

593   A statistical profile of the State of Minnesota, 5th ed., 1971   (Department of Economic
                  Development, St Paul).

594   Mississippi statistical abstract, 1971   (Mississippi State University).

595   Data for Missouri counties, 1970 [Loose-leaf and up-dated]   (University of Missouri, Columbia).

596   Montana data book, 1970   (Montana State Department of Planning and Economic Development,
                  Helena).

597   Nebraska statistical handbook, 1970   (Department of Economic Development, Lincoln).

598   Nevada community profiles, 1970   (Department of Economic Development, Carson City).

599   Economic fact book [for New Jersey] 1972   (Office of Business Economics, Trenton).

600   New Mexico statistical abstract, Vol I, 1970   (University of New Mexico, Albuquerque).

601   New York statistical abstract, 4th ed., 1971   (Division of Budget, Albany).

602   North Carolina State government statistical abstract, 1971   (Department of Administration, Raleigh).

603   North Dakota growth indicators, 7th ed., 1970   (Business and Industrial Development Department,
                  Bismarck).

604   Statistical abstract of Ohio, 2nd ed., 1969   (Department of Development, Columbus).

605   Oklahoma data book, 1968   (University of Oklahoma, Norman).

606   Oregon economic statistics, 1971   (University of Oregon, Eugene).

607   Pennsylvania statistical abstract, 13th ed., 1971   (Department of Commerce, Harrisburg).

608   Rhode Island basic economic statistics, 1970   (Rhode Island Development Council, Providence).

609   Selected South Carolina economic data, 1969   (University of South Carolina, Columbia).

610   South Dakota economic and business abstract, 1971   (University of South Dakota, Vermillion).

611   Tennessee statistical abstract, 1st ed., 1969   (University of Tennessee, Knoxville).

612   Texas almanac, 1972/73   (Dallas Morning News, Dallas).

613   1969 statistical abstract of Utah, 1969   (University of Utah, Salt Lake City).

614   Statistical abstract of Virginia, Vol II, 1970   (University of Virginia, Charlottesville).

615   State of Washington pocket data book, 1970   (Washington State Office of Program Planning and
                  Fiscal Management, Olympia).

616   West Virginia statistical handbook, 1965   (West Virginia University, Morgantown).

617   Wisconsin statistical abstract, 1971   (Department of Administration, Madison).

618   Wyoming data book, 1971   (University of Wyoming, Laramie).

¶   A,   continued

619   Economic report of the President to the Congress.

          Superintendent of Documents, US Government Printing Office, Washington, D.C. 20402.

          1947- 1972.   US$1.50.   304 pages.

          An annual review of the national economy, with a 100-page statistical appendix covering national
              income and expenditure, population, employment, wages, productivity, production and
              business activity, prices, money supply, credit and finance, government finance, corporate
              profits and finance, agriculture, and some international statistics (US balance of payments,
              exports and imports, etc).

          Time factor: the 1972 edition has long runs of figures to 1971 and was published early 1972.

          §   En.

620   Economic indicators   (Council of Economic Advisers).

          Superintendent of Documents, US Government Printing Office, Washington, D.C. 20402.

          1948- (M).   US$0.25; US$3.00 yr (US$4.00 yr abroad).

          Contains indicators of total output, income and spending; employment, unemployment and wages;
              production and business activity; prices; money, credit and security markets; federal finance.

          Time factor: the latest final or provisional figures are given, together with earlier annual and
              quarterly ones.

          §   En.

621   Business conditions digest   (Bureau of the Census).

          Superintendent of Documents, US Government Printing Office, Washington, D.C. 20402.

          1961- (M).   US$1.50; US$15.00 yr.

          Brings together approximately 600 monthly and quarterly economic time series in a form convenient
              to analysts, and also includes other types of data such as foreign trade, Federal government
              activities and international comparisons of consumer prices, stock prices, and industrial
              production to facilitate more complete analysis.   Earlier title was "Business cycle developments".

          Time factor: each issue contains data to the month prior to the date of the issue.

          §   En.

622   Handbook of basic economic statistics   (Economic Statistics Bureau of Washington DC).

          Economic Statistics Bureau of Washington DC, Box 10163, Washington, D.C. 20018.

          1947- (M).   US$72.00 yr.

          A manual of basic economic data on industry, commerce, labour, and agriculture.

          Time factor: data is cumulative (so it is only necessary to keep the current issue), and includes
              statistics from 1913.   Claims to include statistics two to four weeks in advance of official
              publications.

          Note: there is also a 'Quarterly handbook' (US$36.00 yr), and an 'Annual handbook' (US$18.00),
              which both include a monthly supplement service.

          §   En.

¶   A,   continued

623   Business statistics   (Department of Commerce.   Bureau of Economic Analysis).

Superintendent of Documents, US Government Printing Office, Washington, D.C. 20402.
1935- 1969.   US$3.00.   264 pages.

A basic reference volume containing historical data for the series included in "Survey of
current business" and its weekly supplement "Business statistics" (see 624).

Time factor: the 1969 edition, with data from 1939 to 1968, was published early 1970.

§   En.

624   Survey of current business   (Department of Commerce.   Bureau of Economic Analysis).

Superintendent of Documents, US Government Printing Office, Washington, D.C. 20402.
1921- (M).   US$1.00; US$9.00 (US$12.75 abroad) yr.

Includes special articles, a report with charts and graphs on the business situation, and up-to-date
business statistics, including economic indicators, on subjects such as national income,
international transactions, retail and wholesale sales, manufacturers' orders and inventories;
production, prices and shipments in a wide variety of fields such as chemicals, foodstuffs,
metals, leather, paper, printing, textiles, and construction.   Retrospective figures are in
"Business statistics" (623 above), and there is a weekly supplement "Business statistics" which
up-dates some of the information in the monthly, and which is included in the subscription to
that title.

§   En.

625   The U.S. economy in 1980: a summary of BLS projections   (Bureau of Labor Statistics).

Superintendent of Documents, US Government Printing Office, Washington, D.C. 20402.
US$0.65.   59 pages.

Published as Bulletin 1673, this summary contains data on productivity and gross national product,
projected employment by industry and occupation, and projected shape of the labour force.

Time factor: published late 1970.

§   En.

626   A guide to consumer markets   (The Conference Board Inc).

The Conference Board Inc, 845 Third Avenue, New York, N.Y. 10022.
1960/61- 1971/72.   US$5.00 to associates; US$20.00 to non-associates.   246 pages.

Aims to bring together the most important statistical intelligence relating to the consumer, and
includes data on population, employment, income, expenditure, production and distribution,
and prices.

Time factor: the 1971/72 edition contains some data for 1970 but often for earlier years.
Published in 1971.

§   En.

¶   A,   continued

627   OECD economic surveys: United States   (Organisation for Economic Co-operation and Development).
          OECD, 2 rue André-Pascal, 75 Paris 16; or from sales agents.
          1962- 1970/71.   £0.35; US$1.00.   68 pages.
          An analysis of the economic policy of the country which includes statistics showing recent
              developments in demand, production, wages and prices, conditions in the money and capital
              markets, and developments in the balance of payments.
          Time factor: the 1970/71 issue was published in April 1971.
          §   En; Fr.

628   U.S. national income and product accounts ... statistical tables   (Business Economics Office,
              Department of Commerce).
          Business Economics Office, Department of Commerce, Washington, D.C. 20230.
          1958- 1964-67.   not priced.   ii, 43 pages.
          An up-dated version of the 1958 "U.S. income and output".   Includes gross national product and
              national income, personal income and outlay, government receipts and expenditures, foreign
              transactions, and saving and investment.
          Time factor: the 1964-67 edition was published in July 1971.
          §   En.

¶   B - Production

629   Census of manufactures   (Bureau of the Census).
          Superintendent of Documents, US Government Printing Office, Washington, D.C. 20402.
          1810- 1967.   various prices.   3 vols, finally, but issued initially in separate parts.
          Volume I will contain summary and subject statistics, such as size of establishments, type of
              organisation, manufacturers' inventories, expenditure for plant and equipment, power
              equipment in manufacturing industries, fuels and electric energy, selected materials consumed,
              selected metalworking operations, water used in manufacturing, and concentration ratios in
              manufacturing industries.
          Volume II deals with industry statistics, and the final report will be issued in several parts,
              showing for each industry, detailed product shipments and materials consumption, costs of fuels
              and electrical energy, value added by manufacture, employment, payrolls, inventories, and
              capital expenditure.
          Volume III, in two parts, deals with area statistics, showing similar information to the above for
              each State, county and cities with over 10,000 population.
          Time factor: the 1967 census results are now being published.   Each census of manufactures is
              up-dated by "US industrial outlook" (see 630).
          §   En.

¶ B,   continued

630   US industrial outlook   (Department of Commerce.   Bureau of Domestic Commerce).

Superintendent of Documents, US Government Printing Office, Washington, D.C. 20402.

1971- 1971.   US$5.00.   495 pages.

Pinpoints business activity levels for major industries in the US economy, as well as reviewing
   significant development.   Includes a detailed analysis of over 200 individual industries or
   closely related industry groups.   Up-dates much of the information in the "Census of
   manufactures" (623).

Time factor: the 1971 issue, published late 1971, has data for 1970 and projections for 1971,
   1975 and 1980.

§   En.

631   The economy at mid year ... with industry projections   (Department of Commerce.   Bureau of
              Domestic Commerce).

Superintendent of Documents, US Government Printing Office, Washington, D.C. 20402.

1970- 1971.   US$3.00.   66 pages.

Presents significant trends in the economy during the first half of the year, analyses 23 major
   manufacturing and non-manufacturing industries over the past year and projections of activity
   for the future year.   A companion volume to "U.S. industrial outlook", which emphasises
   long range forecasts.

Time factor: the 1971 edition was published in August 1971.

§   En.

632   Annual survey of manufactures   (Bureau of the Census).

Superintendent of Documents, US Government Printing Office, Washington, D.C. 20402.

1943- 1966.   US$6.25.   489 pages.

The survey carries forward from the results of the censuses of manufactures and key measures of
   manufacturing activity for industry groups, important industries, and for geographic divisions.

Time factor: the final report of the 1966 survey was published in June 1969; but preprints of
   chapters of the survey reports are issued as the information becomes available and such preprints
   have already been issued for the 1967, 1968 and 1969 surveys, those for the 1970 survey now
   appearing.

§   En.

633   Industry profiles   (Department of Commerce.   Bureau of Domestic Commerce).

Superintendent of Documents, US Government Printing Office, Washington, D.C. 20402.

1958/65- 1958/69.   US$2.25.   298 pages.

Presents a statistical picture of economic developments in each of 527 manufacturing industries
   and industry groups, by the Standard Industrial Classification.

Time factor: the 1958/69 edition has data for those years, and was published late 1971.

§   En.

¶ B, continued

634   Current industrial reports   (Bureau of the Census).

Bureau of the Census, Department of Commerce, Suitland, Maryland 20233.

(M) or (Q), with annual summaries.   Prices vary.

Contains up-to-date information for particular industries on production, employment, sales, etc.

Titles are:
     Aluminium ingot and mill products   (M).
     Asphalt and tar roofing and siding products   (M).
     Backing of orders for aerospace companies   (Q).
     Carpets and rugs   (Q).
     Clay construction products   (M).
     Closures for containers   (M).
     Complete aircraft and aircraft engines   (M).
     Confectionery (including chocolate products)   (M).
     Construction machinery   (Q).
     Consumption on woollen and worsted systems   (M).
     Converted flexible packaging products   (M).
     Copper base mill and foundry products   (Q).
     Cotton broadwoven gray goods   (Q).
     Cotton, man-made fibre staple, and linters, consumption and stocks   (M).
     Electric lamps   (M & Q).
     Farm machines and equipment   (Q).
     Fats and oils, production, consumption and stocks   (M).
     Fats and oils, oilseed crushings   (M).
     Flat glass   (Q).
     Flour milling products   (M).
     Fluorescent lamp ballasts   (Q).
     Glass containers   (M).
     Heating and cooking equipment   (M).
     Industrial gases   (M).
     Inorganic chemicals   (M).
     Inventories of brass and copper wire mill shapes   (M & Q).
     Inventories of steel mill shapes   (M).
     Iron and steel castings   (M).
     Knit underwear and nightwear   (Q).
     Man-made fiber broadwoven gray goods   (Q).
     Manufacturers' exportsales and orders of durable goods   (M).
     Manufacturers' shipments, inventories and orders   (M).
     Mattresses, bedsprings and sleep furniture   (M).
     Men's apparel   (M).
     Metal cans   (M).
     Metalworking machinery   (Q).
     Nonferrous castings   (M).
     Paint, varnish and lacquer   (M).
     Plastics bottles   (M).
     Plumbing fixtures   (Q).
     Pulp, paper and board   (M).
     Refractories   (Q).
     Rubber, supply and distribution for U.S.   (M).
     Shipments of knit cloth, including interplant transfers   (Q).
     Shipments of thermoplastic pipe, tube and fittings   (M).
     Shoes and slippers   (M).
     Steel shipping barrels, drums and pails   (M).
     Tire cord and tire cord fabrics   (Q).
     Titanium ingot, mill products and castings   (M).
     Tractors (except garden tractors)   (M).
     Truck trailers   (M).
     Typewriters   (M).
     Women's, misses' and juniors' apparel   (M).
     Wool broadwoven goods   (Q).
     Woven fabrics, production, inventories and unfilled orders   (M).

§   En.

¶   B,   continued

635   Federal Reserve bulletin   (Federal Reserve System).

             Division of Administrative Services, Board of Governors, Federal Reserve Service, Washington,
                D.C. 20551.

             1915-   (M).   US$0.60 (US$0.70 abroad); US$6.00 (US$7.00 abroad) yr.

             The standard source of statistics dealing with money and banking.   Also includes important FRB
                indexes of industrial production, in detail; and includes a regular feature "National summary
                of business conditions" (which is also issued as a press release).

             §   En.

636   County business patterns, U.S. summary   (Bureau of the Census).

             Superintendent of Documents, US Government Printing Office, Washington, D.C. 20402.

             1946- 1970.   US$2.25.   ii, 304 pages.

             Indicates the number of business concerns there are in each county or state in each of 100 categories,
                together with statistics on the number of employees and the total payroll for each category.

             Time factor: the 1970 issue was published mid-1971.

             §   En.

637   Census of agriculture   (Bureau of the Census).

             Superintendent of Documents, US Government Printing Office, Washington, D.C. 20402.

             1840- 1964.   3 vols.

             Contains data on the number of farms, types, acreages, land-use practices, facilities, employment,
                expenditure, value of products, etc.   Volume I has state and county statistics, one part for each
                state, Puerto Rico, Guam and the Virgin Islands of the US.   Volume II is a general report, with
                statistics by subject with totals for US regions, geographical divisions and states.   Volume III is
                a series of special reports presenting data for supplementary surveys on farm workers, hired farm
                workers, etc.

             Time factor: preliminary reports of results of the 1969 census are now being published (mid-1972).

             §   En.

638   Agricultural statistics   (Department of Agriculture).

             Superintendent of Documents, US Government Printing Office, Washington, D.C. 20402.

             1936- 1971.   US$2.75.   639 pages.

             Includes data on agricultural production, supplies, consumption, facilities, costs and returns.

             Time factor: the 1971 edition, published late 1971, has data for 1969 or 1970 and some earlier
                figures.

             §   En.

¶   B,   continued

639   Commodity yearbook   (Commodity Research Bureau Inc).

Commodity Research Bureau Inc, 140 Broadway, New York, N.Y. 10005.

1939- 1971.   US$18.95 (US$19.45 abroad); £9.24.   386 pages.

Each of 110 basic commodities has several pages of tabular data arranged in an easy-to-use manner.
Most tables have long runs of retrospective figures, and deal with production, prices, exports,
consumption, and supplies on hand.   For many commodities there are charts of weekly futures
prices for several years, and also monthly cash and spot prices.   An up-dating "Commodity
yearbook statistical abstract service" is published five times a year (subscription US$35.00 yr).

§   En.

640   Fishery statistics of the United States   (Department of the Interior, Bureau of Commercial Fisheries).

Superintendent of Documents, US Government Printing Office, Washington, D.C. 20402.

1939- 1968.   US$5.00.   578 pages.

A general review of landings; processing, canning and packaging of fishery products; the frozen
fishery trade; and the foreign fishing trade.   There are chapters on regional fisheries, including
Puerto Rico.

Time factor: the 1968 edition, with data for that year, was published in 1971.

§   En.

641   Census of commercial fisheries   (Bureau of the Census).

Superintendent of Documents, US Government Printing Office, Washington, D.C. 20402.

1967- 1967.   Currently being published in a number of parts.

Contains data on the number of operators, employment, payroll, operating cost, receipts,
by major type of catch and by regions and selected states.

§   En.

642   Census of mineral industries   (Bureau of the Census).

Superintendent of Documents, US Government Printing Office, Washington, D.C. 20402.

1850- 1963.   US$6.50.   2 vols.

Volume I contains the summary and industry statistics; Volume II the area statistics.   Data include
the number of companies, number of establishments, employment, man-hours, pay-rolls,
value added in mining, quantity and value of products shipped and supplies used, quantity and
cost of fuels and electric energy purchased and quantity produced and consumed, cost of contract
work, cost of purchased machinery, capital expenditures, and horse-power of equipment.

Time factor: the data is first issued in a number of separate reports as the information becomes
available.   The final volumes of the 1963 census were published in 1967.   (Preliminary data on
the 1967 census is about to be issued).

§   En.

¶   B,   continued

643   Minerals yearbook   (Bureau of Mines.   Department of the Interior).

Superintendent of Documents, US Government Printing Office, Washington, D.C. 20402.

1882- 1969.   US$6.00 per volume.   4 vols.

Volumes I and II contain data on metals, minerals, fuels in the United States, including production,
shipping, sales, consumption, etc. Volume III has domestic area reports, with chapters on the
minerals industries in each state.   Volume IV contains international data.

Time factor: the 1969 edition, published early 1971, has data for several years to 1969.

§   En.

644   Annual statistical report   (American Iron and Steel Institute).

American Iron and Steel Institute, 1000 16th Street N W, Washington, D.C. 20036.

1912- 1970.   not priced.   80 pages.

Concentrates on statistics relating to the operation of the iron and steel industries in the USA and
Canada, also US import and export of steel and world production of iron ore, pig iron and
raw steel.

Time factor: the 1970 edition was published in 1971.

§   En.

645   America's textile reporter   (Frank P.Bennett & Co Inc).

Frank P.Bennett & Co Inc, 286 Congress Street, Boston, Mass. 02210.

1887- weekly.   US$5.00 yr.

An annual statistical supplement is published each year in July, giving a wide range of production,
consumption and trade statistics culled from US government publications and other statistical
publications.

§   En.

646   Hosiery statistics   (National Association of Hosiery Manufacturers).

National Association of Hosiery Manufacturers, 468 Park Avenue S, New York.

(A).

Covers all aspects of the industry: production, stocks, exports, imports, manpower and plants.

§   En.

647   Wool situation   (Economic Research Service.   Department of Agriculture).

Economic Research Service, Department of Agriculture, Washington, D.C. 20250.

1964- (Q).   not priced.

Contains data on prices, production, consumption, imports and exports of raw wool, yarns and
fabrics.

Time factor: the data is for two to three months prior to the date of the issue.

§   En.

¶ B,   continued

648   Wool statistics and related data   (Economic Research Service, Department of Agriculture).

        Economic Research Service, Department of Agriculture, Washington, D.C. 20250.

        1920/64- 1930/69.   US$2.25.   294 pages.

        Can be used as a retrospective supplement to "Wool situation", (item above), containing long
            runs of data on the same subjects.

        Time factor: published every two years, with a supplement issued in intervening years, the 1930/69
            edition, with data for that period, was issued in May 1972.

        §   En.

649   Cotton situation   (Economic Research Service, Department of Agriculture).

        Economic Research Service, Department of Agriculture, Washington, D.C. 20250.

        1962- 5 per annum.   not priced.

        Contains data on prices, consumption, imports, exports, and stocks of raw cotton and cotton
            textiles; prices for rayon; and production, consumption, imports and exports of man-made
            fibres and yarns and fabrics therefrom, subdivided by type.

        Time factor: the data is for two or three months prior to the date of the issue.

        §   En.

650   Statistics on cotton and related data   (Economic Research Service, Department of Agriculture).

        Economic Research Service, Department of Agriculture, Washington, D.C. 20250.

        1925/62- 1930/1967.   not priced.   252 pages.

        Contains data on the US acreage under cotton; production, consumption, trade and prices of raw
            cotton; exports and imports of wool, cotton goods, man-made fibre piece goods; production of
            rayon and non-cellulosic fibres by country and type; production of tyre cords and fabrics
            subdivided by fibre; man-made fibre production; and daily rate of man-made staple fibre
            consumption on cotton system spinning spindles.

        Time factor: the 1925/62 and 1930/67 volumes are the basic ones, being up-dated by annual
            supplements, of which the 1971 issue is the latest.

        §   En.

651   Cotton counts its customers   (National Cotton Council of America).

        National Cotton Council of America, P.O.Box 12285, Memphis, Tennessee 38112.

        1956- revised 1969 and preliminary 1970.   not priced.   86 pages.

        Contains data on the quantity of cotton consumed in final uses in the United States.

        Time factor: the revised 1969 and preliminary 1970 issue was published in June 1971.

        §   En.

652   Textile Hilights   (American Textile Manufacturers Institute).

        American Textile Manufacturers Institute, 1501 Johnson Building, Charlotte, North Carolina 28202.

        Contains data on US production and consumption of fibres, yarns and fabrics, with main emphasis on
            cotton.

        §   En.

H

¶ B,   continued

653   Paperboard industry statistics   (American Paper Institute, Paperboard Group).
American Paper Institute, 260 Madison Avenue, New York, N.Y. 10016.
1934- 1970.   not priced.   27 pages.
Contains data on the capacity, production, seasonal trends, companies and equipment, orders,
   paper stocks of the paperboard industry.   Also containerboard production and box plant consumption.
Time factor: the 1970 edition, published mid-1971, has long runs of statistics to 1969.
§   En.

654   Automobile facts and figures   (Automobile Manufacturers Association Inc).
Automobile Manufacturers Association Inc, 320 New Center Building, Detroit, Michigan 48202.
(A) 1972.   not priced.   73 pages.
Contains data on motor vehicle factory sales of passenger cars, motor trucks and buses; production,
   registration, etc.
Time factor: the 1972 edition has long runs of statistics to 1971, and was published early 1972.
§   En.

655   Motor truck facts   (Automobile Manufacturers Association Inc).
Automobile Manufacturers Association Inc, 320 New Center Building, Detroit, Michigan 48202.
(A) 1972.   not priced.   60 pages.
Contains data on motor truck and bus factory sales, production, registrations, etc.
Time factor: the 1972 edition has long runs of statistics to 1971, and was published early 1972.
§   En.

656   Census of the industry   (Vend).
Vend, 165 West 46th Street, New York, N.Y. 10036.
1946- 1971.   US$0.50.   32 pages.
Published in the periodical "Vend" and also available as a reprint, the census shows the market for
   vending machines for drinks, tobacco, confectionery, foods, etc.
Time factor: the 1971 edition of the census was published in the May 1971 issue of "Vend", and
   has data for 1969 and 1970.
§   En.

657   Electronic market databook   (Electronic Industries Association).
Electronic Industries Association, 2001 Eye Street N W, Washington, D.C. 20006.
(A) 1970.   US$15.00.   98 pages.
Contains data of production, sales and foreign trade of electronic products such as television sets,
   radios, record players, tape recorders, computers, testing and measuring equipment for the
   general consumer, industry, government, etc.
Time factor: the 1970 edition, published in 1970, has long runs of figures to 1969.
§   En.

¶   B,   continued

658
      Aerospace facts and figures   (Aerospace Industries Association of America Inc).

Aviation Week and Space Technology, 330 West 42nd Street, New York, N.Y. 10036.

1953/54- 1971/72.   US$3.95.   132 pages.

Contains statistics of aircraft production, missile programmes, space programmes, research and development, foreign trade, manpower, finance and air transportation.

Time factor: the 1971/72 edition, published in 1971, has long runs of statistics to 1970.

§   En.

¶   C - External trade

659
      Foreign commerce and navigation of the United States   (Bureau of the Census).

Superintendent of Documents, US Government Printing Office, Washington, D.C. 20402.

1821- 1965.   Vol I US$7.00; Vol II US$8.25; Vol III US$9.00.

Volume I contains detailed statistics of foreign trade arranged by the SITC and subdivided by countries of origin and destination; Vol II has data arranged by area and country subdivided by the SITC; and Vol III has data arranged by Schedule A and Schedule B commodity subdivided by countries of origin and destination.

Time factor: data was prepared and published annually from 1821 to 1946; then a summary volume was produced to bridge the gap between 1946 and 1963; and the annual volume is again being published from 1964, albeit rather belatedly.   The 1965 edition appeared in 1971.

§   En.

Note: Schedule A is the commodity classification used for imports, and Schedule B the commodity classification used for exports of US foreign trade.

660
      U.S. foreign trade.   FT 135: Imports, commodity by country, general imports, imports for consumption, Schedule A commodity, quantity and value, current and cumulative (Bureau of the Census).

Superintendent of Documents, US Government Printing Office, Washington, D.C. 20402.

(M).   US$1.75; US$21.00 (US$26.25 abroad) yr.

Time factor: each issue has data for the month of the issue and cumulated figures for the year to date (December issue having the annual figures), and is issued about three months later.

§   En.

661
      U.S. foreign trade.   FT 410: Exports, commodity by country, Schedule B commodity, quantity and value, current and cumulative   (Bureau of the Census).

Superintendent of Documents, US Government Printing Office, Washington, D.C. 20402.

(M).   US$2.75; US$33.00 (US$41.25 abroad) yr.

Time factor: each issue has data for the month of the issue and cumulated figures for the year to date (December issue having the annual figures), and is issued about three months later.

§   En.

¶   C,   continued

662
U.S. foreign trade.   FT 800: US trade with Puerto Rico and United States Possessions
(Bureau of the Census).

Superintendent of Documents, US Government Printing Office, Washington, D.C. 20402.

(M) & (A).   Monthly: US$0.20; US$2.50 (US$3.25 abroad) yr.   Annual: US$0.25.

For Puerto Rico and for each Possession (Virgin Islands of the US, Guam, American Samoa) the data
are arranged by commodity subdivided by method of transport.

Time factor: data are not cumulative, and the monthly and annual figures appear about three months
later.

§   En.

663
U.S. foreign trade.   FT 990: Highlights of US export and import trade   (Bureau of the Census).

Superintendent of Documents, US Government Printing Office, Washington, D.C. 20402.

1967-   (M).   US$0.45; US$5.00 (US$6.25 abroad) yr.

Contains seasonally adjusted and unadjusted data by commodity, country and customs district, and
by method of transport.

Time factor: each issue has data for that month and some earlier figures, and is published about
one month later.

§   En.

664
U.S. foreign trade.   FT 150: General imports, Schedule A commodity groupings, world area,
country, and method of transportation   (Bureau of the Census).

Superintendent of Documents, US Government Printing Office, Washington, D.C. 20402.

(A) 1970.   US$2.50.   x, 327 pages.

Time factor: the 1970 edition, with data for that year, was published mid-1971.

§   En.

665
U.S. foreign trade.   FT 450: Exports, Schedule B commodity groupings, world area, country,
and method of transportation   (Bureau of the Census).

Superintendent of Documents, US Government Printing Office, Washington, D.C. 20402.

(A) 1970.   US$2.75.   xiv, 380 pages.

Time factor: the 1970 edition, with data for that year, was published mid-1971.

§   En.

666
U.S. foreign trade.   FT 155: General imports, world area, country, Schedule A commodity
groupings, and method of transportation   (Bureau of the Census).

Superintendent of Documents, US Government Printing Office, Washington, D.C. 20402.

(A) 1970.   US$3.25.   x, 457 pages.

Time factor: the 1970 edition, with data for that year, was published mid-1971.

§   En.

¶ C, continued

667   U.S. foreign trade. IM 150/155. US general imports. Schedule A commodity groupings, world area, country and method of transportation   (US Department of Commerce. National Technical Information Service).

National Technical Information Service, US Department of Commerce, Springfield, Virginia 22151.

Contents:
Table 1   Schedule A groupings of commodities by methods of transportation.
Table 2   Schedule A subgroup by world area of origin and method of transportation.
Table 3   Schedule A subgroup by country of origin and method of transportation.
Table 4   World area of origin by Schedule A subgroup and country of origin, by Schedule A commodity groupings and method of transportation.
Table 5   Number in sample for Schedule A subgroup 990.0 by country of origin   (Note: 990.0 is 'low-valued' shipments excluded from detailed tables).

(M).   Tables 1, 2 and 3 are published in one volume and, together with Table 5, cost US$30.00 yr; Table 4, together with Table 5, costs US$45.00 yr; complete 5 tables cost US$60.00 yr.

Time factor: each issue has data for the month and cumulated data for the year to date, and is issued very quickly after the end of the period covered.

§   En.

668   U.S. foreign trade. EM 450/455. US exports. Schedule B commodity groupings, world area, country and method of transportation   (US Department of Commerce. National Technical Information Service).

National Technical Information Service, US Department of Commerce, Springfield, Virginia 22151.

Contents:
Table 1   Exports of domestic merchandise, Schedule B groupings of commodities and method of transportation.
Table 2   Exports of domestic merchandise, Schedule B subgroup by world area of destination and method of transportation.
Table 3   Exports of domestic merchandise, Schedule B subgroup by country of destination and method of transportation.
Table 4   Exports of domestic merchandise, world area of destination by Schedule B subgroup and country of destination, by Schedule B commodity groupings and method of transportation.
Table 5   Exports of domestic merchandise, number in sample for exports to Canada by Schedule B subgroup.
Table 6   Exports of foreign merchandise, Schedule B subgroup totals and method of transportation.
Table 7   Exports of foreign merchandise, country of destination totals and method of transportation.

(M).   Tables 1, 2 and 3 are published in one volume and, together with Table 5, cost US$40.00 yr; Table 4, together with Table 5, costs US$70.00 yr; Tables 6 and 7 cost US$10.00 yr together; complete 7 tables cost US$100.00 yr.

Time factor: each issue has data for the month and cumulated data for the year to date, and is issued very quickly after the end of the period covered.

§   En.

669   U.S. foreign trade. FT 210: imports for consumption and general imports, SIC-based products and area   (Bureau of the Census).

Superintendent of Documents, US Government Printing Office, Washington, D.C. 20402.

1970.   US$2.25.   307 pages.

Time factor: the 1970 edition, with data for that year, was published mid-1971.

§   En.

¶   C,   continued

670   U.S. foreign trade.   FT 610: Exports of domestic merchandise, SIC-based products and area
           (Bureau of the Census).
         Superintendent of Documents, US Government Printing Office, Washington, D.C. 20402.
         1970.   US$5.25.   xii, 604 pages.
         Time factor: the 1970 edition, with data for that year, was published mid-1971.
         §   En.

671   U.S. foreign trade.   FT 246: Imports for consumption and general imports, TSUSA commodity and
           country   (Bureau of the Census).
         Superintendent of Documents, US Government Printing Office, Washington, D.C. 20402.
         1970.   US$5.25.   606 pages.
         Time factor: the 1970 edition, with data for that year, was published mid-1971.
         §   En.

672   Foreign agricultural trade of the United States   (Department of Agriculture.   Economic Research
           Service).
         Economic Research Service, Department of Agriculture, Washington, D.C. 20250.
         (M).   not priced.
         Contains detailed statistics of imports and exports of agricultural products.
         §   En.
         Note: this publication is supplemented by the annual publications: "U.S. foreign agricultural
           trade statistical report"; "U.S. foreign trade by countries"; "U.S. foreign agricultural trade by
           commodities, (fiscal year)"; and "U.S. foreign agricultural trade by commodities, (calendar
           year)".

         Refer also to 082 and 083.

¶   D - Internal distribution

673   Census of business   (Bureau of the Census).
         Superintendent of Documents, US Government Printing Office, Washington, D.C. 20402.
         1929- 1967.   prices vary.
         Covers the retail, wholesale and service trades and includes data such as number of establishments,
           employment and payroll, and receipts.   The preliminary reports appear first and then the final
           volumes for the United States as a whole and for each separate state, including Puerto Rico,
           Guam, and the Virgin Islands of the United States.
         Time factor: the results of the 1967 census are now being issued; 1963 was the date of the previous
           census, but in future a census will be taken every five years.
         §   En.

         Refer also to 568.

¶   E – Population

674   Census of population   (Bureau of the Census).

            Superintendent of Documents, US Government Printing Office, Washington, D.C. 20402.

            1790– 1970.   prices vary.   not complete as yet.

            A large number of preliminary and final reports have been or are to be issued.   The major reports
              so far published are:
                 Final population counts.   Series PC(v1) in which there is one report for each state, the District
                    of Columbia, and the US as a whole. Data are for states, counties, minor civil divisions,
                    all incorporated places, and unincorporated places of 1000 or more inhabitants.
                 General population characteristics.   Series PC(v2) in which there is again one report for each
                    state, D.C., and the US.   Selected data on age, sex, race and relationship to head of
                    household are included.
                 Volume I.   Characteristics of population.
                    Contains separate reports for US, each state, D.C., Puerto Rico, Guam, Virgin Islands
                    of the United States, American Samoa, Canal Zone, and Trust Territory of the Pacific.
                    Each report was first issued as four separate chapters, and then assembled and issued in
                    hard cover:
                              Number of inhabitants   PC(1)–A
                              General population characteristics   PC(1)–B
                              General, social and economic characteristics   PC(1)–C
                              Detailed characteristics   PC(1)–D.
                 Volume II. Subject reports.
                    Detailed information on cross–relationships for the US, regions and some states, etc, on
                    such subjects as national origin and race, fertility, families, marital status, migration,
                    education, employment, occupation, industry, and income.
            §   En.

            Refer also to 568.

¶   F – Standard of living

675   Handbook of labor statistics   (Bureau of Labor Statistics).

            Superintendent of Documents, US Government Printing Office, Washington, D.C. 20402.

            1947– 1971.   US$3.25.   xii, 369 pages.

            Incorporates the major series produced by the Bureau, and related series produced by other US
              government departments and foreign countries.   Contains tables dealing with the labour force,
              employment, unemployment, labour productivity, compensation, consumer price index,
              living conditions, and similar subjects.

            Time factor: the 1971 edition, issued as the Bureau's Bulletin no.1705, has data for several years
              to 1970, and was published in December 1971.
            §   En.

676   Monthly labor review   (Bureau of Labor Statistics).

            Superintendent of Documents, US Government Printing Office, Washington, D.C. 20402.

            1940–.   US$0.75; US$9.00 (US$11.25 abroad) yr.

            Includes a detailed breakdown of the consumer price index (cost of living) and also important
              statistics on wholesale prices, earnings of workers, employment and unemployment.
            §   En.

¶   F,   continued

677   Current population reports P-60: consumer income   (Bureau of the Census).

               Superintendent of Documents, US Government Printing Office, Washington, D.C. 20402.

               1948- (irr).   prices vary.

               The reports contain information on the proportion of families and persons at various income levels.
                  They also contain data on the relationship of income to age, sex, colour, family size,
                  education, occupation, work experience, and other characteristics.

               §   En.

678   Consumer price index: US city average and selected areas   (Bureau of Labor Statistics).

               Bureau of Labor Statistics, 415 5th Street N W, Washington, D.C. 20212.

               1953- (M).   free.

               §   En.

679   Household food consumption survey, 1965-66   (Agricultural Research Service, Department of
                  Agriculture).

               Superintendent of Documents, US Government Printing Office, Washington, D.C. 20402.

               US$1.00 each report.   10 reports.

               A series of 10 reports on food consumption of households in the United States as a whole, the
                  northeast, north central, south and west regions; and on dietary levels in these same areas.

               Time factor: the survey reports were published in 1970 and 1971.

               §   En.

680   Statistics of income: individual income tax returns   (Internal Revenue Service, Department of
                  the Treasury).

               Superintendent of Documents, US Government Printing Office, Washington, D.C. 20402.

               1954- 1969.   US$3.75.   vi, 426 pages.

               Time factor: the 1969 edition, with data for that year, was published in December 1971.
                  Preliminary volumes are published earlier.

               §   En.

681   Current population reports: P-65: consumer buying indicators   (Bureau of the Census).

               Superintendent of Documents, US Government Printing Office, Washington, D.C. 20402.

               1963- (Q).   prices vary.

               Contain information on the proportion of households reporting intentions to purchase automobiles,
                  houses and household equipment within a particular period of time.

               §   En.

Central statistical office

682   Dirección General de Estadística y Censos   [General Office of Statistics and Censuses],
             Cuareim 2052, Montevideo.
             t   290734.

             The Dirección General de Estadística y Censos is responsible for the collection, analysis and
publication of the official statistics of Uruguay, other than statistics of foreign trade.
             Unpublished statistical information may be supplied on request when available, and there is a
photocopying service for which the cost of production of copies is charged.

Another organisation publishing statistics

683   Centro de Estadísticas Nacionales y Comercio Internacional del Uruguay (CENCI)
                [Centre for Uruguayan National Statistics and International Trade],
             Misiones 1361, Montevideo.
             t   953-56   cables CENCIURU.

             The Centre is responsible for the compilation of the official foreign trade statistics of Uruguay.

Libraries

             The Dirección General de Estadística y Censos (see above) has a library which is open to the
public for reference to statistical publications.   The headquarters of the Banco Central in Montevideo
also has a library.

Libraries and information services abroad

             The Uruguayan embassies abroad receive the official statistical publications of the country;
embassies include:

United Kingdom	Uruguayan Embassy, 48 Lennox Gardens, London SW1X 0DL
	t 01-589 8835/6.
USA	Uruguayan Embassy, 2362 Massachusetts Avenue N W, Washington,
	D.C. t HU3-7266.
Canada	Uruguayan Embassy, 124 Springfield, Ottawa. t 745-9664.

Statistical publications

¶   A – General

684   Anuario estadístico de la República Oriental del Uruguay   [Statistical yearbook of Uruguay]
          (Dirección General de Estadística y Censos).
          Dirección General de Estadística y Censos, Cuareim 2052, Montevideo.
          1884- 1964-1965-1966.   not priced.   2 vols.
          Fascicule I contains data on territory and climate and population; fascicule II contains data on the
              economy, including livestock and agriculture, fishing, industry, and energy.
          Time factor: the 1964–1965–1966 edition, covering those three years, was published in 1968;
              and edition covering the years 1967 to 1969 is to be published shortly.
          §   Es.

685   Boletín estadístico mensual   [Monthly statistical bulletin]   (Banco Central del Uruguay).
          Banco Central del Uruguay, Departamento de Investigaciones Económicas, Montevideo.
          1942/44-.   not priced.
          Contains data on money and credit, balance of payments and foreign trade, public finance,
              prices and price indices (including cost of living), and production (agriculture, livestock,
              and manufacturing industry).
          §   Es.

686   Basic data on the economy   (US Department of Commerce, Bureau of International Commerce).
          US Department of Commerce, Sales and Distribution Branch, Washington, D.C. 20230.
          US$0.15.   8 pages.
          Issued as 68-113 in the series "Overseas business reports", this report presents selected basic data
              useful in the analysis of Uruguay as a market for US exports.   Data include statistics of population,
              structure of the economy, agriculture, manufacturing, construction, power, etc.
          Time factor: published in December 1968, the report contains data for several years to 1967.
          §   En.

¶   B – Production

          Refer to 684 and 685 for industrial production.

687   Censo general agropecuario   [General census of agriculture and stockbreeding]   (Ministerio de
              Ganadería y Agricultura).
          Ministerio de Ganadería y Agricultura, Montevideo.
          1961.   not priced.   55 pages.
          Contains data on the utilisation of the land, crops, livestock, employment, etc.
          §   Es.

          Refer also to 684 and 685 for agricultural production.

¶   C - External trade

688   Analisis estadístico: Uruguay. Importación-exportación   [Statistical analysis: Uruguay. Imports-
            exports]   (CENCI).

            Centro de Estadísticas Nacionales y Comercio Internacional del Uruguay (CENCI), Misiones 1361,
            Montevideo.

            1957- 1970.   not priced.   269 pages.

            Contains tables of trade by country and detailed tables of imports and exports arranged by commodity
            subdivided by countries of origin and destination.

            Time factor: the 1970 edition, published mid-1971, has data for 1970.

            §   Es.

689   Importación   [Imports]   (Importación).

            Importación, Colon 1580 esc.7, Montevideo.

            (M).   U$ 550.00.

            Contains detailed statistics of imports arranged by commodity and subdivided by port of entry and
            country of origin.

            Time factor: each issue has data for the date of the issue and is published one or two months later.

            §   Es.

690   Exportación   [Exports]   (Importación).

            Importación, Colon 1580, esc.7, Montevideo.

            (M).   U$ 450.00.

            Contains detailed statistics of exports arranged by commodity and subdivided by port of exit and
            country and/or port of destination.

            Time factor: each issue has data for the date of the issue and is published one or two months later.

            §   Es.

691   Exportación cumplidas estado por país y producto. Exportación cumplidas estado por producto
            [Exports by country and product. Exports by product]   (Banco Central del Uruguay,
            Departamento de Investigaciones Económicas).

            Banco Central del Uruguay, Departamento de Investigaciones Económicas, Montevideo.

            (M).   not priced.

            Detailed statistics of exports arranged by commodity and also arranged by country subdivided by
            commodity.

            Time factor: computer-printout for the month of the issue and cumulated figures for the year to
            date, published three or four months later.

            §   Es.

¶   C,   continued

692   Importaciones cumplidas estado por país, rubro y subrubro   [Imports by country, commodity group
          and sub-group]   (Banco Central del Uruguay, Departamento de Investigaciones Económicas).

       Banco Central del Uruguay, Departamento de Investigaciones Económicas, Montevideo.

       (M).   not priced.

       Detailed statistics of imports arranged by country of origin, subdivided by commodity groups and
          sub-groups.

       Time factor: computer-printout for the month of the issue and cumulated figures for the year to
          date, published three or four months later.

       §   Es.

¶   E – Population

693   Censo general de población y vivienda   [General census of population and housing]
          (Dirección General de Estadística y Censos).

       Dirección General de Estadística y Censos, Cuareim 2052, Montevideo.

       1963.   not priced.

       The results of the census include a final definitive volume for the whole country and separate
          volumes for each of the 19 regions.

       §   Es.

       Refer also to 684.

¶   F – Standard of living

694   Indice de los precios del consumo   [Index of consumer prices]   (Dirección General de Estadística
          y Censos).

       Dirección General de Estadística y Censos, Cuareim 2052, Montevideo.

       (Q).   not priced.

       §   Es.

       Refer also to 685.

Central statistical office

695   Dirección General de Estadística y Censos Nacionales   [General Office of National Statistics and Censuses],
Ministerio de Fomento [Ministry of Development], Esquina de Cervecería, Caracas 101.
† 55 21 13-19.

     The Office is responsible for the collection, analysis and publication of official statistical publications of Venezuela.

     Publications other than those described in the following pages include:
       Boletín trimestral de estadísticas demograficas y sociales   [Quarterly bulletin of demographic and social statistics].

Libraries

     The Dirección General de Estadística y Censos Nacionales, referred to above, has a library which is open to the public for reference to statistical publications.

Libraries and information services abroad

     Venezuelan Embassies abroad have copies of Venezuelan statistical publications including:
       United Kingdom   Venezuelan Embassy, 6/3 Hans Crescent, London SW1X 0LX.
                   † 01-584 4206.
       USA   Venezuelan Embassy, 2409 California N W, Washington, D.C.
                   † CO5-7323.
       Canada   Venezuelan Embassy, 140 Wellington Street, Ottawa.   † 234-2340.

Statistical publications

¶   A - General

696   Anuario estadístico de Venezuela   [Statistical yearbook of Venezuela]   (Dirección General de Estadística y Censos Nacionales).

     Dirección General de Estadística y Censos Nacionales, Ministerio de Fomento, Esquina de Cervecería, Esquina Cervecería Este 2, Caracas 101.

     1887- 1968.   not priced.   xxxi, 721 pages.

     Main sections:

Geography & meteorology	Finance & banking
Demography	Foreign trade
Production & consumption	Education & employment
Prices & price indices	Justice
Transport, communications & telecommunications	Miscellaneous.

     Time factor: the 1968 edition, published late 1971, has data for 1968, and for three or four or more earlier years.

     §   Es.

¶ A,   continued

697   Compendio estadístico de Venezuela   [Statistical compendium for Venezuela]   (Dirección General
de Estadística y Censos Nacionales).

Dirección General de Estadística y Censos Nacionales, Ministerio de Fomento, Esquina de
Cervecería, Esquina de Cervecería Este 2, Caracas 101.

1968.   not priced.

A less detailed edition of 696 above.

Time factor: the 1968 edition, published in 1970, has data for 1968 and some earlier years.

§   Es.

698   Informe económico   [Economic report]   (Banco Central de Venezuela).

Banco Central de Venezuela, Caracas.

1950- 1969.   not priced.   239 pages.

Apart from data on money, finance and banking, this report has chapters and tables on prices,
national production and income, capital formation, and foreign trade.

Time factor: the 1969 edition, published in 1970, has data for 1968 and earlier years.

§   Es.

699   Basic data on the economy   (US Department of Commerce, Bureau of International Commerce).

US Department of Commerce, Sales and Distribution Branch, Washington, D.C. 20230.

US$0.15.   23 pages.

Issued as 71–058 in the series "Overseas business reports", this report presents selected basic data
useful in the analysis of Venezuela as a market for US exports.   Data include statistics of
population, structure of the economy, agriculture, manufacturing, construction, power, etc.

Time factor: published in December 1971, the report contains data for several years to 1970.

§   En.

¶ B – Production

700   Boletín trimestral de estadísticas industriales   [Quarterly bulletin of industrial statistics]
(Dirección General de Estadística y Censos Nacionales).

Dirección General de Estadística y Censos Nacionales, Ministerio de Fomento, Esquina de
Cervecería, Esquina Cervecería Este 2, Caracas 101.

1941-.   not priced.

Contains data on production (agriculture, forestry, hunting and fishing), mines and minerals,
manufacturing industry, electricity, consumption, economy and finance.

Time factor: each issue has long runs of figures up to the date of the issue, and is published
some months later.

§   Es.

¶ B, continued

701   Anuario estadístico agropecuario   [Statistical yearbook of agriculture and stockbreeding]
       (Ministerio de Agricultura y Cría).

       Ministerio de Agricultura y Cría, Caracas.

       1961- 1969.   not priced.   714 pages.

       Contains statistical data on crops, forestry, fisheries; including production, prices, trade,
       use of equipment, etc.

       Time factor: the 1969 edition, published late 1970, has data for 1969.

       §   Es.

702   Petróleo y otros datos estadísticos   [Statistical data on petroleum, etc]   (Ministerio de Minas e
       Hidrocarburos   [Ministry of Mines and Minerals]).

       Ministerio de Minas e Hidrocarburos, Caracas.

       1952- 1968.   not priced.

       Contains statistical data on petroleum and other minerals.

       Time factor: the 1968 edition was published in 1970.

       §   Es.

703   Monthly bulletin   (Ministerio de Minas e Hidrocarburos).

       Ministerio de Minas e Hidrocarburos, Caracas.

       1966-.   not priced.

       Includes a section of statistics on drilling operations, drilling rigs, petroleum produced (crude oil
       and refined products), and exports.

       Time factor: each issue has data for a period up to about three months prior to the date of the issue.

       §   En.   An edition in Es is also available.

       Refer also to 696 and 697

¶ C – External trade

704   Boletín de comercio exterior   [Bulletin of foreign trade]   (Dirección General de Estadística y
       Censos Nacionales).

       Dirección General de Estadística y Censos Nacionales, Ministerio de Fomento, Esquina de
       Cervecería, Esquina Cervecería Este 2, Caracas 101.

       1959- (Q).   not priced.

       Main tables show exports, imports and re-exports arranged by commodity and subdivided by
       countries of destination and origin.

       Time factor: each issue has data for the period of the issue and cumulated figures for the year to
       date, and is issued about six months later.

       §   Es.

¶ C, continued

705   Comercio exterior de Venezuela   [Foreign trade of Venezuela]   (Dirección de Comercio Exterior
         y Consulados   [Ministry of Foreign Affairs]).

       Dirección de Comercio Exterior y Consulados, Caracas.

       1962- (M).   not priced.

       A survey of Venezuelan industry and trade, including production of commodities, development
         possibilities, tourism, and export potentials.

       §   Es.

¶ E - Population

706   Censo general de población y de vivienda   [General census of population and housing]
         (Dirección General de Estadística y Censos Nacionales).

       Dirección General de Estadística y Censos Nacionales, Ministerio de Fomento, Esquina de
         Cervecería, Esquina Cervecería Este 2, Caracas 101.

       1873- 1961.   not priced.   2 vols.

       Includes data on the general, educational and economic characteristics of the population.

       §   Es.

       Refer also to 696 and 697.

¶ F - Standard of living

       Refer to 696 and 697.

Central statistical office

707   Bureau of the Census,
        Department of Commerce, Washington, D.C. 20230, USA.
        t (202) 735 2000.

        The Bureau is responsible for the collection, analysis and publication of economic statistics for the Islands.

Statistical publications

¶   A – General

708   Annual report: Virgin Islands   (US Department of the Interior).
        Superintendent of Documents, US Government Printing Office, Washington, D.C. 20402, USA.
        1926– 1970.   US$0.70.   iii, 170 pages.
        The annual report of the Governor of the Islands, containing general information.
        Time factor: the 1970 edition was published in June 1971.
        §   En.

¶   B – Production

709   Censuses of business, manufactures, and mineral industries: Virgin Islands of the United States
            (US Bureau of the Census).
        Superintendent of Documents, US Government Printing Office, Washington, D.C. 20402, USA.
        1957– 1967.   US$0.50.   21 pages.
        Contains data on the number of establishments, sales, receipts, payrolls, employees for each
            industry or kind of business for each individual territory (Municipality of St Thomas & St John,
            Municipality of St Croix, Charlotte Amalie, Christiansted, and Frederiksted).
        Time factor: published in August 1969.
        §   En.

        Refer to 637 for census of agriculture.

¶   C – External trade

710   External trade statistics with foreign countries   (Department of Commerce).
        Department of Commerce, P.O.Box 1692, St Thomas, Virgin Islands 00801.
        1969.   not priced.   60 pages.
        Contains statistics of imports and exports of commodities subdivided by countries of origin and
            destination.
        Time factor: the 1969 edition, with data for that year, was published early in 1970.
        §   En.

¶   C,   continued

711   U.S. foreign trade.   FT 800: US trade with Puerto Rico and United States Possessions
                   (Bureau of the Census).

              Superintendent of Documents, US Government Printing Office, Washington, D.C. 20402.

              (M) & (A).   Monthly: US$0.20; US$2.50 (US$3.25 abroad) yr.   Annual: US$0.25.

              For Puerto Rico and for each Possession (Virgin Islands of the US, Guam, American Samoa) the data
                   is arranged by commodity subdivided by method of transport.

              Time factor: data is not cumulative, and the monthly and annual figures appear about three months
                   after the period covered.

              §   En.

¶   E – Population

              Refer to 674.

References are to the serial numbers used in the text;
an asterisk (*) following a serial number indicates
that the title is listed under its publishing organisation
at that number but not further described.

INDEX OF TITLES

INDEX OF TITLES

INDEX OF ORGANISATIONS